Spiritual Citizenship

SPIRITUAL

TRANSNATIONAL PATHWAYS from

CITIZENSHIP

BLACK POWER to IFÁ in TRINIDAD

N. FADEKE CASTOR

Duke University Press   Durham and London   2017

Designed by Heather Hensley
Typeset in Chaparral Pro by Copperline Books

Library of Congress Cataloging-in-Publication Data
Names: Castor, N. Fadeke, [date] author.
Title: Spiritual citizenship : transnational pathways from
black power to Ifá in Trinidad / N. Fadeke Castor.
Description: Durham : Duke University Press, 2017. |
Includes bibliographical references and index.
Identifiers: LCCN 2017021994 (print) | LCCN 2017036667 (ebook)
ISBN 9780822372585 (ebook)
ISBN 9780822368731 (hardcover : alk. paper)
ISBN 9780822368953 (pbk. : alk. paper)
Subjects: LCSH: Trinidad—Religion—African influences. | Blacks—
Trinidad and Tobago—Trinidad—Religion. | Cults—Trinidad and
Tobago—Trinidad—African influences. | Ifa (Religion)—Trinidad
and Tobago—Trinidad. | Orisha religion—Trinidad and Tobago—
Trinidad. | Black power—Trinidad and Tobago—Trinidad.
Classification: LCC BL2530.T7 (ebook) | LCC BL2530.T7 C378 2017 (print) |
DDC 299.6/972983—dc23
LC record available at https://lccn.loc.gov/2017021994

Duke University Press gratefully acknowledges the support of the
Melbern G. Glasscock Center for Humanities Research, which
provided funds toward the publication of this book.

Cover art: Shrine establishment for Asewele (the spirits of lost
travellers), dedicated especially to Africans who died in the slave
trade and during slavery. Pictured from left to right are: Ifetayo;
Oubi Kumasi-Ka; Patricia Ifagbamila Gibbons; Iya Akinde Rudder;
Baba Ifasuen Norbert Bell; Iyanifa Ọmọlaṣọ Annette Thompson;
Iya Ifabunmi Rhonda Valentine-Charles; Rawle Afuwepe Gibbons;
Chief Alagbaa Awo Ifa Tayese Erinfolami. Ile Eko Sango/Osun Mil'osa,
Santa Cruz, Trinidad, 2015. Photo by N. Fadeke Castor.

This book is for all those who came before,
who paved the way,
whose footsteps I walk in,
and shoulders I stand on.

This is for you.

Mo dupe lopo lopo.

CONTENTS

Yorùbá is one of the four official languages of Nigeria and is a member of the Niger-Congo family of languages. About thirty million people speak forms of Yorùbá, from nations in West Africa (e.g., southwest Nigeria, Benin, Togo) to nations throughout the Americas (e.g., Brazil, Trinidad, and the United States).[1]

Continental Yorùbá

Yorùbá is a tonal language with three tones: high, mid, and low. High tone is indicated by an acute accent. Low tone is indicated by a grave accent, and mid tone is left unmarked. Continental Yorùbá has seven vowels. Continental Yorùbá spelling uses an underdot to distinguish the sixth and seventh vowels with the following American English pronunciation equivalents:

a   father
e   bait
ẹ   bet
i   beat
o   boat
ọ   bought
u   boot

For consonants, Continental Yorùbá spelling uses the underdot with the letter s to distinguish the alveolar and palatal voiceless fricatives spelled with an 's' and 'sh' in English. The only consonantal pronunciations unfamiliar to speakers of Spanish, Portuguese, and English are /k͡p/ and /g͡b/. What distinguishes them from their European-language counterparts is simultaneous closure. Because Yorùbá does not have a /p/, the orthography spells these phonemes using 'p' and 'gb' respectively.

Diasporic Yoruba

Throughout the African diaspora, members of Yoruba-based religious communities speak forms of Yoruba, including in Cuba a creole mixed with Spanish (Lucumi). Although Continental Yorùbá is a tone language, most Diasporic forms of Yoruba have suprasegmental systems based on those of the dominant languages in those countries, i.e. Spanish, Portuguese, and English. To reflect this reality, I do not mark tone in Diasporic Yoruba spellings.

Like Spanish, varieties of Yoruba spoken in Spanish-speaking countries only have five vowels, so the spelling of those varieties does not employ the underdot. It is helpful to add a note here on the variability of spelling norms. For example, in the diaspora, key terms like Òrìṣà (Continental Yorùbá orthography) may be written as Orisa, Orisha, Oricha, or Orixa depending on the orthography of the dominant language. The first two spellings are most common in English, the third in Spanish, and the last in Portuguese. When writing about Yorùbá-based religions in the diaspora, many authors use the spelling that corresponds to that tradition. For example, when writing about Brazilian Candomblé in English, many authors use standardized Portuguese spellings of Yorùbá words, such as Oxum and Orixa.

In this text I use Diasporic Yoruba when discussing Yorùbá-based religious communities and their ritual practices in the Americas. The titles and names of diasporic individuals will remain unmarked (no diacritical marks).

In the case of naming Yorùbá elders from West Africa, all efforts will be made to use the correct marks for their names. Yorùbá place-names and terms, when referencing Continental Yorùbá, will also reflect standard Yorùbá orthography.

"Save her, she's mine." Those words have haunted me for years. And in responding to their call, I have been on a long journey—a journey that has taken me to this place of making an offering; an offering to the ancestors and an offering to you, my readers. In doing so I find myself being called to come out of the "spiritual closet," as it were, for as M. Jacqui Alexander reminds us, "pedagogies of the Sacred" are needed for us to make sense of ourselves (2006, 15). The spiritual teachings and initiations that brought about this work will come as no surprise to those I have worked with over the years in Trinidad, even as they may be news to some people in the academy. Unlike many Western academics who have studied the Yoruba religion, I did not answer the call of Spirit while conducting research in the field. It was in fact the other way around for me. The spirits, specifically the ancestors, sent me to graduate school to study them.

When I was in graduate school, a faculty member warned me that studying the Yoruba people, their culture, and traditional religion could come with a stigma because academics would question my subjectivity if I came to follow the Yoruba spirits, the Orisha. "Too late," I thought. They were among the spirits who had sent me to graduate school and started me on the path that eventually led me here, to this work that you are reading. Leading me to this place of stark vulnerability where I tell my stories and in doing so offer a secret that I had tucked away back when I started school. Holding on to it until I was ready to take it out and put it on, simultaneously coming out of the spiritual closet and embracing my power. As Audre Lorde tells us, "The woman's place of power within each of us is neither white, nor surface; it is dark, it is ancient and it is deep" (2007, 37). It is from this deep space that I move forward on this journey (for it is ongoing) to answer Oshun's call. This offering began a long time ago.

Standing behind the counter in a pagan bookstore, surrounded by herbs, candles, and crystal balls, I had no idea that the next few moments would be critical to changing my life. I didn't know enough to recognize the voice of God/dess talking to me, talking about me. I couldn't have named that voice. I couldn't have named her if I'd been asked. I did know enough to be aware that something was happening—and that it was an important happening.

From my black combat boots and up through the many piercings, I looked like any other Bay Area punk rocker. (This was the early 1990s. Were we post-punk yet? We certainly didn't think so at the time.) Well, maybe with the exception of my darker skin and nappy hair. There weren't many black punk rockers then (or now). And there was definitely no Afro-punk scene back then. This was back in the "primitive" times of no popular Internet (sure, DARPA existed, but who knew about that?!). Strangely enough, for all my uniqueness, the woman standing next to me could have been my twin—another pierced black woman dressed head to toe in black. She was my coworker, my neighbor, and my best friend. And she was my coconspirator in all things not good for us.

So what was going on that day? How did two disaffected black punk rockers come to the attention of God/dess? This may be hard to believe, but it started with a candle. You know those seven-day candles in glass you can buy at the grocery store? Among many other "magical" supplies, the store where I worked sold these candles. And for a small fee the candle could be dressed. "Dressed" here does not refer to putting on clothes but rather to anchoring a blessing with glitter and oil. I would take a candle, say green for wealth, and sprinkle glitter on top from a shaker. Gold glitter would go first—for money again. Then maybe some blue (the color associated with Jupiter, for luck in material endeavors). And then an added dash of silver for blessings of spirit. The color associations were seemingly personal and arbitrary. Everyone had his or her own system, yet the associations were only somewhat arbitrary—they were linked into a larger system of signs drawing heavily on astrology and pagan cosmologies.

So on that day I dressed a candle; yellow, I think. After sprinkling the glitter, I added a few drops of oil. I don't remember which oil, but it would have been one labeled something like "Attraction," "Court Case," "Fire of Love," "Job," or "Money Drawing." These oils are another level of dressing designed to attract specific energies (as clearly designated by their names) to that candle. Once the glitter and oil are added, a prayer can be said, and then a film of wax stretched over the top seals the newly "consecrated" candle. This keeps the energies (and glitter and oil) in place until the customer activates them by lighting the candle. All this for less than $2.50! Which was a bargain even in 1990s dollars.

How, then, did dressing this candle for someone else lead to God/dess talking about me and to me? How did this change my life and put me onto the path that would lead to this book, this story? All I can say is that opportunity presented itself: opportunity for the divine to lay a claim and give a charge. And I was not completely unaware. I felt the tremors of energy then. Even now, twenty years later, I can remember how that buildup of energy felt.

I had recently been reading from the books that we stocked mainly on Wicca and other forms of European paganism. Among the very few titles on African diasporic religion and spirituality, I recognized the book *Jambalaya* (1985) by Luisah Teish. The cover, with its drawing of a snake encircling a black woman's head, was memorable. I knew this book from my college days. One of my classes was Womanist Theology, with visiting scholar Carol P. Christ. Though the class was largely focused on European paganism, we had read parts of this book based on New Orleans voodoo and drawing on Afro-Caribbean/West African Orisha religions. *Jambalaya* was a groundbreaker when it came out in the mid-1980s. Nothing like it could be found in bookstores—a strong black woman's voice asserting the power of her ancestral traditions. In the calls to listen to "she who whispers," that inner voice (or spirit guide), she addressed the power in her own voice. And while doing so she asserted the power of women's voices everywhere, especially the voices of women of color.

Yes, I'm still talking about how dressing a candle led me to hear the voice of God/dess. Remember that in that moment I had felt a charge of energy, which I largely attributed to dressing the candle. As I bagged the candle and rang up the sale, I marveled, "I just dressed a candle for Luisah Teish. She wrote that book, *Jambalaya*. Wow!" Left there, I would have taken it as a good sign, as a shift in fortunes perhaps. Maybe better things were coming?

I had just recently come back. For I had run away from Oakland. You know, the fight-or-flight response? Mine had been triggered, and I had fled— all the way to Los Angeles! All the way to the home of my former college, tucked in the San Gabriel Valley. What would cause me to fly so far? In those days I had little to no money from my part-time, seven-dollar-an-hour cashier job at the pagan bookstore. And keeping up my bad habits took most of that. As broke as I was, LA was really far (and to this day I have no idea how I got there and back; for sure it wasn't by plane, so I must have gotten a ride somehow). What was I running from? Mookie died. Rather, Mookie was killed. Run over by a car on Martin Luther King Drive, five times. They hit him, backed over him, and then did it again and again. Living on the margins, Mookie had crossed the wrong person. He was my friend and his death filled me with horror and fear. A fear for him, already realized. And a fear for me, a fear for my future. Is this how little his life, our lives, my life was worth?

So I had fled to the last safe place I knew. I went south to SoCal and away from this place where my friend was run down in the streets. After seeing old friends, old haunts and getting grounded in affirmations of life I came back to Oakland and my shared apartment, to my part-time job, and to my best friend and partner in crime. The fall of 1993 was an unsettled time for me, to say the least. I would later recognize this as a period of liminality,[1] where I was not what I had been but not yet what I would become. Or, in less abstract terms, I was ready for a change.

This context frames this moment when God/dess talked—and, more important, when I listened. "Thank you for your purchase. Please come again." I imagine that I said something this innocuous to Luisah Teish as I handed her the brown bag wrapping her dressed candle. And I am sure that she thanked me before she turned to leave. A tall, beautiful woman, she had a strong presence even in the mundane movement of walking to the exit. Part of the grace in her bearing came from a background in dance, including time studying with Katherine Dunham. Maybe this was why I was watching her. And maybe it is why when she turned it was so fluid. As if she was dancing, her lifted leg leading her body 180 degrees to face the counter.

And then again, maybe it was the God/dess in her. Literally the God/dess in her.

"Save them!" a voice cried from where she stood. And there was a look on her face that I had never seen. Her eyes were wide, fixed, and bright. As she stared straight ahead, her hand lifted to point a finger, first at me and then at my friend. Swinging toward a third person, our senior coworker, she commanded again, insistently, "They are my children. Save them."

With her message delivered, all the energy left the space, like a light going out. She was Teish again. She looked at our coworker, her goddaughter, we would learn later, as if to say, "You hear?" Glances were exchanged. Seemingly satisfied, she turned and departed. Teish/Oshun had left the building, but she had left behind a charge—in fact a divine charge. And that meant it was not to be questioned, it was to be obeyed. Our coworker was an "older" African American woman, and she let out a loud sigh as she came to this realization. (I must remark that my friend and I were both in our early twenties, and at that point everyone seemed older. Our coworker could have been thirty or fifty!) She turned to us, her skeptical gaze looking us up and down, then said, "That was Oshun who spoke. And whether I like it or not, I'm going to have to try." We didn't know what she felt compelled to try. And we also didn't know at the time that she was an Orisha devotee and served that Yoruba feminine energy called Oshun, the energy of fresh water, creativity, and women's power.

The "save them" part remained unspoken between us. Again she sighed and looked us up and down, taking in our black boots, our artfully torn black jeans, and the flashes of metal from our piercings—nose and belly buttons hinting at others unseen. She was dressed all in white, making for a sharp contrast, one echoed by the difference in our energies, like the difference between a gentle breeze and the storm winds of a tornado. Her repeated sighs conveyed both her distress and her submission—distress at the task in front of her and simultaneous submission to Oshun's charge. Working together until our shifts ended and the last customer left, we locked the door and turned the battered "Open/Closed" sign in the window. It was then that she addressed us: "Look, I'm going to invite you to my house, to a ritual. And before you come you'll have to do what I say." The instructions that followed would turn out to be a litmus test. Were we committed? Were we up to the challenge? Were we ready?

I offer this story, one of my more precious memories, as the turning point. This was the key that led me to this journey of spiritual citizenship. Oshun provided the key, but it took me (and my Ori, or personal divine consciousness) to turn the key in the lock and then go through the opened door. Since then, I have walked a path illuminated by the ancestors, those upon whose shoulders I stand. Orisha, divine emissaries of God/dess (Olodumare), and Ifá (wisdom of Olodumare) have provided help along the way. And twenty-plus years into the journey, Ẹgbẹ́ Ọ̀run (spiritual comrades from heaven) revealed the direction, gifts, and company that had been mine all along. Indeed, it turns out that Spirit has been with me all along.

ACKNOWLEDGMENTS

I give thanks to those who have come before me, to my ancestors: *Mo juba Egun, Mo Dupe*. A special note of recognition and honor to those who made the passage to the spiritual realms as this project was under way and whose unconditional love smoothed my path: Aldwyn Clarke, my uncle; Charlene Beckles, my childhood friend; Hilda Castor, my paternal grandmother; and Ivy Carmen Walke, my maternal great-aunt. This book is dedicated to them and to all the ancestors upon whose shoulders I stand. I would not be here without them. Included among the ancestors are many scholars who paved the way. I drew on their energy, words and spirits, including (and this is by no means a complete list) Audre Lorde, Frantz Fanon, Zora Neale Hurston, Katherine Dunham, and Stuart Hall. Special mention of my mentor who inspires me every day and left us too soon, Michel-Rolph Trouillot; while his name may not be on every page, his spirit is. I hope that he would be proud. *Mo juba Egungun.*

The roots for this project took shape while I was a graduate student at the University of Chicago. Thanks to my doctoral committee (Andrew Apter, Jean Comaroff, Michel-Rolph Trouillot, Stephan Palmié) and the faculty of the Department of Anthropology at the University of Chicago for providing me the space and intellectual nourishment to grow as a scholar and into an anthropologist. Special thanks go to John Comaroff for encouraging me to stay in the field as long as I could (three years!). That one remark at just the right time was a true gift. No thank-you to Chicago Anthropology would be complete without recognition of Anne Ch'ien and her remarkable support. Truly generations of us, myself included, would not be where we are or have accomplished half as much without her. Thank you, Anne! And last but in no way least, at UC, Michael Dawson and the Center for the Study of Race, Politics, and Culture provided me an intellectual home, engaging work, occasional funding, and safe harbor. Much thanks.

I gratefully acknowledge fellowship awards from the Wenner-Gren Foundation (Grant 6956) and the Fulbright-Hays Doctoral Dissertation Research Abroad Program that supported portions of my fieldwork. Additionally, funding from the Tinker Field Research Grant, Center for Latin American Studies; African Language Grant, African Studies Committee; Research Grant, Center for the Study of Race, Politics and Culture; and the Division of Social Sciences at the University of Chicago facilitated fieldwork in Trinidad, which provided the initial research for this book. At Texas A&M University, I received funding from the Office of the Vice President's Program to Enhance Scholarly and Creative Activities grant, which supported additional and important fieldwork research in Trinidad; I am thankful for that support at a critical time. Funding at Texas A&M University was also provided by the College of Liberal Arts, the Africana Studies Program, and the Department of Anthropology. Special thanks to the Glasscock Center for the Humanities for consistently supporting this project, especially with a research grant that supported my fieldwork in Nigeria. Importantly, the Glasscock Center provided a grant toward the publication of this volume. Thank you.

Texas A&M University has provided me with an academic home and supportive environment to finish this manuscript. My thanks go to the faculty and staff (especially, Annette Jackson, for always being there) of the Department of Anthropology and to the Africana Studies Program, core members including Adrienne Carter-Sowell, and Alain Lawo-Sukam, with a special mention to my colleagues David Donkor and Phia Salter, who kept me company and saw me through. The special energy, intellect, and commitment of Kimberly Brown brought me to Texas A&M, which I will never forget; much thanks for her unflagging faith in this work. At Texas A&M, my colleagues Rob Carley, Donnalee Dox, Dan Humphrey, Shona Jackson, Kathi Miner, Rebecca Hankins, Wendy Leo Moore, and Jason Parker were generous interlocutors, always willing to offer an ear or a shoulder. My appreciation to my graduate student and research assistant, Myeshia Babers, for sharing large parts of this journey with me, being there in a pinch, and helping with copyediting at several crucial moments.

I extend my thanks to the TAMU students who assisted me with interview transcription, including Myeshia Bobers, James Johnson, Karen Martindale, and Taylor Rhoades. My thanks to Marcy Haltermann and Celeste Riley, who are a central part of my support community in BCS that kept me together body and mind while I wrote. In Texas, my family away from family are the Myers family: Jesse, Marilyn, Stephen, and all the Myers out of state—thank you for being there for me. Large parts of this book were written in cafés throughout the Bryan/College Station area. A big shout-out and thank-you to all the baristas, counter folks, and other good people who kept me in decaf (so I could drink plenty!) and company over the long hours. Café encounters with numerous folks provided sustenance and at times inspiration; I owe a special debt to Negar Kalantar and Alireza Borhani, who recognized the universal aspect of my work and mirrored it back to me at critical moments. Many thanks.

Portions of this book have benefited from warm receptions and generous critiques at various conferences, seminars, and workshops: African Studies Workshop, University of Chicago; Glasscock Center for the Humanities, Texas A&M University; Harvard University; Obafemi Awolowo University, Ilè-Ifè, Nigeria; North Carolina Central University; Philosophical Society of Trinidad and Tobago; University of California, Berkeley; University of Texas at Austin; University of the West Indies at Mona, Jamaica; and University of the West Indies at St. Augustine, Trinidad and Tobago.

I owe a special debt of gratitude to Tommy De Frantz, E. Patrick-Johnson, Tavia Nyong'o, Jason King, Jennifer DeVere Brody, Venus Opal Reese, Anna Scott, Omi Osun Joni Jones, Anita Gonzalez, Hershini Bhana Young, Harvey Young, Koritha Mitchell, Omise'eke Natasha Tinsley, Matt Richardson, Melissa Blanco Borelli, Rashida Braggs, Uri MacMillan, Sarah Jane Cervenac, Grisha Coleman, Yolanda Covington Ward, Raquel Monroe, Stephanie Batiste, Jayna Brown, Daniel Alexander Jones, Tamara Roberts, Racquel Gates. The Black Performance Theory working group: Thanks to Anne-Marie Bean for inviting me in, to everyone for welcoming me, and to Tommy for mentoring me at crucial junctures. Special thanks to Jeffrey McCune, a journey mate in the BPT community and beyond, for being kinfolk in its most important sense. Whenever and wherever I go, I will work to pay forward the invaluable lessons that have helped me on my way—lessons in creating generative space, witnessing, and the power of embodiment in the creation and negotiation of theory.

It is hard to list all the scholars whose questions, encouragement, support, and inspirational example contributed to the completion of the manuscript. Please forgive any omissions; they only reflect my own absentmindedness and not a lack of deserved gratitude. I give thanks for being in the company of, and sharing in this academic journey with, amazing scholars: the Florida International University Interrogating the African Diaspora crew, including

Jean Rahier, Carole Boyce Davies, Barnor Hesse, David Goldberg, Philomena Essed, and Michael Hanchard; at Williams College, Michael Brown, Olga Shevchenko, Joy James, Gretchen Long, and Kenda Mutongi; African and African Diaspora Studies faculty at Duke University, including Mark Anthony Neal, Wahneema Lubiano, Maurice Wallace, Lee Baker, Michaeline Crichlow, Anne-Maria Makhulu, Charles Piot, and Bayo Holsey (now at Rutgers); members of the Association of Black Anthropologists, especially Deborah Thomas, John Jackson, Aimee Cox, Patricia Van Leeuwaarde Moonsammy, David Simmons, Gina Athena Ulysse, Jafari Allen, Bertin Louis, Elizabeth Joy Chin, and Faye Harrison; and my African and Diasporic Religions Association crew, Funlayo E. Wood, Deanna Oyafemi Lowman, Lisa Osunleti, Nzinga Oyaniyi, Khytie Brown, Okomfo Ama Boakyewa, and Koko Zauditu-Selassie. Many thanks to the dialogue, in person and through their work, who have contributed to this project, including: M. Jacqui Alexander, Kai Barratt, Ryan Bazinet, Kamari Maxine Clarke, Renee Alexander Craft, Dianne Diakité, Maarit Forde, Laurie Frederik, Lyndon Gil, Tracey Hucks, Yanique Hume, Erica James, Keith McNeal, Achille Mbembe, Lisa Outar, Rachel Afi Quinn, Barbara Ransby, Neha Vora, and Meccasia Zabriskie. Special thanks to Aisha Khan for her generous mentorship and friendship.

Truly this book is the product of a widespread community, in this realm and others: *Ese pupo gbogbo*! Much of the credit for this project goes to the many friends who held my hand and walked with me on this journey. They spent countless hours on the phone and on the computer with me, alternately sharing, grousing, and commiserating. A shout-out to the Chicago Trini Posse, with a special note of gratitude to Denise Borel-Billups, Marlon Billups, and Lima Redhead for being there through thick and thin. Fellow travelers on this journey who started in Chicago, though some of us ended up in faraway places, were wonderful companions: Meida McNeal, Beth Buggenhagen, Chris Corcoran, Alice Jones-Nelson, and Paul Ryer; many thanks for all the late-night calls and last-minute critical support at various stages along the way. Thank you, my friends, for always being there with just the right word of encouragement at just the right time.

Three people supported me during revisions to the book's completion. Without their critical input and invaluable feedback on numerous manuscript drafts, this book would not be what it is (and, of course, all mistakes are my own). *Mo dupe*, Eniola Adelekan, Colleen Madden, and Andrew Nolan. Saying thank you is inadequate for the energy that you have put into this book. I hope that you see your efforts reflected in these pages!

This project would not have happened without the entry, at different times and to different extents, that I was granted into the kind hearts, creative communities, sharp minds, and open homes in Trinidad. Those who helped me are too numerous to name individually, but let me offer here a collective thank-you! I owe much to Burton Sankeralli, a friend and guide from the first, and our many hours of conversation and limes. At the University of the West Indies (UWI), support for this project came from the Center for Creative and Festive Arts and Rawle Gibbons. Patricia Mohammed contributed insightful comments and guidance at various stages. An extended community of scholars and artists at UWI, from the St. Augustine campus to the Mona campus, provided inspiration as well as critiques on different versions of this project, often in the context of a good lime: Ella Andall, LeRoy Clarke, Makemba Kunle, Carolyn Cooper, Gabrielle Hosein, Maureen Warner-Lewis and Rupert Lewis, Earl Lovelace, Peter Ray Blood, and Gordon Rohlehr.

In Trinidad, many members of the Orisha community—too many to name here—helped me along the way. I give honor and praise to all those who shared their spirits with me over the many years of this project. Special mention must be made of Iya Sangowunmi, Iyalode Loogun Osun Sangodasawande, who appears in these pages, for opening her home, shrine, family, and heart to me. *Mo dupe Iyalode.* There would be no project without her active intellect, warm heart, and open arms. My thanks extend to the members of Ile Eko Sango/Osun Mil'osa and to her entire family, especially those who have returned home to the ancestral realm: I.T. McLeod, Curt McLeod and Charlie McLeod. My spiritual family in Trinidad extends far and wide. At the core there are those I shared the mat with: Marc Awosope La Veau, Nadine Omallo (iba), Marvin George, and Dominique Braud. In the wider Orisha community my path has crossed those of many who lent assistance—whether by listening to the project and providing feedback, feeding my spirit, or both. *Ese pupo gaani.*

Much gratitude is extended to the elders who have helped to shape this project, many of whom generously shared their spiritual journeys in interviews: Oba Adefunmi II, Awo Ifa Korede, Baba Sangodele, Iya Amoye, Baba Clarence Forde, Baba Sam Phills, Iya Osunyemi, Chief Abiodun, Chief Ogunbowale, Iyanifa Bangela, Iya Omilade, Iya Ajiwenu, Iya Turunesh Raymond, Baba Avery Ammon, Baba Afuwape, Baba Ogunkeye, L'Antoinette Stein (of Jamaica, though our paths crossed as much in Trinidad), Chief Oludari Olakela Massentugi, Iyalode Awo Agbaye Ifakorede Oyayemi Aworeni (Mother Joan); Agba Ifagbola, Agba Ifasina Oyabinde, Agba Makanjuola, Awo Ifakolade Atinumo, Baba Menes de Griot, Oba Kiteme, Babu Ketema, Rubadiri Victor. Baba Ifakunle deserves special mention here for his support and generosity of spirit; even though he is the *babalawo* of Harlem, NY, whether here or there our interactions were always grounded in Trini soil. Special thanks go to Chief Alagba Erinfolami for generously sharing his stories and wisdom.

Thanks to all the soca artistes whose music fed my spirit and fueled my writing, reminding me of "home" all the while, wherever my body may have been in the moment. A special thanks to Machel Montano for the music, the work, and the friendship. You were there when I needed you, and I give thanks for our time working together; even though the soca research we did is not included in this volume, the spirit of your work runs throughout.

I was blessed to be cared for not only by spiritual family but also by, as they say, "blood" and "pumpkin vine" family in Trinidad. My family there all took care of me: the Castors, especially Uncle Keith and Uncle Philip; and the Walkes, especially Aunt Ivy, Aunt Grace, Aunt Mona, my cousin Michael, and his family: Rosemary, Christian, Samuel, Karin, David, and Faith; my godfather, Uncle Boykin, and my cousins George, Nardie, and Kieko Daniel. The Clarke family embraced and encouraged me while providing unflagging support: Tricia (and Marvin, Ethan, and Samantha), Kevin and Hazel, Aldwyn Jr., Aunt Judy (and all her sisters, Aunt Cheryl, Aunt Simone, Aunt Pat, and Aunt JoAnne, thanks for being my aunts), Aunt Vera, Aunt Lynette, Uncle Erwin, and Dionne Boissiere. And a special mention for someone who always loved me up and always knew that I could do it, Aldwyn Clarke Sr. The Clarkes took me into their family and treated me as their own; they have my eternal gratitude and love. My love and thanks to other branches of my Trini family, including Michel and John Andrews, Curtis Bachan, George Henry, Fayola Kunle, Natasha Mark, LouAnna Martin, and Bert Seales.

The spiritual community of Ile Oshun Orunmila provided me the solid foundation from which I stepped forward on my path. I would not be where I am without the initial guidance and teachings of Yeye Oshunmiwa Luisah Teish, Awo Falokun David Wilson and Iya Oshogbo Uzuri Amani. *Mo dupe.* I continue to walk my path alongside a diaspora of godbrothers and godsisters, all of whom have enriched my journey: Awo Fasegun Falokun (aka Baba Earl), Baba Alalade (Watts then, Andrew now), Iya Selena Allen, Iya Risha Henry, Iya Omisade Amy Gerhauser, and Iya Ifalola Omobola. I give great respect to all the spiritual brethren and sistren whom I have met along the way.

My gratitude also follows the transnational paths that I document, crossing the Atlantic to Nigeria. I am forever grateful for the hospitality, teachings, and fellowship provided by Oloye Ṣọlágbade Pópoólá and his family in Odewale Town, Ogun State, Nigeria. That will always be a special spiritual home to me. A major part of this journey was finding my voice, and a major part of that was finding my Ẹgbẹ́ Ọrun. *Ese pupo* to Oloye Pópóọlá for opening that door and to my Iya Egbe for guiding me. I could not have gotten by without the care of all the Iya, especially Iya Alaje, Iya Ṣola, Iya Iyabo from Togo and Iya Adeyosola. I received guidance, instruction, and much patience from Awo Alaje, Ojugbona, and the other priests of the Ogbè Alárá temple. *Aburo aboye.* Thank you to all the omo awo, who endured my many questions, showed me around, and took such good care of me: Omo Awo Ifagbemileke, Omo Awo Nimbe, Omo Awo Ṣola Pópóọla, Omo Awo Awolola, Omo Awo Fasegun, and Omo Awo Taiye. *Ese pupo gaaaaani!* Throughout Nigeria, I was met with kindness and hospitality. Special thanks in Oṣogbo to Awodiran Agboola, Agbongbon Fakoyade Faniyi and his family, and Iya Doyin and to the numerous priests who located keys and opened up shrines for me to visit, pray, and make offerings in Ilé-Ifẹ̀. I know that the spirit of Oluorogbo helped me to finish this book; I give thanks.

This project has come to fruition in large part due the discerning critical input and unflagging support of Ken Wissoker over many years. Thank you, Ken, for believing in this project when it was just a thought, and for meeting me vision for vision in what it could (and would) come to be. The two anonymous reviewers for Duke University Press could not have been more on point and helpful as they provided needed truths, pushes, and affirmations. This book is the better for their suggestions, guidance, and calls for clarification or elaboration. I am blessed, as this was truly an exemplary review process. My gratitude also for the great team at Duke University Press, project editor Sara Leone, editorial assistants extraordinaire Maryam Arain, and Jade Brooks, and copyeditor Susan Ecklund for their wonderful mix of insight, kindness, and professionalism.

I would like to give special thanks to my family for their infinite love, support, wisdom, and patience: Mom (thanks for all the prayers and one-day-at-a-time and first-things-first pep talks) and Leighton; Dad and Judith Mom, and my brothers Justin and Trevor. I am very grateful for their unwavering faith that I could finish what I started; it has been a continuous source of support.

And last, but always first, I say a singular thank-you to my husband, Awo Ifásèyítán Taiwo Thompson, my partner in this marketplace. I am so grateful for the day that we met and decided to join our journeys together. Your unflagging support and wise counsel have meant everything in the final stages of this project. Mo dupe.

An earlier version of chapter 2 appeared in *Cultural Anthropology* as "Shifting Multicultural Citizenship: Trinidad Orisha Opens the Road" (2013). Though many hands have helped me on this journey, I take full responsibility for any errors or shortcomings that may appear in this text.

Pathways to Spiritual Citizenship

"You will travel widely, all over the globe." I heard these words with a disbelief that must have shown on my face. "Really, this is what Ifá says," the babalawo said in a thick Nigerian accent. In that moment I didn't know who or what a babalawo was or what Ifá was. I just knew that they were wrong. I had little more than the change in my pocket to my name, and none that I could spare. I had no official identification let alone a passport. I could barely afford to get a ticket to ride the train across the Bay, from Oakland to San Francisco.

"Who do you think you are?" Those were the words that went through my head. And I am sure they were visible on my face. Across from me the Ifá priest looked at me with a kind and knowing appraisal. He had seen this before with other clients. And having divined for me, he had seen aspects of my destiny. Looking down at the mat, he told me, "Ògún is very important for you." I wrote "Oggum" in my notes, a misspelling that reflected my lack of knowledge. I had never heard that word before. And of the many ways to spell Ogun in the diaspora, that is not one of them.

Only a few weeks earlier I had been at work when Oshun, the Yorùbá Orìsà of creativity, fresh water, and women's power, had manifested (see appendix II). In the middle of the day she had possessed one of her priests in a pagan bookstore. Oshun claimed me as her own that day, "Save her," she commanded, "She's mine." That mandate had brought me to a small apartment above a garage in Oakland where I sat across from a Nigerian

FIGURE INTRO.1 His Royal Majesty Oba Adébólú Fátunmise, the Àdàgbà of Iyánfowórogi (then Chief Fátunmise) in Port of Spain, Trinidad for the Sixth World Congress of Orisha Tradition and Culture, 1999. Photo by N. Fadeke Castor.

elder, who introduced himself as Bólú Fátunmise.[1] I would later learn that he was an eighth-generation Ifá priest, or babaláwo, from Ilé-Ifè, Nigeria (and it would be many more years before I started to grasp the implications of this).

In that moment, hearing that Ogun was important to me, I was lost. Lost and uncomfortable, sitting there in borrowed and ill-fitting light-colored clothes. For all my own clothes were black. I had been instructed to wear white if possible, light colors even, but under no circumstances black! Over the next several months I would learn that for this group black cloth was associated with negative energy as they believed it absorbed all energies—both good and bad. Right then I just felt annoyance piled on top of the discomfort. I was way outside my comfort zone. And that annoyance was linked to my feeling that these people thought there was something wrong with me, something unclean.

It was the instructions to take a bath that had started my journey to that living room where I sat while a stranger told me unbelievable things about my future. Or, more accurately, the journey had started with the decision to take a "spiritual" bath. I still distinctly remember standing in my kitchen talking to my roommate. I tried to explain the experience of being commanded by a voice from God/dess. And described my dilemma: "They want me to take a bath before I go to this thing. With milk. And then dress in white." I shook my head not only at the milk bath but also because I wondered where would I, who wore only black, get white clothes?

"I don't know why. I just feel that this is important," I explained that I was at a crossroads saying, "If I do this everything will change." I can still feel the sink pressing into my back as I took in the liminality, the in-betweenness, of the moment. Do what I had been doing (with grimmer and grimmer consequences visible all around me) or make this change? Take a bath? There was a deep breath, a shrug, and then a decision that a bath couldn't hurt. Even if it seemed kind of weird to bathe in milk and flowers, I had done stranger things. Just this one little step, and then I would see. That one decision, to take that bath, put my feet on the path to uncovering my destiny and learning to hear from and speak to God/dess in one of her many forms. A path that over two decades led me home to the land of my ancestors, to my own initiations, and to membership in a transnational spiritual community. Just as Awo Bólú Fátunmise told me, I would indeed "travel the globe." Taking that bath was a critical decision, an opening to a new path.

Later I would learn that the event I was spiritually cleansing for was a ritual celebration of a new Orisha priest. One of Luisah Teish's godchildren (in this religion relations are mapped through terms of spiritual kinship) had received initiation to Obatala, the Orisha of creation and wisdom, whose symbol is white cloth. On the day that I went, the new initiate, or *iyawo,* was being presented to the community. She was not allowed out from her corner (or "throne") as the initiation was not yet complete (it would be finished later in the week). Her rite of passage still had more phases to go; as of that moment when I saw her, she was still liminal (Turner 1969). I was not the only person experiencing liminality.

On the day I went, I found myself drawn in by the beating of drums as I walked into the house nervous as could be. My late arrival meant that I entered a room bursting with people and energy. On one end of the room was a space blocked off by white fabric, which surrounded and supported piles of fruit, food, and flowers. To my uneducated gaze there was a jumble of things around a seated figure clothed in white, a strange figure hidden from full view by the veil of her crown. Decades later, I can still remember the eerie calm and serenity of this person in the middle of a room of pulsing energy. Overcome by all that energy, feeling both invisible and out of place, I fled outside. There I reached for a familiar comfort and lit a cigarette.

"No, no, no—none of that. You can't do that here," came the loud reprimand from one of the many people dressed elegantly in all white. And standing there in my ill-fitting borrowed clothes, I knew no one. And I was being admonished for doing the one thing that gave me comfort, smoking. Just then a man, dressed in bright, rich colors, came to my rescue. "It's okay, just take it away from the house. Come down here to the end of the driveway." Looking at the other person, he quickly added, "She meant no harm. I don't think she knew." From the other person's reaction, who quickly backed down, I could tell my defender was a person of status. And from the style of his colorful clothes I took him to be a foreigner. And from his accent I guessed he must be from somewhere in West Africa.

That was how I met my first Ifá priest, Awo Bólú Fátunmise, and got my first Ifá reading. That was how I ended up in the garage apartment hearing that I would travel the world. As a visiting Nigerian elder, Awo Fátunmise was conducting Ifá divinations. This divination is a core ritual of Ifá priests in which clients receive answers to questions, remedies to problems, and information about their future. (While writing this, I realized that he must have been charging for those divination sessions. I have no memory of paying, however, or even of being able to pay had I been asked.)

I still have the few words jotted down on a torn piece of pink notebook paper. Those were my very first notes on an Ifá reading and possibly my first notes for the project that ultimately gave birth to this book. For, indeed, I would stay and join that spiritual community. This reading would be my introduction to the cosmology of Yorùbá traditional religion and the ritual practices of serving the divine forces of nature and deified ancestors known as Orisha (in both the singular and the plural). I would learn that the Yorùbá referred to an ethnic group in West Africa with a complex history going back a thousand years (a history much older than the label "Yorùbá").[2] And that in the contemporary moment there were thirty million Yorùbá-language speakers throughout West Africa, with the majority of them residing in southwest Nigeria (a cultural region called Yorubaland). I would sort out my confusion after some time, for Yorùbá can refer to people, culture, religion, and/or language. And at a later moment I would learn that many African diasporic religions from Candomblé and Umbanda in Brazil to Santería in Cuba, identified with Yorùbá culture and religion (among other nations, notably the Kongo/Congo). Adding to my confusion was that the "Yorùbá" identified from the diaspora could be imagined, historical, contemporary, or a mix of all three!

Taking the bath, going to the ritual in borrowed whites, going for a "reading," as divinations are called, were all moments of spiritual praxis, even though I was unaware of this at the time. They were actions of cleansing, prayer, and sacrifice, all central to African diasporic religions (called alternatively Yorùbá, Òrìṣà/Orisha, or Ifá throughout this text). From taking a bath, to going to a ritual *bembe*, *feast*, or *tambor* (terms for the gathering where the gods are called with offerings, prayers, drums, dance, and song), to getting a reading and making offerings: these are all fundamental rituals. Elders would later teach me that the foundations of Yorùbá ritual include elements of cleansing or washing, prayers or invocations, divination or reading, and appeasing through offerings. In that first week I had done or seen several of these things. I would go on to eventually do all of them. And in doing so, my life would intersect with the lives of other travelers on this spiritual journey—travelers in Oakland, California; in Santa Cruz, Trinidad; and in Ilé-Ifè, Nigeria—and with the numerous spirits who accompanied me to the many places in between.

I would learn many names for these spirits that drew on Yorùbá cosmology, the chief among them Òrìṣà/Orisha (referred to as Orisha throughout the text). These supernatural and at times historical figures are the approachable aspects of God, evident in the forces of nature all around us. We have already met Ogun, who is the original ironworker, a surgeon, a warrior, and a king (among his many mythic aspects). Òṣun/Oshun, who in her way has brought us—writer and reader—here together, is the fresh water of the river, women's power, and the creativity of reproduction. She is all these things and much more. They say that there are 801 Orisha, with the 1 being the plus of infinity. Every aspect of God's creation is sacred, and every aspect of her creation can be encountered as an Orisha. It is because of this complexity and this magnitude that many call the Yorùbá religious tradition, on the continent and in the diaspora, the Orisha religion (or the plural "Orisha religions" to encompass the diasporic diversity).

Spiritual Citizenship is about the power of the sacred to inform new ways of belonging to community, the nation, and the transnational. In this book I engage the critical knowledge systems and ritual practices of African-based religions in the African diaspora. I locate contemporary Trinidad's Orisha and Ifá communities as inheritors of the promise of the 1970s Black Power movement.[3] From the turn of the millennium I draw on ethnographic materials to illuminate Orisha as engaged in the performance and practice of an emerging spiritual citizenship. The liberatory process of decolonization I identify draws on a spiritual praxis grounded in non-Western cosmologies and transnational spiritual networks that are embedded in a dynamic mixture of the historical, imagined, and contemporary Yorùbá. Informed by Yorùbá cosmology and a newly planted Ifá lineage, Orisha communities in Trinidad have embarked on a pathway of community building guided toward ideas of freedom, liberation, and social justice.

Trinidad and Tobago is a twin island nation-state whose society, culture, politics, and economics all bear the hallmarks of a colonial legacy. While independence in 1962 occurred politically and symbolically on many levels, decolonization (which I understand as a process and not a singular event) did not "naturally" occur as a consequence. The Orisha religion in Trinidad informs a *spiritual citizenship*, rooted in the African diaspora, that critically engages with inherited hierarchical legacies of identity and distinctions of difference. I found these critical engagements to be visible in both religious and performance practices, from aspects of the annual Carnival celebrations to everyday reconfigurations of time and space (e.g., the national pasttime of hanging out with friends, involving storytelling, music, and often libations known as *limin'*, that exists in a now-for-now moment).[4] I focus on spiritual practices of African religions as a form of critical engagement and performance rooted in the African diaspora and the black radical tradition. This engagement with a wide diasporic horizon that joins people beyond the local, the national, or even the regional into a series of global relations, I refer to as "transnational spiritual networks."

By spiritual citizenship I mean the rights and responsibilities of belonging to community, informed by spiritual epistemologies, that is, not limited to the national but also inclusive of the diasporic, global, and transnational. I draw on Aihwa Ong's definition of cultural citizenship as a point of departure, which refers to "the cultural practices and beliefs produced out of negotiating the often ambivalent and contested relations with the state and its hegemonic forms that establish the criteria of belonging within a national population and territory" (1999a, 264). Where Ong speaks of this culture, I expand the concept to include both the spiritual and the cultural. My identification of spiritual citizenship also encompasses "a dual process of self-making and being-made within webs of power linked to the nation-state and civil society" (264) while extending the scale of this formulation. I do so first by moving across space to both the smaller level of local communities and the larger level of the transnational and global communities. Then the scale also expands across time to deploy responsibilities across generations, both to those who are yet to come and to those who have come before. In forming diasporic community that draws on the resources of transnational spiritual communities to support and build locally and nationally, Yorùbá cosmology and ritual practices provide methods to access past generations (the ancestors) and heal historical wounds. This in turn informs a spiritual praxis that extends the healing to current and future generations.

Historically in Trinidad, spiritual citizenship has roots in the early British colonial period where individual and collective relation to the state (i.e., colonial governance) was informed, at least in part, by a religious understanding of the world. An early example of this was the organization of Yorùbá families in Diego Martin to purchase burial land for members of the African community. These families pooled their resources for this as many repatriated, indentured, and enslaved Africans were not Christian and thus, were barred from burial in church graveyards (Warner-Lewis 1996). While examples of spiritual citizenship such as this can be seen throughout the colonial period, my project here focuses on postindependence developments.[5] Specifically, the discourses of the 1970s Black Power movement in Trinidad (called a revolution by many) introduced critical questions aimed at changing inherited social relations that reproduced inequities along lines of race, class, color, and gender. Emergent from these conversations—and the social unrest that accompanied them—was a revalorization of non-European heritages, specifically the overgeneralized idea of "African." In the quest for non-European knowledge systems, values, and beliefs, many turned to African religions, both those at home and those from the African continent. This book explores this turn and how it has come to inform the understanding of belonging to community, asking: What is expected from belonging to a religious community? How does this inform the rights and responsibilities of belonging to the national community (being a Trinidadian) or to a larger global community (being a member of the African diaspora)? How do these levels of belonging then impact other facets of identity, be they race, color, class, or gender?

In exploring these questions, *Spiritual Citizenship* draws attention to critical cultural and spiritual practices. I match the spiritual together with citizenship as a means for understanding modes of belonging and the building of community informed by the sacred.

Rhizomatic Reflections

"Ogun onire, ogun onire." These words were still swirling in my mind as I left the Ile Eko Sango/Osun Mil'osa (IESOM) shrine, where I had just performed my duty as a child of Ogun (so I had been told). I had sung to Ogun to clear the road and open the way for the twenty-four-foot wood carving of Shango's sacred double-headed ax (*ose*) to get seated upright. As a crew of men worked the makeshift scaffolding and ropes to raise the statue into its fifteen-foot concrete base I had circled around and around, singing all the time, "Ogun onire, ogun onire."

After this spiritual labor, I was riding home over the hills, from one valley to the next, and reflecting on how the linear narrative that writing conventions demand fails to accommodate the nonlinear contradictory and polymorphous flow of Trinidad's cultural practices. The moving of the two-story carving from horizontal to vertical so that it could be seated in a fifteen-foot cement base was truly remarkable as it was done by six men with only ropes and shaky scaffolding (figure Intro. 2). I had been anxious to catch a ride home with Curt McLeod, the son of the shrine's spiritual mother. His SUV greatly facilitated the journey over curving, narrow roads, taking only forty-five minutes instead of the two to three hours that "traveling" (hailing route taxis on the road) through the capital of Port of Spain would have taken. And I needed to get ready for the other activities scheduled for later that same day.

For the raising of Shango's ose was happening during Carnival 2003. The day of the raising was a Sunday, when fetes are scheduled during the day or early evening to accommodate a Monday morning work schedule for most attendees (and organizers). I was attending, with some of my non-Orisha friends, a fete where I was sure to run into Iya Sangowunmi and other people from the shrine. For this was the McLeod Fete, hosted and organized by the McLeods' family business, led by I. T. McLeod and Pat McLeod (aka Iya Sangowunmi), the same couple that owns the several acres at the base of the Santa Cruz Mountains that are home to the IESOM shrine. Iya Sangowunmi leads IESOM and devotes her time, energy, and family resources to building a spiritual community there in order to fulfill her destiny (as outlined by her *ita*, the divine plan of her destiny) of bringing Orisha festivals to life in Trinidad.

I mention this story here to emphasize that the relation between Trinidad's cultural and spiritual practices, which at first glance are seemingly

FIGURE INTRO.2 Ile Eko Sango/Osun Mil'osa shrine members work together to place the twenty-four-foot statue of Shango's sacred double-headed ax (Ose Ṣhango; made by Yorùbá carver Hassan Olánipẹ̀kun) into its fifteen-foot base. Santa Cruz, Trinidad, 2003. Photo by N. Fadeke Castor.

separate and discrete, fold back on themselves to become self-referential. That is, they move away from the neat linearity largely privileged in Western narratives. After we had elevated Shango's ose, I left Iya at the shrine, garbed in ritual wear and ase (spiritual energy), only to meet her later that night at a middle-class outdoors nightclub set on a pier over the water of the Chaguaramas peninsula. All of this was on my mind as I looked out the window, as Curt deftly maneuvered over winding roads. Rather than focusing on the precipitous drop below, mere feet away from our tires, I concentrated on the equally tricky and fraught task of presenting a singular narrative of this Orisha religion in Trinidad as my ethnographic experiences presented me with everyday lived realities challenging to many accepted academic boundaries and categories.

Diasporic Articulations: Race, Citizenship, Religion, and Freedom

Spiritual Citizenship examines the performance of religion and ritual as situated within the context of transnational flows—that is, within the African diaspora. Critical to my study are understandings of the dynamics of diaspora as central to community; the centrality of spirit to the black radical imagination (freedom and liberation); identity and belonging (race and citizenship); and a recentering of difference that shifts the frame of multiculturalism from the exceptional to the everyday.

In my work on Trinidad's African diasporic religions, I have repeatedly observed the importance of the "diasporic horizon" (P. C. Johnson 2012). Diaspora is a complex term that references both community and identity, beyond its initial meaning in "dispersal." This key term has been widely discussed and analyzed in the academic literature (Clifford 1994; Hall 1999, 2003; P. C. Johnson 2012; Kelley 2000; Palmer 2000; D. Scott 1991).[6] I do not represent or restate this literature here. Rather, my intent is to highlight the facets of diaspora (and its theory) in relation to religion, which contributes to my argument on spiritual citizenship. The African diaspora is more than a community created through dispersal from a homeland. Diasporas are "social identifications based on shared memory bridges linking a lived space and a left-behind place" (P. C. Johnson 2007, 48). Diasporas, then, are performative communities invested in creating, negotiating, and traversing "bridges" between space and place.

This is especially true when diaspora is linked to religion. I find Johnson's conceptualization of "diasporic religions" useful for understanding the intersection of diaspora and religion that is so central to Trinidad Ifá/Orisha. When it comes to African diasporic religions, the possibility of doing away with diaspora is complicated by its widespread use throughout these communities. Thinking of diasporic religions as "the collected practices of dislocated social groups whose affiliation is not primarily or essentially based on religion but whose acts, locutions, and sentiments towards a distant homeland are mediated by, and articulated through, a religious culture" is particularly useful for my work (P. C. Johnson 2007, 258). This works very well with Trinidad's African diasporic religions, whose religious culture routinely and substantively performs diaspora. Through this performative they link disparate social groups to create communities, build networks, and inform identities. I am particularly cognizant of how diasporic religion works in Trinidad as "having family tree 'elsewhere,'" which engages historical memory (say, of the slave trade and colonialism) to reinforce for Orisha and Ifá devotees "a double consciousness in relation to place" that contributes to "an awareness [that] is central, even actively conjured in their lived experience" (P. C. Johnson 2007, 31).

For the people I work with, the diasporic elsewhere is a lived everyday reality, much more than an abstract concept. It is a far-flung and wide network of spiritual family and community members in an "imagined community" that operates materially, virtually, and in the imaginary (Anderson 1991). The diasporic religious community or, using my preferred term, transnational spiritual networks offer sources of knowledge, access to global hospitality (before Airbnb), connections for work and business, and opportunities to exchange spiritual fellowship. Much of this is standard to immigrant communities, usually characterized by nationality. The difference here is that this community operates across nationalities, even as its members are locally grounded in their respective nation-states (and bound by laws governing border crossing, such as those related to visas, which will be seen in chapter 5).[7]

I envision spiritual citizenship as part of the numerous visions of "the imagination of both political and social life beyond the territorial boundaries of the nation-state" (D. A. Thomas and Clarke 2013, 309) that have emerged in the shadow of modernity and the dispersion of millions of Africans that we understand as the African diaspora. I argue for a conceptualization of citizenship that exists beyond the nation-state, even as it works with, and through, the nation-state. And I claim this wider frame of citizenship as part of the heritage of Pan-Africanism, Black Power, Négritude, and other politically engaged conceptualizations of the African diaspora (or other black radical traditions). Thus, I do not separate diaspora from a global formulation of citizenship; the two go hand in hand for an understanding of how people of African descent make community and negotiate systems of power (including the nation-state) while also working toward liberation and freedom.

I understand Ifá/Orisha in Trinidad as a form of black liberation and as part of "black internationalism" that consists of global black movements with a history that predates the "new" globalization (West, Martin, and Williams 2009). These various movements, from Pan-Africanism to Négritude and beyond, engage what we now typify as the black radical imagination to embrace the "possibility of new social worlds" (West, Martin, and Williams 2009, 2; see also Apter 2016). In positioning the emergent spiritual citizenship of Trinidad's Ifá/Orisha community as part of the "globally connected waves of struggle by African peoples over the past two and half centuries" (West, Martin, and Williams 2009, 3), I reintroduce the spiritual and the religious to the political. Audre Lorde tells us, "The dichotomy between the political and the spiritual is also false" (2007, 56). An examination of important moments of historical conjuncture, such as the Black Power movement in Trinidad, reveals the importance of continuing to break down artificial divides, like that between the sacred and the secular. The ability to draw on a rich source of knowledge and understanding, outside of the Western canon, is the dividend of opening up our approach to struggles for black liberation. As M. Jacqui Alexander reminds us, "We were political *because* we were spiritual" (2006, 323).

We would be mistaken to reduce emancipation and freedom to the singular frame of national liberation (Wilder 2015, 3). My approach to Ifá/Orisha in Trinidad centers on conceptualizing the community as part of the wider wave of black internationalism, "a product of consciousness, that is the conscious interconnection and interlocution of black struggles across man-made and natural boundaries—including the boundaries of nations, empires, continents, oceans and seas" (West, Martin, and Williams 2009, 1). That is, the model of spiritual citizenship that I locate envisions layers of belonging, and a multiplicity of communities with their attendant roles and responsibilities. National citizenship does not preclude or compete with spiritual citizenship; rather, it is one facet within the entanglement of belonging. These entanglements are scalar, moving from the local to the national, regional, and global. And in doing so they create dynamics of belonging that span constructed borders and boundaries. Thus, I find spiritual citizenship, which I delimit here as diasporically grounded and tied to black liberation, to be supranational, containing and encompassing the national while also focused on a diasporic horizon.

Any examination of political belonging from a diasporic frame raises issues not only of citizenship but also of identity. I consider this work a contribution to the "new analytic frame" called for by Thomas and Clarke in "considering the vexed relationships between race and global formations today" (2013, 307). Attention to the history of race and citizenship in the Americas reveals the too often obscured (or softened) historical fact that citizenship was not meant for Africans or their descendants (and this sentiment could extend to all non-Europeans). This history also reveals the survival against all odds of enslaved Africans and their strivings to be full citizens (never three-fifths of a person; see Kantrowitz 2012). In a by now well-known narrative, those of African descent in the Americas are largely the legacy of those not meant to survive.[8] And Africans in the Americas must negotiate an inherited Western citizenship that was constructed for Europeans, and landholders at that (Kantrowitz 2012). This is important as a point of departure to understand these negotiations of citizenship in the diaspora and its provenance. Certainly citizenship as it is largely understood is not a concept exclusive to the West, nor is it strictly tied to belonging to a state, or bounded territory. Just as subjects of the nation are produced as citizens, so then can opening up the concept of citizenship inform new forms of subject making and identity.

I agree with Sheller, in her investigation of Caribbean "counter-performances of citizenship" that come "from below," that "to become a citizen is also to become a gendered, racialized and sexed subject" (2012, 26). I would add to this that subjects are constructed as secular or religious (and at times both) depending on the nation-state. This was especially true in the colonial project with the construction of colonial subjects, who were often enslaved and indentured. This recalls that subject construction is often not free and certainly not free of power relations. Here I return to Sheller, who reminds us, in speaking of Haiti but applicable throughout the diaspora, about "the limits of self-determination and autonomy in a world in which the meanings of 'blackness,' and the legitimacy of black citizenship, are still overdetermined by forms of structural violence that transcend the postcolonial state" (2012, 186). This speaks powerfully to what is at stake in an emergent spiritual citizenship: the freedom to construct liberated subjectivities that radically imagine (by going outside of strictly Western thought) ways of belonging, being, and becoming. This would include a freedom to struggle against inherited colonial hierarchies of difference and move toward decolonized identities of race, class, color, gender, and sexuality. While in this book I focus predominantly on performances of race and class, these do not, and cannot, operate without gendered and sexualized intersections. In my offering here I hope to initiate a dialogue on how spiritual praxis and citizenship can open up new horizons of possibility for all our many distinctions of difference, our many identities.

Trinidad's multiculturalism is not one based only on a diversity of race or ethnicity (though it is also that). Religious diversity is an important facet in today's society, in a nation where the minority position is agnosticism or atheism. There is a rich array of religious believers in Trinidad, from Protestants to Sathya Sai Baba, Muslims to Seventh-Day Adventists, Catholics to Hindus, Rastafari to Mormons, and the African diasporic religions of Ifá/Orisha and Spiritual Baptists. Among all these religions it is hard to find a public nonbeliever in Trinidad. As mentioned earlier, Trinidad is not a secular nation. In fact, the leadership of postindependence Afro-Trinidadian politics was a mainstream Christian leadership, even among the diversity of the nations' religions.

In defiance of the orderly classification of race and religion, Indo-Trinidadians participate in and contribute actively to what is commonly labeled as the "African" Orisha tradition. Houk (1995, 135) describes these Indo-Trini participants as mainly interested bystanders, though he estimates their presence as being up to 10 percent of the Orisha tradition, including notable shrine leaders and drummers. The influence from Indo-Trinidadian culture moves beyond the individual level of participation in community to theological influences from Hinduism. Aiyejina and Gibbons remark, "So strong is the inter-penetration of Africa and India in Trinidad that, in the context of the Orisha tradition, Osayin is perceived by some Orisha practitioners as having an Indian dimension and Hindu deities are represented in many Orisha *chapelles* or in separate Hindu chapelles within the same yard" (1999, 198).[9] In addition to there being Indo-Trinidadian adherents to Ifá/Orisha and the theological influence of Hinduism, there also exist cultural and political sites of support between sectors of the respective communities.

Locating Myself, Locating the Ancestors

In engaging a reflexive ethnographic practice, I position myself in the "writing against the grain" project of a decolonized anthropology (Harrison 1991, 2008). Doing so puts me humbly following the footsteps of those who broke ground in what is now recognized as black feminist anthropology. From the pioneering work of Zora Neale Hurston and Katherine Dunham to today's elders, notably A. Lynn Bolles, Faye Harrison, Irma McClaurin, and Sheila Walker, to name but a few (for more, see McClaurin 2001). In conjunction with other critical voices in ethnography, from feminist anthropology to the postcolonial, I understand my location as being simultaneously inside American systems of power by citizenship and geography and yet outside these same systems by the marginality of both my race and gender. Thus, my insider/outsider status was already a complicated one before I set foot in the "field." Adding to this complexity are my familial relationships in Trinidad which brings with it more valences, locally and globally inflected, of race, gender, and class. Now add to this a mix of religion and nationality, and one has a true postcolonial, postmodern brew of contested subjectivities. In many ways and places, the often-fraught complex of anthropologists' subjectivity has been addressed at length.

And certainly being an African American woman of Trinidadian descent impacted my entry into and experiences in the field. Over the course of three years, I increasingly became viewed as a native born Trini who had returned after a long time in "foreign" (the local term for locations outside of Trinidad, usually in North America or Europe). This shift coincided with the movement of my racial designation, in which I began to see myself more as "red" (my local category in Trinidad) than as "black" (my category in America). None of these shifts existed in isolation. They all mixed together with my family's middle-class background in Trinidad to complicate my positions further.

A pivotal moment for me in Trinidad's Orisha religion brings to the forefront some important dynamics of the "betwixt and between" that is the methodological and ethnographic position of the insider/outsider. I was deep in the Santa Cruz Valley at the base of the mountain at the IESOM shrine for the international Alásùwadà Ifá conference (more on this in chapter 5). After two days of presentations where spontaneous rituals shifted the schedule, I was the first person to speak on the final day. As I walked up to the stage, my mind was whirling—how would this audience of Ifá priests, mostly from Trinidad, Venezuela, and Los Angeles, respond to my presentation? Newly initiated to Ifá (in that very location), I had made the decision to draw on my larger expertise and present on my journey. How had I become both an Ifá priest and an ethnographer/academic? This required me to go back over twenty years to my first steps into Orisha. My path has been the opposite of numerous other academics who became involved in the Yorùbá religion through their studies. As I began to detail in my opening stories here, it was my involvement in the Yorùbá religion in the mid-1990s that had brought me to graduate school, to ethnographic research, and ultimately to that conference on Ifá in the Santa Cruz Valley of Trinidad. And there I stood on the IESOM stage, looking out at a truly diverse audience of Ifá priests and devotees.

I began, "The ancestors brought me here. They brought me home. But first the ancestors sent me to graduate school. And it is through that path that I stand here today as an Ifá initiate of the Irentegbe Shrine, Little Oyo, Shrine Gardens, Santa Cruz. And it is through that path that I stand here today holding a PhD in cultural anthropology. That is the short story. "

I continued to tell how, in 1999, I arrived in Trinidad for the Sixth World Congress of Orisha Tradition and Culture to conduct my initial research in what ultimately became this book. It was then that I re-met family, who shared love they had been holding onto during my absence in the many years since my childhood visits. And I re-met the land, the society, the culture, all of which answered a call that I had felt deep down in my spirit. It was while I was at the Sixth World Orisha Congress, a global gathering of African diasporic religious practitioners and academics, that I met the conference organizer. Iya Sangowunmi, a newly initiated priest of Shango (who would become the shrine leader of IESOM), instantly recognized my family name and would later come to embrace me as her own (more on this in chapter 3). This relationship would serve as my entry into Trinidad Orisha, a network of Yorùbá-oriented shrines and a community of amazing people whose stories I try to do justice to throughout this text.

The ancestors brought me home to Trinidad, and it is there that I would later be initiated to Ifá. I would have the blessing of living in Trinidad to do my research as a Fulbright fellow and Wenner-Gren grant recipient from 2002 to 2005. During this time a divination reading from a visiting Ifá priest would lead to my getting a hand of Ifá (initial initiatory introduction to Ifá) in Chicago, where I was put under Ifá's protection. The spiritual genealogy of this ritual introduction to Ifá serves as an example of the transnational spiritual networks central to African-based religious community in the diaspora. I received my hand of Ifá from Awo Ifawole Keita, spiritual godson of Baba Medahochi, who was one of the original members of South Carolina's Oyotunji Village (a community informed by diasporic approaches to African religions, including Yorùbá Ifá and Orisha, and Benin Vodou).[10] Baba Medahochi's own initiation was in Togo to Ajá (another version of Ifá), which means that when I went back to Trinidad with my hand of Ifá, I carried the ase of Togo, via Chicago, back with me. I had become the very example of the transnational spiritual networks that I was studying!

At the Ifá conference deep in Trinidad's Santa Cruz Valley, I spoke that day in 2012 to an audience of Ifá priests and devotees (from Los Angeles, California; Ibadan, Nigeria; and Caracas, Venezuela) about being humbled and blessed to have completed the PhD, to have been initiated right there at the IESOM shrine, and then being well on my road to writing a book on Orisha in Trinidad (this book), all under the direction and at the behest of the ancestors. I stood there in front of my elders and gave thanks. I gave thanks for the very dilemma that I would like to touch upon here. In many ways I walk—as I suspect many of us do—"betwixt and between" (Marcus 1998; Turner 1986). That is, I am both an insider and an outsider. Of Trini parentage, I grew up in the United States. Even though I have come to see Trinidad as my home, since my "navel cord" was not "bury in de yard" (the local measure of belonging), many would say that I'm not a true Trini (and to them I say, "Who you?").

Throughout my graduate training as a cultural anthropologist, I was never at ease with the Eurocentric Western modalities of academic discourse. (This unease informed my development of a critical and decolonial tool kit; see Harrison 1991, 2008.) Not to mention my disquiet at the centering of the Western atomized view of the individual, so contrary to Yorùbá philosophy, largely at the core of the theory I was learning. And here I come to my project and the questions at the crux of the matter. How to speak to the Ifá/Orisha community and my ancestors in a language that will be seen and heard by my academic community as well? How do I negotiate the precepts of Ifá in the seemingly secular world that is based on such different and often opposing values? In striving to answer these questions, my ethnographic explorations identified an emancipatory potential, a radical way for people to reimagine themselves and the world around them, how they live together in the world, in a tradition that builds upon those who have come before—with both roots, as in a tree, and routes, as in pathways to the continent, to West Africa. I located this in Trinidad: in Orisha, in Ifá, and at the IESOM shrine—all places that I have called home. On that day, as I stood on the stage, I looked out at the Ifá people gathered from across the diaspora and declared, "The ancestors brought me home."

Spiritual Citizenship emerges from a deep engagement with Trinidad over fifteen-plus years, including thirty-six months of consecutive field-based research on Afro-Trinidadian ritual and festival events. This book is based in part on an ethnographically grounded study of several Canboulay cultural practices (Carnival and emancipation celebrations, in addition to the Orisha religion).[11] That study focused on the Afro-Trinidadian middle class and their differing expressions of cultural citizenship.[12] I recuperated a tradition of intensive ethnographic work to ground a growing body of theory on race, difference, nationalism, and postcolonialism. In focusing on these festive practices, I engaged cultural practices as a field illuminating the theoretical concerns of race, ethnicity, class, and nationhood, an approach that is shared with this work.

My ethnographic work on Orisha rituals and community building explores the dynamics of cultural performance and identity that constitute spiritual and cultural citizenship. In approaching the shrines and events of Trinidad Orisha, I paid particular attention to the spaces and places that religious identity intersected with, and informed, spheres of social and political life. It was in the process of mapping these intersections that the spiritual and cultural citizenship that informs this work became clear. Careful attention to ritual, festival, and everyday practices revealed the artificiality of dividing life into these separate categories largely created by the ethnographic gaze.

After I moved back to the States in 2005, changes in my "field" compelled me to seek additional funding and conduct new research. Over the summers of 2010, 2011, and 2012, I researched the recent establishment of Ifá initiatory lineages in Trinidad Orisha (see especially chapters 4 and 5). I worked with sixteen Ifá priests to create in-depth oral histories. These sessions focused on spiritual and religious pathways and genealogy: How did they come to the Orisha religion? How did they then come to Ifá? In asking these seemingly simple questions stories emerged of identity, family, politics, culture, and travel (to name just a sample of topics). From this rich archive I was able to map the recent emergence of Ifá in Trinidad.

Mapping the Journey

In *Spiritual Citizenship: Transnational Pathways from Black Power to Ifá in Trinidad*, my approach to African diasporic religions is diasporic, transnational, and global; even as people's spiritual experiences are locally grounded, they are always also globally informed. Thus, I find the study of Africans and their descendants in the Americas to be embedded in transnational spiritual networks. I divided this work into two parts as it moves from a focus on the black cultural citizenship visible in political engagements within the national frame (part I) to an emergent spiritual citizenship that becomes evident in a wider transnational frame (part II).

In part I, the first chapter opens with a story of spirits interceding in human affairs, literally sending "people to the streets." This is followed by another call, that of the drums that center spirit and agency. I move on to map the unfolding of the 1970 Black Power movement in Trinidad when frustrations literally burst into the street as critiques that had been building for years became direct challenges. This confrontation of the postcolonial state was a moment in which the nation both visibly imagined more and demanded more for itself. And in that moment the privileging of European everything—from aesthetics to economics—was questioned. And the African (imagined and otherwise) was reconsidered, reevaluated, and reengaged. In this critical space that called for new ideas of freedom and belonging, new ideas of community, and new ideas of citizenship, many looked for new forms of the spiritual and the sacred. Many people then turned to African diasporic religions, visibly bringing together the secular and sacred, the political and religious (or, indeed, as said by many, these were never separate).

Following Black Power, the African religions in Trinidad moved from the margins of society and entered mainstream politics in unprecedented ways in the following decades. In chapter 2, I examine the emergence of the Orisha religion in the public sphere, with state sponsorship, and its relationship to Trinidad's cultural politics of multiculturalism. The chapter situates the Indo-Trinidadian political sponsorship of African religions in Trinidad within the larger framework of multiculturalism. I argue that this sponsorship enabled a shift in discourse from an Afro-Euro continuum that privileges a "Creole" multiculturalism to one that is based on the contribution of particular elements. This shift then makes room for Indo-Trinidadian contributions to the nation, including the non-Christian religious and cultural contributions of Hindus.

Chapter 3, the opening chapter of part II, marks the transition from a spiritually informed black cultural citizenship to an emergent spiritual citizenship through an exploration of local institution building and shifting practices. The chapter begins with the close reading of a prayer that maps diasporic geographies and locates the local within larger transnational networks while performing spiritual labor for the nation. These themes of interplay between the local, the national, and the transnational are explored in the context of a global Orisha conference, shifts in ritual practices, and a case study in the spiritual politics of Carnival. The closing section examines an annual festival as an exemplar of the transitions in Trinidad Orisha practice, in part informed by an increasing exposure to new lineages and ritual knowledge from Yorubaland.

I consider the emergence of Trinidad Orisha into transnational Ifá/Orisha networks in chapter 4. This shift brings into focus polarities of the Orisha religion in Trinidad between local ancestral practices and those shrines orientated toward Ilé-Ifè, Nigeria. In several sections I document the travels of Ifá/Orisha priests and devotees between Trinidad and Nigeria. These travels reinforce the place of Trinidad Orisha (and the emerging local Ifá) in transnational spiritual networks. The relationships that were formed through these journeys facilitated the exchange of spiritual knowledge, rituals, and ase that would continue to have a profound effect on the Trini Orisha community (explored further in the following chapter).

Using ethnographic and historical material on the establishment of "Ifá in the ground," chapter 5 explores how Trinidad became the newest home for Ifá in the diaspora and how this development illuminates an emerging spiritual citizenship. Sections explore how conferences arise as important transnational sites for institution building informed by new spiritual knowledge, praxis, and ase where newly articulated ideas of a global spiritual citizenship engage with ideas of social justice and freedom. In a personal narrative on Aséwẹlẹ, a ritual to settle the souls of those lost in the slave trade and in slavery, I offer an ethnographic vignette that highlights the responsibility of spiritual citizenship not only to those who are here now, or to those in following generations, but also to those who have come before. In this ritual we witness the enacting of spiritual citizenship as offerings are made to appease and settle the lost souls. As an Ifá elder asks, "With the rites not done for them, how could anyone expect peace and progress in its real sense on both sides of the Atlantic?" (Pópóọla 2007, 35). The closing section focuses on the 2012 Alasuwada conference, which through spiritual praxis and an emerging spiritual citizenship endeavored to bring Ifá to bear directly on how people live together in community through a focus on developing an Ifá-informed social policy.

Throughout the text I play with the boundaries and borders of language use in how I present the Yoruba language, at times with diacritical markings indicating tone, and at other times with no markings. Rather than capricious or random, there is a pattern to the play (as is often the case in diasporic/Caribbean play). I have named the atonal use of Yoruba in the Americas as

"Diasporic Yoruba." This is also reflected in my own Yoruba language use, which is largely for sacred contexts and atonal (i.e. without diacritics). I apologize for any errors in the Continental Yorùbá. Full diacritical markings are attempted to properly convey tone for Continental Yorùbá names and context.

I felt that this contextual representation was important to try in a text that argues for decolonial approaches to ethnography, religion, and politics. Thus, I strategically present the full markings of the profound and beautiful language of Yorùbá (while recognizing that its written orthography is deeply intertwined with a history of colonialism and Christian missionaries). I have taken some liberties when the contexts overlap (as they often do) and for common terms that have a consistent understanding on both sides of the border (babalawo, ase). I have adopted the hybrid form of Ifá/Orisha to reference the African diasporic religion in Trinidad that is primarily informed by Yorùbá religion. I chose to combine the Continental Yorùbá spelling of Ifá (which is universally understood and employed) with the Diasporic Yoruba spelling of Orisha (another universally understood spelling) as a reflection of the interplay of the two streams—continental and diasporic—in Trinidad's African diasporic religion. For more linguistic details please see the Note on Orthography.

PART I

Spiritual Engagements with Black Cultural Citizenship

CHAPTER 1

The Spirit of Black Power

An Ancestral Calling

"The Orisha manifest in the *palais* to send us on the streets . . . [calls of *ekuse* (well done) and the rattle of *iroke Ifá* could be heard] . . . Manifest in the parties and in the drums at the corner." With his piercing gaze, Baba Erinfolami brought us all into that moment. We could hear the drums, ringing out to call the people to the streets, going back thirty-five years to what we now call the Black Power revolution in Trinidad. His words rang out at the Sixth Annual Rain Festival at Ile Eko Sango/Osun Mil'osa, up in the back of the Santa Cruz Valley. Onstage in traditional African top and pants (*buba* and *sokoto*), with his iconic red velvet *fila* (a traditional Yorùbá brimless hat), Baba Erinfolami continued to weave a narrative that spanned decades, pulled spirits forward as active agents, and tied the present moment in 2005 to the protests and consciousness-raising of Black Power. He pointed to Khafra Khambon, a former student leader of the 1970 Black Power movement who was in the audience, and said, "We were fighting an uphill battle for those who went to prison, look two them sitting here." My mind lingered on the power of drums and how the spirits were not only called by the drums, but also on how the spirits used the drums to call us; the communication line worked both ways.

"I needed to find the source of the drums." Iya Sangowunmi recalled the urgency she felt when hearing the drums in her early childhood. She shared how that moment came around full circle for her in the early 1980s. When she planned the launch of her new organization, the African Women's Association, Iya asked someone to find a drummer to play at the opening. As she recalled:

> He went and brought a man, now deceased, name Isaac Lindsay. . . . And when we went down to the place on Sixth Street there, to the community center, this man came with his drums and started beating. *It was such an awakening. It touched something in me that I didn't even know was there. . . . It just was a different thing.* And I became so interested in what was going on, 'cause I asked him what it was he was doing, and he said he was clearing the place before we could start and do whatever it was we were doing.
>
> So on the actual family day I sat down to talking with him as they were beating drums . . . and he told me about Orisha. He gave me enough to pique my interest, and I wanted to find out further. Because the only thing I had ever heard or known in that way when they started to tell me about Orisha.

It was those drums that brought back for her a half-buried memory of running up the hill in search of the source of the drums, of being caught and switched by her aunt, and then of quietly waiting for her mother to come home. (More discipline to come!) And it was in the conversation between her mother and her aunt that she heard the term for the first time:

> Gyal—that is the first time I hear that word, I hear Baptist, eh, but I never hear Shango. Those Shango people beating drum whole night, whole day.
>
> That name Shango remained with me for a long, long, long time. Because I didn't know what it was. You know? When she said "Shango people," what made them different from other people?
>
> As a grown-up I forget about it. So when I came back, the whole thing with the Shango came back to me, and I started interacting with the tradition. It was almost like, well *I know now that it was an ancestral call.*

The drums had called out to the child, reaching something deep inside her. Decades later, hearing the drums again, Iya was able to reconnect to that moment and realize that the ancestors had been calling her. She was able to draw on her knowledge of Yorùbá cosmology, understand the collapsing of time and space, to place that early moment within a larger spiritual context. For it is not only we who reach out to the spirits, spirits reach out to us.

The ancestral call was a call to people in both the spiritual and the material realm, birthing spiritual citizenship out of a critical moment in the

FIGURE 1.1 Iyalode Loogun Osun Sangodasawande, Iya Sangowunmi, founder and leader of Ile Eko Sango/Osun Mil'osa, at the Orisha Family Day festival held at the Lopinot Ancestral Grounds, Arouca, Trinidad, 2003. Photo by N. Fadeke Castor.

black radical tradition. I would hear different versions of this story, of the drums calling people to the Orisha, over and over again. And many of these stories were in the context of the 1970 Black Power movement. The years surrounding 1970 were a time when people could hear drums playing at night from the hills and valleys surrounding Port of Spain (Pantin 1990, 71). One way to understand this was as a shift of consciousness, a new awareness of a diasporic historicity tied to a newly valorized blackness. From another perspective, the spirits reached out to their children and called them home. Both readings lead to a singular outcome: social change had come with a fire of critique burning in the spirit of African ancestors.[1]

Creolization of African Religions

An understanding of the emergence of African diasporic religions as a force of black liberation and decolonization in Trinidad calls for a necessary grounding in historical context. And central to the history of the Caribbean is creolization. As Édouard Glissant remarks, "The Caribbean is an archipelago of countries born of creolization" (quoted in Hiepko 2011, 256). While I agree that creolization is central to the history of the Caribbean, I seek to locate an earlier moment of creolization as vital to African religions in both West and Central Africa and the Caribbean. The creolization that I reference is not only of the European-African mixing of languages and cultures that is prominent in both the literature and the imaginary (Bernabé, Chamoiseau and Confiant 1993; Glissant 1997; Khan 2007; Palmié 2006; Price 2006; C. Stewart 2007; Trouillot 1998). Rather, these African diasporic religions first emerged from the creolization of numerous African groups, whose historical interactions from the continent were intensified in new configurations during the Atlantic slave trade, during slavery, and under colonialism (Adderley 2006; Gomez 1998; Mintz and Price 1992). This continental cultural and religious mixing laid a common groundwork for the new wave of creolization that was to occur across the Atlantic.[2]

The Orisha religion in Trinidad is a renaming of what used to be called Shango in Trinidad and in the academic literature until the latter part of the twentieth century (for examples that use the term "Shango," see Herskovits and Herskovits 1947; Mischel 1957; Simpson 1965, 1978; Smith, M.G. and Paul 1963). Regardless of the name, African-based religious forms have been practiced in Trinidad since the relatively large settlement of African slaves at the end of the eighteenth century. These slaves mainly hailed from the French colonies, whose planters were fleeing their fear of an increasingly unsettled and rebellious slave population, and ultimately the Haitian Revolution. This later African "Creole" population became one of the important historical antecedents in the development of Trinidad's Orisha religion, contributing practices that are often more associated with Haitian Vodou.[3] Among the other historical contribution to the multifaceted field of spiritual and religious complexes (interchangeably referred to as Trinidad Orisha or Orisha Work) include repatriated African captives that settled in Trinidad.[4] Among the numerous African ethnicities that settled in Trinidad were "the Mandingo, Fulbe, Susu, Temne, Kissi, Kwakwa, Kromantee, Mine (Minre), Allada, Chamba, Hausa, Popo, Igbo, Northwestern Bantu, Ibibio, Kongo and

Yoruba" (Lum 2000, 204–5), with the prominent African cultural groups being the Kongo, Yorùbá, and Rada (Adderley 2006, 159; Howard 2004, 161; Warner-Lewis 1991).[5]

The Orisha tradition in Trinidad emerged, like so many Afro-Atlantic religions, within transnational spiritual networks that had touched ground at a particular historical conjuncture (see Hall 1995, 1999, 2003; Matory 2005; D. Scott 1991, 1999). In this specific colonial conjuncture at the turn of the nineteenth century, a large influx of French planters and their slaves settled in Spanish Trinidad. As described by Higman, "From a mere 1,500 (including only 200 slaves) in 1780, the population of Trinidad grew to 17,500 (10,000 of them slaves) by 1797" (1984, 44). Among this population were both African and "Creole" slaves who practiced varying versions of African religious traditions (Trotman 2003). Many of these practices drew on religious traditions from the west coast of Africa (what was then the Bight of Benin and the Gold Coast), what Houk has called "a family of religions" (1995, 53). Throughout the diaspora, African descendants have remembered, created, and passed on spiritual practices and doctrines that have been called by many names in Trinidad over the years: Shango (often confused with Spiritual Baptist names like Shango, Shouter, or Shaker Baptist) and finally, in contemporary times, Orisha and most recently Ifá or the compound Ifá/Orisha (which I use most often throughout the text).

African Religions in Trinidad: Spiritual Baptist and Orisha

Trinidad's colonial history shapes the contemporary cultural politics of nationhood, including changes in the Spiritual Baptist and Orisha religions and their relationship to the social and political order. In the 1800s, French planters and British colonial elites competed for control of the political, social, and economic resources of a country populated primarily by the descendants of African slave and free laborers and Indian indentured laborers. In the early and mid-1800s, the struggle between the dominant (Spanish/French) Roman Catholic Church and the (British) Anglican Church for the social and religious patronage of the elites provided a limited opportunity for the African and Indian populations to practice their own religious traditions in relative peace. However, by the late 1800s, both elites and the Creole middle class perceived the African-based traditions of Spiritual Baptist and Orisha as threats to a "civil" society modeled on European manners and customs.

By the late 1800s, the British claimed dominance in legal and social spheres, if not in the cultural and religious spheres, which were still dominated by a "Creole" culture and Catholicism. A principal site for the contestation of dominance was the church. The appearance of Christianity, in this case Catholicism or to a lesser extent Protestantism, was vital for many Africans (and Indians) to have social and economic security, or even the limited available mobility. Forms of masking deities and the blending of rituals have all been documented in Trinidad Orisha. This syncretism would be visible in a form familiar to Melville Herskovits and Frances Herskovits, American ethnographers who researched "African traits" in the Caribbean in the 1930s, including Trinidad's association of Orisha with the saints. This Roman Catholic iconology persists into the contemporary moment in Orisha religion, though it is fading even as the church loses its long-held spiritual dominance in Trinidad (figure 1.2). On the other hand, the Protestant tradition has contributed to a great extent to the Spiritual Baptist (also known as Shouter Baptist) and to a lesser extent to the Orisha faith. One consequence of the dual Christian influence in Trinidad is the existence of two interlocking but doctrinally distinct African religious traditions, Spiritual Baptist and Orisha.

Spiritual Baptists practice a Christian doctrine centered on the Bible as the source of the divine word. Congregations meet in a church and hold services in front of an altar. The embodied practices of worship resemble numerous Christian practices, but with their own particular form. Most important in locating Spiritual Baptists as a Christian practice is their acceptance of Jesus as the son of God, a savior who has come and will come again (with echoes of Shango myths of sacrifice and rising). Orisha also exhibits aspects of Protestantism, though mainly through the Spiritual Baptist rubric. The relationships between these two religions are complex, intertwined, and not fully documented; both Stephen Glazier (1983) and Kenneth Lum (2000) treat the religions as being predominantly separate.[6] Glazier puts forth that "although there are many differences between Baptist rites and those of Shango, many assume that these two ritual forms are similar" (1983, 39). Sankeralli sums up the dynamic between the two: "It should be understood that for the most of the 20th century the major articulations of African 'religion' by this emergent community were the Spiritual Baptists and a 'folk' religiosity where the African appropriation of Catholicism was central, the latter directly related to Trinidad's Yoruba. . . . Here Protestant Psalms or Catholic novenas can be used to pelt spiritual forces" (2002, 26).

FIGURE 1.2 This Oshun shrine is located in an Orisha chapelle in the hills of Laventille, Port of Spain, Trinidad. The lithograph and statues of Catholic saints represents a syncretism more pervasive in the older generations of Trini-centric Orisha devotees, 2004. Photo by N. Fadeke Castor.

In Trinidad, as elsewhere in the Caribbean, the theologies of dominant imposed religions such as Protestantism and Catholicism can be used to express the logics of African diasporic religions. So Christian prayers can throw negative energy at someone or, as Sankeralli states, "be used to pelt spiritual forces." Throughout Trinidad, regardless of religious adherence, there exists a widespread belief in supernatural forces (Khan 2000). These forces, be they a *jumbie* (spirit) in the night or the calling of *goat-mouth* (bringing something into being by saying it), are part of the cultural fabric.

In analyzing the relationship dynamic between the Spiritual Baptist and Orisha religions, thinking that depends on polarities to place the religions into neat categories obscures rather than clarifies.[7] That is, the religious practices are not "either/or" but rather are "both/and." Another way to think of this is that Spiritual Baptist and Orisha are two branches of a shared root that are more rhizomatic than representative of the two ends of a continuum or spectrum. Houk, in his largely demographic work *Spirits, Blood, and Drums* (1995), estimates that "well over 50% of orisha worshippers are also Spiritual Baptists and participate in the activities of both religions on a regular basis" (36). Based on my fieldwork experience, I would concur with Houk and add the caveat "recognizably" Spiritual Baptist. This nuance reflects my experience that the majority of Orisha practitioners either are, or have been, Spiritual Baptists. Whether or not they currently practice in a recognizable manner (attend church, hold positions in the Spiritual Baptist theocracy, etc.), the doctrines of Spiritual Baptists are often apparent in the practices of the Orisha tradition, and at times vice versa. In fact, for the most part, there is a shared doctrine that is manifested in either the churchyard (recognizable as Spiritual Baptist) or the *palais* (recognizable as Orisha) and sometimes in both. Though the two manifestations are then representative of a shared body of beliefs, there is not a cohesive unanimity. Substituting Yoruba for Orisha (as is often done locally), Sankeralli states, "Yoruba and Baptist share a community and a cosmology and have profoundly defined each other, even though their respective work have remained distinct, many are indeed involved in both. This close association has in recent times given rise to the popular misnomer—'Shango Baptist,' a confused but very widespread reference to those involved in the 'complex'" (2002, 26). Differences in interpretation, as in all religions, often create oppositional views that become the source of conflict between different branches. However, there is a contemporary branch of Orisha in Trinidad that is breaking away from this shared foundation of beliefs. I elaborate on these divisions and this Yorùbá-centered branch of the Orisha faith in later chapters.

The Years of Persecution

The state in Trinidad, whether colonial or postcolonial, has had a contentious history of relations with both the Spiritual Baptist and the Orisha communities that until recently were characterized by persecution and inequities going back to the mid-1800s. In 1917, British colonial authorities passed the Shouters Prohibition Ordinance (SPO), which outlawed the practices of the Spiritual/Shouter Baptists (bell ringing, shouting, etc.), criminalizing this African diasporic religion faith alongside other practices associated with "Africa" (i.e., drumming and dancing).[8] This law was just one example of the persecution of non-European cultural expressions (Indian and, especially, African) justified in the British colonial promotion of the "civilizing mission." Throughout the first half of the twentieth century people perceived to practice African-based religions were subject to criminalization and discrimination, losing homes, jobs and at times their freedom. These persecutions were met with resistance and an organized lobbying campaign in the 1930s and 1940s to change the laws.

In the eyes of the law, the two faiths, Spiritual Baptist and Orisha, were largely indistinguishable. Legislation was largely written with reference to practices that were being proscribed or prohibited (e.g., the beating of drums) rather than with specific reference to either faith. However, in those instances (such as the SPO of 1917) where the police specified one faith for persecution, the courts and society made no such distinction. Until recently, in the years approaching and directly after the millennium, the conflation of the two faiths has continued within the state and the public sphere (from this confusion arose the hybrid term "Shango Baptist," largely rejected by Orisha and Spiritual Baptists alike, even as the term has been embraced by the general public). This conflation becomes important on an analytic level when considering the persecution of these African diasporic religion faiths and their concomitant responses.

The negative attitudes against both African-based religions from colonialism continued into the 1960s, only to be challenged during the 1970s Black Power movement. The challenges of Black Power emerged from the failure of the state, society, and business sectors to meet the expectations raised by independence in 1962. This laid the groundwork for shifts in the cultural and religious field to manifest in the 1980s and beyond that would have serious implications for the Orisha religion and its followers. These challenges, and subsequent changes to the Orisha religion in Trinidad, are detailed in the following sections.

B(l)ack to Africa: From Legal to Official

The Black Power movement would come on the heels of independence to engage the demonization and criminalization of African-based religious and cultural practices, which was a major inheritance of the colonial era. The colonizers' attempt to create a hegemonic field of Eurocentric values

FIGURE 1.3 A close-up of a Spiritual Baptist street altar, that includes the iconic Baptist bell, olive oil, various bottles of perfume, bay rum, water, and a vase filled with local decorative foliage. Toco, Trinidad, 2005. Photo by N. Fadeke Castor.

and norms would become visible in the contestations over religious freedom. It was after the repeal of the SPO in 1951 that there was a gradual emergence of African diasporic religions into the public sphere.[9] Further, it would take decades for the older leadership, conditioned to secrecy and shame, to pass on the reins to a younger generation. Eventually, by the 1960s, one could go into town and see a group of Baptists on the corner with their iconic bell, water, and the Holy Bible singing the gospel and praising God's name (figure 1.3). At this same time, however, Orisha devotees still practiced in quiet, often retiring to the "bush," and largely remaining outside of the public eye. All of this would change with the upcoming cultural upheaval of the 1960s and 1970s, including independence, and even more so with the subsequent Black Power movement.

The transition from marginalized and persecuted to state-sanctioned and publicly recognized religion was catalyzed, in large part, by the emerging African consciousness of the Black Power movement (Glazier 1983, 127; Henry 2003, xxiii; Hucks 2006, 31; Sankeralli 2002, 30). As mentioned earlier in the chapter, "The hills of Port-of-Spain . . . would reverberate at nights to the crackling of drums; old African rituals, like the Shango, ignored by a younger generation, now became symbols of pride" (Pantin 1990, 71). The impact of those "crackling" drums would be felt in the following decades as increasing numbers of both the lower working class (grassroots) and the middle class would be attracted to the tradition and slowly become willing to associate with it publicly as a source of African pride. Aiyejina and Gibbons address this conjuncture of politics, religion, race, and class:

> In spite of the association between leading political figures and African-inspired religious traditions, the public acceptance of such traditions did not begin to gather pace until after the mass protests of the 1970s. These protests which have gone down in history as the Black Power Movement encouraged racial pride and the embrace of African names and fashions. Indirectly, the interest which this movement initiated extended into the area of religion and encouraged many closet devotees of these traditions to come out in the open. This period also signaled the public participation in these traditions by African middle-class with the result that middle-class professionals have become influential members of the socio-political leadership of the more prominent Orisa shrines in Trinidad. (1999, 206)

From the 1970s into the contemporary moment, a growing number of middle class participants have contributed their economic and social capital to the campaign to revalorize African religious and cultural practices. What had been persecuted prior to the 1950s and demonized up into the 1970s became less marginalized and tolerated in the 1980s. This direct outgrowth of Black Power, as noted by Gibbons, both brought members of the Orisha faith into the public sphere and opened entry to new adherents, crossing what were previously prohibitive boundaries of class (and in some instances color).

Springer situates the Orisha tradition within the struggle for African consciousness in the Black Power movement: "In the aftermath of the failure of the National Joint Action Committee many of us came to the traditional African religion as an act of political and ideological self-expression. It is indeed my conviction that the recognition of African religion is the ultimate step in the reclamation of self for the diaspora African" (1995, 91). Her sentiment was echoed by many priests in the oral religious histories that I collected. Awo Eniola speaks of a now elder priest Babalorisa Olakela Massetungi, who in the 1970s was "part of a group of people who shared the idea that in order to accomplish the total liberation of the African person, African spirituality. . . certainly could not be left out. And so I think that the people who he was involved with at that time became very active in trying to research African spirituality and disseminate information on African spirituality." Trinidadians who were abroad would be impacted by the circulation of ideas on civil rights, Black Power, Pan-Africanism, and Black Nationalism in England, Canada, and the United States and be inspired to examine the connections between religion, race, and politics.

As evidenced in recollections by elders in the Orisha religion the social critique and protest of the times broke the illusion of a separation between the three categories of religion, race, and politics. Iya Sangowunmi recounts from her time in England during the late 1960s and early 1970s, "Religion for that time started to be politics. I became very active in Pan-African issues." Or, as Babalorisa Olakela (aka Oludari) succinctly put it, "So I was a Catholic until the 1970 uprising. By 1971, I became embroiled in African traditional religion." People from both the grassroots and the middle class would respond to the social critiques of neo-colonialism and political unrest of the time with a search for ancestral roots that often took the form of an interest in African religions and their local expressions. For many, their political consciousness and religious consciousness were so intertwined as to be inseparable. Rather than a neat linearity of radical politics leading people to explore alternatives to mainstream Christianity, the lived reality was more complicated. Each individual I spoke with about this time located him or herself at various points along a continuum of politics and religion. Included in the mix were political and religious positions so varied that any map making begs for more than two dimensions. Among the Orisha and Ifá priests whom I interviewed, many came to political consciousness, whether in Black Power or Pan-Africanism, during the 1970s. This in turn led them to African-based religions that became their primary focus and identity. In contrast, Oludari was clearly on the other side (plate 3). As he described it, "I am a Pan-Africanist and I am a revolutionary first before I am a priest." Oludari is not alone in this sentiment. His history of more than four decades in the Orisha religion (or "African Sacred Science," as he prefers to call it), with the majority of that time in a leadership position, points to the need to complicate our typologies that forcibly separate religion and politics. Spiritual citizenship as an argument of critical consciousness rejects the Western division of religion, politics, and culture into artificially separate spheres (Asad 1993).

The Black Power movement would challenge class biases and the cleavages of racial politics. As described by Rohlehr, "The 1970 'revolution' . . .

signaled the presence of a gulf *within* Creole society that was as profound as the parallel gulf that separated Creole from what came to be termed the 'alienated and marginalized' Indo-Trinidadian" (1998, 869). The rallying cries of Black Power called attention to the conflicts of capitalism that replicated the colonial order of power relations, even as they replaced colonial elites with Afro-Creole elites (who Lloyd Best would refer to as "Afro-Saxons" and the "Afro-Saxon regime"; Best 2004). Prime Minster Eric Williams's emphasis on education and history would come to fruition in a most unexpected manner, producing the leaders of the Black Power movement who brought a critical analysis, with historical roots in Trinidad's academics and labor activists, to bear on the nascent postcolonial moment.

Reports from the time indicate that prominent black radical figures, such as Stokely Carmichael and Walter Rodney, were capturing the imagination of "grassroots" youth. Pantin's recollection focused on the critical rhetoric heard on the corner from portable radio sets, "Glib of tongue, angry, hurling invective in every direction, Carmichael would quickly emerge a hero to the black youth of Trinidad and Tobago" (1990, 8). Carmichael's youthful experience of a colonial Trinidad combined with his experience in black America provided him a wider diasporic frame. In his book *Black Power: The Politics of Liberation in America*, he reflected on the legacy of colonialism: "The colonial power structure clamped a boot of oppression on the neck of black people and then, ironically, said, they are not ready for freedom . . . and no-one accepted blame. And there is no white power structure doing it to them. And they are in that condition because they are lazy and don't want to work, and this is not colonialism and this is the land of opportunity and the home of the free. And people should not become alienated but people do become alienated" (Ture and Hamilton 1992, 22–23).[10] Alienation was clearly evident in the streets, in the palais, and in the heart of Trinidad's cultural expression, Carnival. This latter was in part evidenced by the themes of the masquerade bands in the 1969 and 1970 Carnival. The moment that would become understood as Black Power was characterized by a rapid exchange between the circulation of ideas (from texts, speeches, and broadcast media—mainly through the radio and somewhat the news from limited TV broadcasts) and their analysis and expression. In conversations, people recounted frequent gatherings under the corner streetlight to read the latest political tract or listen to a speech being broadcast on the radio. Among these, texts such as Frantz Fanon's *Wretched of the Earth* (1963) and *Black Skin, White Masks* (1967) were in wide circulation. Fanon's analysis of colonial structures of violence on psychological, cultural, and structural levels struck a chord with the youth. As reported by Pantin, "By their reasoning, the government of the day was only a 'front' for an elite 'white' establishment that manipulated the strings from behind" (1990, 10).

In addition to radio broadcasts of Black Power speeches and news of unrest in the United States, Europe, Africa, South America, and the Caribbean (especially Jamaica),[11] there is evidence that the events and discourses of the moment captured the imagination of Trinidad's lower- and working-class communities. This would spread to the sons and daughters of the middle class, who, with the recent opening of access to tertiary education provided by Williams, were in attendance at the University of West Indies (UWI), St. Augustine, in increasing numbers. According to Pantin, "Black Power would come close to toppling the government of the People's National Movement (PNM) in 1970 and the great irony of this was the PNM had spawned such a movement" (1990, 10). The newly opened educational opportunities produced the leaders of the Black Power movement, who brought a critical analysis, with historical roots in Trinidad's academics and labor activists, to bear on the nascent postcolonial moment. It was from this population of Afro-Trinidadian middle-class students, alongside people, young and old, from the Afro-Trinidadian grassroots, that Black Power organizations would coalesce and find their way onto the streets. And from their experiences on the streets, in marches and protests, many people would become galvanized to rethink their relations to the large social categories that impacted their everyday lives: race, religion, politics, culture, and the nation.

The critical view and voice that would take a lead role in Black Power emerged over decades in political, cultural, and spiritual spheres. The critical and decolonizing force that was increasingly visible in the 1960s had roots in the cultural practices of the previous decades. An elder in Orisha reflected on the time by stressing the importance of being on the streets with steel band and Carnival masquerade (*mas'*), and *jouvay* (late night mas' on Dimanche Gras) in the 1940s and 1950s and emphasizing that it was the Orisha folks who were doing this. The African communities central to Black Power were the same communities central to Carnival and Orisha. In Trinidad, critical cultural politics center on these core practices of Carnival, the steel pan and the opening moment of Carnival with its dirty masquerade in oil, mud, and paint in the depths of the night (jouvay). The interplay of these performatives often obscures the shared community in which these cultural and religious expressions are based. In Trinidad, any developing form of spiritual citizenship has roots that must be recognized in the locally embedded festival epistemologies of Carnival, in all its critical force, as well as in the historical conjuncture of Black Power.

Carnival 1970: Black Power Mas'

Trinidad's son Stokely Carmichael had been banned from Carnival in 1969 at the height of the years of social upheaval and turbulence worldwide (and would be banned from countries throughout the British Caribbean, including notably Jamaica and Guyana). However, Carnival 1970 dawned with little anticipation of trouble (other than the normal bacchanal), let alone a dawning revolution. Though it was largely uneventful, in retrospect, Carnival in 1970 was marked by several signs of the impending tumult; it is due mainly to the diligence of reporters that with hindsight we can read the signs of change in that year's Carnival. Raoul Pantin, at the time a reporter for the establishment paper, the *Trinidad Guardian*, wrote in his memoir on the Black Power revolution:

> The first thing that was unusual, was immediately striking about the J'Ouvert morning of February 9, 1970, was the sudden, spontaneous outpouring of Black Power bands. As if by some mysterious pre-arrangement, more than a dozen bands appeared on the streets, waving posters of Stokely Carmichael, Che Guevara; young men in black berets and black shirts punched their fists at the soft morning sky. And the largest of these bands was called "One Thousand and One White Devils" (an American black Muslim pejorative term for "white people"). These bands drew a flicker of recognition in the press but the Carnival of 1970 passed without incident. (1990, 44)

Only in retrospect would these portrayals in the 1970 Carnival be seen as harbingers of the social protest and turmoil to come. In a 1971 memoir on 1970 Black Power in Trinidad the sociologist Ivar Oxaal reflects on the 1970 Carnival. In his initial passage he describes an idealistic and romantic vision of past Carnivals:

> In the beginning there was the Carnival, neatly poised between madness and the sanest possible exaltation. A profound and singular inwardness which was yet a complete loss of self in the communal flow through the day, and days, toward an ending, "the last lap," which on Tuesday eve-

ning became a dusky mosaic. Last Lap: a myriad mingling of retreating but undefeated armies which never fought a battle; of butterflies, kings, planets, fruits, flowers—of all Creation recreated and put on willing legs to be borne in a state of levitation through the town, paraded in front of the Governor or Prime Minister, before this final wending homeward behind one's favorite steelband. (1971, 27)

Oxaal follows this with his observation of the transformation that Black Power both brought to and signaled by Carnival: "In 1970 this beautiful but escapist miracle was broken. Miracles would no longer suffice. A break-out from traditional form occurred which would be repeated in the violation of other mental structures of the colonial period: reified concepts of social geography—who can go where—were shattered as well, as we will see" (27). His observation that "reified concepts of social geography . . . were shattered as well" would prove to be optimistic as over the following decades Carnival would become increasingly commodified on the level of both economic and social capital, further reifying the social geography that directs "who can go where" (Castor 2009). Though the effects of Black Power would not completely overturn the existing social order, Carnival in 1970 was "a political carnival *par excellence* as bands of young people lampooned the absurdities of the social system" that initiated ripples in the culture and politics that would be felt for decades to come (Ryan 1972, 367n11).

I quote at length an article from the establishment newspaper, the *Trinidad Express*, from the week of Carnival 1970. This report is worth drawing attention to as an important first-person account of the secondary historical material available on Black Power. The specifics of this accounting also speak to Oxaal's observation of the "break" that combined the political with the aesthetic:

The J'ouvert crowd in Independence Square was taken by surprise, first by the presentation of "The Truth about Blacks" from Pinetoppers, Inc., and then by "King Sugar" put out by "The U.W.I." "Truth" had been described as a band put out by Black Power militants in Port-of-Spain to voice their protest against the harassment of militant black leaders abroad, and the banning of Stokely Carmichael by the Trinidad and Tobago Government from entering this country where he was born. The marchers carried huge portraits of Eldridge Cleaver, the Black Panther leader; the late Malcolm X, Carmichael, and others. There was also a caricature of Prime Minister, Dr. Eric Williams, looking somewhat like a pig.

And there were lots of slogans, mainly calling for solidarity among the black people of the world. "King Sugar" recreated the hardships suffered by the workers in the sugar industry from slavery and indentureship up to the present day. The message the band was striving to put over was scrawled on its banner—"Black blood; black sweat; black tears—white profits." The Cedros band was a different matter. It was a dramatized indictment against the government for years of neglect. And although the Parliamentary Representative for the area assured them before Carnival that all their problems were being looked after, the people decided they would still bring out their band. This is in itself a measure of the confidence they have in the promises of politicians. And who can blame them? Why should they believe that promises made now will be fulfilled when those made 13 years ago remain promises?

But the one thing in common about these three bands is that they might have started a trend. And if we are to have another Carnival before elections, we may find politics more strongly represented on both days than ever before. (*Express*, February 15, 1970; quoted in Oxaal 1971, 28)

While observing that in 1970 "Carnival for once had failed as catharsis," Khafra Khambon (née Dave Darbeau) would also note: "The St. James village drummers had not so much played 1001 WHITE DEVILS—the Klu Klux Klan, Enoch Powell, Vorster, etc,—as they had performed a public ritual of exorcism" (1995a, 220). The (spiritual) power of Carnival to express, and release, the greater tensions of society was expected, perhaps even taken for granted. However, the events following Carnival would take the government, business leaders, and the greater public in Trinidad by surprise, because, rather than dissipating or being "exorcised," tensions gathered force and spilled out into the streets, catalyzed by events both at home and abroad. Chief among these events was the Sir George Williams Affair, which occurred in Montreal, Canada.

NJAC and the Sir George Williams Affair

Events in North America played an important role as catalysts for Trinidad's Black Power though not so much those in the United States, such as the mid-1960's struggles over voting rights in Selma, Alabama or the 1970 arrest and persecution of Angela Davis. Rather, it was the experience of Caribbean students (mostly of African descent) with racism in Canada, a fellow Commonwealth country, that would lead to protests in sympathy and ultimately to Black Power Day. As one Orisha elder and Black Power activist commented to me, "Canada in some ways seems to have impacted on Trinidad and Tobago politics and history even more than we will recognize or give credit to."

Trinidad's Black Power movement originated in the coming together of people from UWI, St. Augustine and the labor movement to protest the arrest of Caribbean students at Sir George Williams University in Montreal, Canada (Pantin 1990; Ryan and Stewart 1995). The National Joint Action Committee (NJAC) was formed on February 26, 1969, from a "loose confederation of groups," including Black Power groups like the Black Panthers and supposedly radical trade unions (Oilfield Workers' Trade Union, Transport and Industrial Workers Union). Two NJAC student organizers stood out: Dave Darbeau (now Khafra Khambon) and Geddes Granger (now Makandal Daaga; Pantin 1990, 51). The committee would be remembered as the public face of the Black Power movement and played a critical role in galvanizing public support through a series of rallies and marches ranging from an initial dozen participants to a peak in the tens of thousands. Narrative accounts of the Black Power movement all point to an incident at Sir George Williams University (now a part of Concordia University) in Montreal as a catalyst for the formation of NJAC and galvanization of Black Power in Trinidad.

In January 1969, talks between the university students (mainly Caribbean) and the administration broke down following a series of attempts within the institution to address the unresolved and long-standing allegations of racism against a biology professor. Attempts to resolve the conflict between students of color and the professor at a hearing were disrupted by student protesters and their supporters, who then took over the university's computer center on the ninth floor of the main campus building. The sit-in served as a catalyst on campus with an occupation of the faculty club by hundreds of white students six days later (Belgrave 1995, 127). Negotiations came close to successful resolution on February 10, but ultimately the administration rejected the students' terms. The next day police were called out in force as the students barricaded themselves in the computer center, where a fire "mysteriously" broke out. The students, fleeing smoke and flames, were rounded up and arrested (128).

The following arraignments and trial were heavily publicized and watched closely in both Canada and the Caribbean. Protests were organized on the UWI campus to support the ten Trinidadian students, who, as the largest group from a single country, were the first to go to trial. In Montreal, the office of the Trinidad High Commission was occupied (in part by the same Trinidadian students) where demands to speak with Prime Minister Eric Williams were met (by phone), leading to the Trinidad government's agreement to pay the students' legal fees and fines (131). Out of the Sir George Williams Affair would come increasing mobilization and organization around issues of Black Power and civil rights. February 26 was declared an International Day of Solidarity and in Trinidad would become known as Black Power Day, which, "effectively localized the struggle and heralded the real start of the 1970 revolution in Trinidad" (131).

Black Power Day: February 26, 1970

"The God we served, in His Whiteness seemed to mock us" (Springer 1995, 90). So said black activist, poet, and Orisha elder Eintou Pearl Springer, reflecting on the events of Black Power Day, a day that would see a march against "white power structures," targeting both businesses and the church. In the first major Black Power demonstration in Port of Spain, two to three hundred UWI students marched on the Canadian High Commission along the South Quay in protest of police and racial violence against black students at Sir George Williams University. Though the arrests had taken place the year before, the arrested students (among them several Trinidadians) were facing trial for property damage in early 1970. The South Quay demonstration was planned to coincide with the one-year anniversary of the February 2, 1969, demonstration in which UWI students had successfully blocked "visiting Canadian Governor-General Roland Michener from entering the St. Augustine campus" (Pantin 1990, 50–51). Students headed up to Independence Square and the Royal Bank of Canada and then went up along Frederick Street, with their numbers growing by the minute. According to Pantin, "The student leaders stopped outside well-known stores, singling out their owners by name for 'oppressing black people'" (51).

Next the crowd went to the Cathedral of the Immaculate Conception, "the biggest symbol of the 'white power structure' where they proceeded to throw black cloth and flags over the several white statues" (52). This last act, the very fact of entering into and demonstrating in a Roman Catholic Church, sparked public outrage and resulted in the arrest of eight men who were charged with "disturbing a place of worship and incitement" (53). Years later, Eintou Pearl Springer would write of that day, "Our first act of defiance, our first blow for liberation was to enter the Roman Catholic Cathedral and drape the images in black. In our youth, we did not fully understand the depth of that symbolism. All we knew was that anger and frustration had reached boiling point. The God we served, in His Whiteness seemed to mock us. He seemed to represent everything that was unattainable" (1995, 90). Among the protesting students who were arrested that day was Valerie Belgrave, a middle-class Afro-Trinidadian who would become a locally noted novelist (Pantin 1990, 70).[12] Decades after her experiences in Canada and in the Black Power movement she wrote, "The importance of the Sir George Williams incident, however, is that it united the black community in Montreal and it served as the rallying point which united various radical and progressive groups hear [sic] in Trinidad" (Belgrave 1995, 120). From these events in Canada and the response to them in Trinidad, the diasporic frame of Black Power becomes very clear.

Woodford Square Goes on the March

In March 1970 the demonstrations would continue with gatherings in Woodford Square organized by NJAC, marked by red, black, and green flags flying to accompany the raising of a black and African consciousness.[13] Geddes Granger proclaimed with his characteristic charismatic and fiery delivery, "If Massa Day was truly done, then Black Power Day must come!" (quoted in Pantin 1990, 54). He spoke in the same space where Eric Williams had delivered historical and political lectures less than a decade earlier, declaring "Massa Day done," to mobilize an emerging new electorate at the dawn of Independence. While Williams had inspired the people during the transition from British Colonialism his political leadership in the early years of Independence was critiqued by Granger and other leaders of the Black Power movement. As Pantin observes, "where Williams had stirred the crowd passions of the 1950s—anti-colonialism, Independence—Granger addressed the passions of a post-Independence generation" (54). Where Williams embraced the Afro-Creole middle class, Granger drew upon his roots in the grassroots community of Laventille and his background in the arts. Granger founded and ran a community center from the early to late 1960s focused on education, culture, and the arts called Pegasus in Laventille before taking advantage of the PNM's education program and enrolling in UWI, St. Augustine. There he would become the president of the Students' Guild and a lead organizer of NJAC (56).

"We shall walk without speaking, without shouting, without smiling, but we shall walk in anger," shouted Granger (Pantin 1990, 59). The first week of March 1970 would see a huge protest march of more than 10,000 people who walked from Woodford Square, down Frederick Street, to the Beetham 'Shanty Town' with Granger declaring, "Every black man in this country is a shanty town" (57).[14] I am excerpting a brief section from an evocative accounting of that day that was published in the *Trinidad Express* which brings us into the crowds where, "Deafening shouts of 'power, power' filled the tense afternoon air as six flags—three red, two black and green, and one green—were planted before the building by six serious-faced young, black, men and women. And Granger, his voice resounding from a microphone, interpreted the meaning of the colours for the crowd: 'The red flag is a declaration of war; black is for victory; for black unity; and green is for peace after we have achieved victory'" ("Black Power Stuns the City,"*Trinidad Express*; quoted in Oxaal 1971, 31). In a prescient echo of how many Black Power events in the United States and the Caribbean would unfold,

> He urged the crowd to move in peace, cautioning that there were dissident elements who had a plan to incite the marchers into violence. "There is a plan to brutalise you. We are not yet ready for violence. We are not ready for the confrontation—but it will surely come," Granger shouted. . . . And the march grew to almost unimaginable proportions. Up South Quay, around the Fly-Over Roundabout—many thought the demonstration was heading to San Juan. It stopped, however at Shanty Town which NJAC Chairman Geddes Granger identified as a symbol of the "Government indifference" to black people.
>
> Granger told the milling thousands that the plight of the people in Shanty Town was their plight, and he reminded the many who were muttering about the smell of the place that the people in Shanty Town had to live in it everyday [*sic*] of their lives. Along the Beetham Highway cars slowed to listen as "power" shouts greeted every speaker. University students, members of the National African Cultural Organization (Sangre Grande), Joint Action Committee, the African Cultural Association (St. James), the Black Panthers (North and South Trinidad and Tobago), Afro Turf Limers (San Juan), African Unity Brothers (St. Ann's), Southern Liberation Movement (San Fernando), Pinetoppers Incorporated (East Port-of-Spain) and National Freedom Organisation—each mounting the makeshift rostrum to say his piece. "Power! Power!" the crowd shouted

after almost every line. As one onlooker said: "I have never seen anything like this." (31–32)

On the following day, Thursday, March 5, hearings in Canada were held against the eight students arrested there. This drew another large crowd in Port of Spain. The riot squad was called out, marking the first night of Molotov cocktails. NJAC, led by Granger and Darbeau at Woodford Square, would declare "war" on Friday, March 6. This was a war against the racial ideologies and economic relations inherited as part of the colonial legacy. Pantin quotes Granger as saying, "The conviction derived from our historical experience that once our people are re-educated to liberate their minds from domination of the racist capitalist ideology of white Western civilization, they can forge the institutions and organization necessary for our complete liberation" (1990, 58). Over the following weeks there would be an increasing number of protests, growth in the numbers of Black Power groups, and increased circulation of publications such as broadsides and pamphlets (59).

March to Caroni

While demonstrations and marches would continue, the March to Caroni was a major turning point for race relations and the possibilities of class-based coalitions in the burgeoning social movement. Under "the slogan borne by some NJAC flags: INDIANS AND AFRICANS UNITE," the march was held on Thursday, March 12, 1970 (Pantin 1990, 64). Starting from Woodford Square, approximately ten thousand people gathered and marched down the Eastern Main Road several miles to Curepe, where they turned and headed south on the Southern Main Road (64–65). In a notably quiet and violence-free protest, thousands upon thousands of mainly Afro-Trinidadians "marched into the heart of the largely Indian sugar belt of Caroni in Central Trinidad, to actively demonstrate for racial unity between African and Indian 'black people'" (Meeks 1996, 21). The days leading up to the march were highly charged, as leaders from NJAC reached out to religious and labor leaders of the Indo-Trinidadian community, while the "establishment" watched with growing apprehension.

Members of the business community, especially the Port of Spain Chamber of Commerce and the PNM, the ruling government, watched closely for the potential of the movement to develop into an even greater threat. A coalition that brought together both grassroots Afro- and Indo-Trinidadians, including both Afro- and Indo-Trinidadian labor unions across divides would present a formidable force. All of this was at stake in the moments leading up to the March to Caroni. Pantin reports his own encounter with these politics, as Bhdase Sagan Maraj, head of Sanatan Dharma Maha Sabha, "virtual leader of the Hindu community," called him, initially happy to welcome Black Power demonstrators, and then called back hours later, suddenly opposed to the march (1990, 61). However, though the march took place without violence, it did not fulfill the promise of coalition building. Small numbers of Indo-Trinidadians joined the march, but the Indo-Trinidadian leaders and their large numbers of followers failed to materialize. As Warner writes of the events of 1970, "The revolution . . . took on a mantle of blackness as a symbol of the plight of a struggling Third World nation, and the Indians found it difficult to throw their full support behind it, viewing the blacks' sudden interest in the East Indian sugar worker with suspicion" (1993, 281). Even with this outcome, the establishment remained nervous. Management of the national newspaper the *Guardian* ordered that mention of the size of the crowd be eliminated from reporters' reports, and that no pictures of George Weekes (a labor leader), Geddes Granger, or Dave Darbeau be printed (Pantin 1990, 66, 68).

The promise held by the March to Caroni, which was the "creation of a unified mass movement that could put the fear of the Lord in any incumbent government," was forestalled (Pantin 1990, 61). The Black Power movement strove to speak to issues of both class *and* race in the postcolonial environment of a generally stagnant economy with the failure of new jobs to materialize, alongside insignificant changes in the elite and foreign ownership of corporations. An important part of this dynamic was to define blackness by using economic conditions in an attempt to widen the meaning of the term.[15] However, as the Indian leadership's lack of support for the March to Caroni indicated, this broadening of the term largely failed. As Rohlehr states, "The class basis of the 1970 protest movement was always very clear, even though the protest was articulated through the then current vocabulary of Black nationalism and in the process frightened and alienated people from the same class and with the same problems, but who were of different ethnicities and generally resented being termed 'black'" (1998, 871). Thus, the potential for mobilization on a class basis, across race and ethnic lines, which the establishment so feared, never materialized. As Meeks notes, "Despite NJAC's broad definition of 'black' to include Africans and Indians, many Indians refused to identify with the slogan of Black Power, and ended up being even further alienated from the movement" (1996, 22). Leaders of Black Power, throughout the Caribbean and notably in Trinidad, were inspired by Walter Rodney's writings, especially his book *The Groundings with My Brothers* (1969). In that volume Rodney confronted directly the issue of blackness as inclusive, writing, "I maintain that it is the white world which has defined who are blacks—if you are not white then you are black. However, it is obvious that the West Indian's situation is complicated by factors such as the variety of racial types, and racial mixtures and the process of class formation. We have, therefore, to note not simply what the white world says but also how individuals perceive each other. Nevertheless, we can talk of the mass of the West Indian population as being black—either African or Indian, Portuguese or Chinese" (Rodney 1969, 6; also quoted in B. J. Thomas 1992, 396). According to Thomas's description of Rodney's position: "Black Power was meant to include everyone" (396), though it was up to each group to determine its own participation.

There were, however, important shifts within the dynamics of Afro-Trinidadians from the exclusive hold of Afro-Creoles ("Afro-Saxons" in Lloyd Best's terminology) to pride in an African ancestral heritage. During March and April 1970, Orisha drums could be heard at night, from the east side to the west side of Port of Spain, as the marches and gatherings continued. This shift in cultural practice and consciousness would have reverberations through the society for the decades to come, far outstripping their immediate impact. In a volume that came from a retrospective conference on the 1970 Black power "revolution," held in 1990 at UWI, St. Augustine, political scientist Selwyn Ryan recalls,

> Broadly, the argument of Daaga [Granger] and others was that blacks were powerless in their own land and that the time had come to alter the historically defined hierarchical status system which had contrived to relegate them to the cellar place in the economic and social system even though they controlled the formal levers of political power and official patronage. There was also the view that the time had come for diaspora based Africans to embrace the African past and to take pride in their "negritude" and the "beauty" of being black. Mental emancipation was an essential part of the struggle. (1995, 695)

In the chapters to follow, it will be seen how an African consciousness, based in the grassroots Afro-Trinidadian community, would also take hold in portions of the Afro-Trinidadian middle-class community, informing religious and cultural practices and social relations.

Momentum in the movement waxed and waned over March and April, with flare-ups of activity and violence. After the March to Caroni, there continued to be marches every day to different communities with smaller and smaller crowds (Pantin 1990, 72–73). Subsequently, the arrested Sir George Williams University students came home, and Prime Minister Eric Williams spoke publicly on Black Power for the first time. Toward the end of March, things became violent, with protests on Charlotte Street and the riot police storming Woodford Square in downtown Port of Spain (74). It is interesting to note that Pantin's narrative, published twenty years after the events, includes his first-person accounts of feeling safe from the violence, knowing that the police would not hit him because of his conservative dress and because he was "fair-skinned" (75). The racial logics of the colonial era that privileged whiteness, and in its absence "lightness," remained salient through independence and Black Power. Beyond this, these racial logics continue to organize social relations into the twenty-first century throughout the Caribbean and the greater postcolonial world.

The month of April saw Black Power come back to public awareness with several major events, from coalitions to tragic violence. On the positive side was support for the Black Power movement from two closely linked communities that shared a dependence on the oil industry: the steel band movement and the Oilfield Workers Trade Union (Meeks 1996, 26–27). In sharp contrast, twenty-four-year-old Basil Davis was shot in the back by a policeman, becoming, "the 'first martyr of the revolution'" (27); this tragic event further catalyzed support for the movement. With support coalescing, the visible high mark of numbers came on Thursday, April 9, when Basil Davis's funeral procession went from Woodford Square to Barataria Cemetery and an estimated 30,000 or more people (some estimates going as high as 100,000) lined the streets for miles (many more than the 10,000 who marched to Caroni; Meeks 1996, 27; Pantin 1990, 77–78).

In this critical moment of resurgence in Black Power, the governing party split into liberal and conservative wings. The instability of the PNM's division was underscored by A. N. R. Robinson's resignation from his position as external affairs minister in protest of the PNM government's lack of response to the Black Power demands (Meeks 1996, 27; Pantin 1990, 80).[16] Adding to the major events of April was a tragic fire in San Juan in which four Indian girls died; the fire was blamed on arson by Black Power activists, which served to increase racial tensions. The last straw for the beleaguered government was a strike by more than six hundred workers (almost all of them Indo-Trinidadians) at Brecchin Castle, the Couva sugar factory. With escalating tensions on the streets, increasing agitation in the industrial sector, and dissension among political leadership in the government, the country was, indeed, in crisis. While there were a number of contributors to the upheaval, it was the threat of labor uniting across diverse industries, from sugar to oil to water, that would generate a government response. This in turn further catalyzed events, moving Black Power to an even greater level of social upheaval and, ultimately, cultural (if not political) change.

Mutiny and Curfew

Events in April would continue to escalate, ultimately involving threats to national security and international calls for help. On April 21, a nationwide state of emergency was declared, with a dusk-to-dawn curfew. Key Black Power leaders were arrested before dawn and taken to a "hastily put together" detention camp (Pantin 1990, 81). A tumultuous riot in the heart of downtown on Frederick Street arose that morning as police told crowds that, under the new state of emergency, it was illegal to gather. Two young lieutenants at the Teteron National Defense Force Base (located at the site of the former U.S. naval base, on the peninsula of Chaguaramas, about ten miles west of the capital) turned their guns on their superior officers and mutinied. This surprising event would be compounded by a mutiny at Camp Ogden, St. James (the base located at the edge of Port of Spain; Pantin 1990, 86). Reaction to the tense events of that day was swift, with several international governments calling to inquire about the possibility of military support. Venezuela and the United States sent warships to Trinidad, with the U.S. carriers being turned away and the two Venezuelan ships asked to stay off the coast as a show of force, in case of further armed conflict.

Over the next weeks, rebel demands were negotiated with the Williams government, including bringing back formerly ousted leader Lieutenant Colonel Joffre Serrette into command (Oxaal 1971, 39). After about two weeks, Serrette would lead the mutiny leaders Raffique Shah and Rex LaSalle to Port of Spain for "questioning," where they were arrested on charges of mutiny and treason (Pantin 1990, 94). Eventually eighty mutineers, including Shah and LaSalle, would be tried by a Commonwealth military tribunal.[17] Shah and LaSalle, sentenced to twenty and fifteen years, respectively, would be freed two years later (alongside many of the mutineers) by the Trinidad and Tobago Court of Appeal on "legal technicalities" (Pantin 1990, 94). By May 1970, according to Meeks, "After the arrest of the mutineers and the prolonged dusk to dawn curfew which followed, the revolutionary movement, demoralized and without leadership, seemed to crumble and disintegrate as though it had never really existed" (1996, 34). The state of emergency was lifted on November 20, 1970 (though there would be intermittent states of emergency throughout the early 1970s).[18] As the gatherings of thousands faded from public memory alongside the shouts of "Power to the people!" so too would the shift of consciousness the Black Power movement had engendered in Trinidad fade, only to reemerge in different religious and cultural forms over the subsequent three or four decades.

Many of the leaders and organizations that had been active in 1970 would refocus their energies along the lines that "any political change which is to be meaningful for the black man must have a cultural base" (Darbeau n.d.; reprinted in Oxaal 1971, 63–64). Geddes Granger felt strongly that through, "the arts . . . the spirit of the people would emerge and develop" (Pantin 1990, 56). He identified that the grassroots communities of Laventille in the hills above Port of Spain "constantly buoyed its spirit its own music and song, calypso and steelband, feeding off the older Baptist and Orisha music remembered from Africa." (55) What he had started in his cultural work in the Laventille community arts organization of Pegasus in the late 1960s would reemerge years later from of a reorganization of NJAC as a renewed focus in culture. In Trinidad's Black Power movement politics, culture, and spirituality were always closely intertwined. And all three were in critical relation to economics (and remain so into the contemporary moment, as true in Trinidad as throughout the post-colonial countries of Africa and Caribbean). Reflecting on this complex dynamic Rhohler states,

> The National Joint Action Committee, which had spearheaded the Black Power rebellion of the youth, was politically neutralized by detentions, frequent police harassment, armed searches for arms and seditious literature, the 1971 State of Emergency, but most of all by the Prime Minister's Special Works project which employed the technique of making block leaders and potential insurgents foremen and checkers on Special Works. Rebels became the clients of the State, whose patronage began to define and influence the direction of power on the blocks.

In the midst of such manipulation, the National Joint Action Committee (NJAC) established and maintained a forum for what they called Black Tradition in the Arts in which they featured the leading protest poets, calypsonians and musicians. (1998, 874)

Other organizations would emerge in the 1990s, including the National Action Cultural Committee that sponsored "the annual series of calypso competitions: Young Kings and Young Queens, focusing on newcomers to this peculiarly Trinidadian craft," directed especially at grassroots black youth and Carnival (Pantin 1990, 113). Additionally, under the leadership of Khafra Khambon (née David Darbeau), politically informed mobilizations of culture would coalesce around the commemoration of emancipation into the Emancipation Support Committee.

In the postindependence politics that focused on the development of a national community, culture and politics would be firmly conjoined. Political tensions of neocolonialism that erupted in 1970 Black Power were only partially resolved by the changing policies of the PNM government. Social tensions revealed in 1970 were ameliorated as much by the subsequent oil boom as by a substantive shift in government policies or business ownership. Into the 1980s and 1990s, much of the political critique and protest of the 1970s era moved into social and cultural spheres. Specifically, the Afro-Trinidadian middle-class leadership was tasked with consolidating a "national culture" in the midst of negotiations between tensions of a multicultural rhetoric informed by a Creole discourse that overlooked the position of Indo-Trinidadians. As Rohlehr assessed, "The 'Creole' intelligentsia from which Williams recruited his political directorate had defined both 'nation' and 'culture' in terms of 'Creole' imperatives to the exclusion of other ethnic groups" (1998, 875). These negotiations played out in the arena of public culture, as evident in the politics surrounding Carnival (a long-term and perennial site of political negotiation). In the 1990s and into the new millennium, neoliberal economics have shaped institutions of Carnival, such as fetes and mas' bands, increasingly sorting people into separate categories along lines of race, class, and color.[19]

The dilemma of the middle class was rooted in the challenge of creating a national culture and being charged with leadership in a system that gives them the appearance of power without actual power. This created the basis for cultural capital being a source of power (e.g., providing status and access to political leadership) within the middle class and the national public sphere. Moments such as the 1970 Black Power movement in

Trinidad reveal portions of the African middle class moving out of their comfort zone and traditionally held position of political conservatism that protected their class interests. This "traditional" political position of the Afro-Trinidadian middle class had contributed to the reproduction of power structures inherited from the colonial regime where social stratification organizes and polices social, political, and economic opportunities for people along lines of race, class, color, and ethnicity. Black Power threatened to disrupt these social categories and the political, social, and cultural systems that supported them. Arising out of a radicalized student body at UWI, NJAC was largely made up of the children of the middle class and upper class (with few exceptions to the rule, such as Geddes Granger). Though the followers of Black Power came largely from the grassroots, that much of the impetus and leadership came from the middle class made many of the power brokers in Trinidad very uncomfortable (seen largely in the reaction of the Port of Spain Chamber of Commerce and the establishment newspaper, the *Guardian*, as documented by Pantin [1990]).

The immediate legacies of 1970 Black Power were challenges to stereotypes of blackness, where the shame associated with being African was replaced with an opposite reaction that reversed the polar associations of white/good and black/bad (rather than transcending or decentering the symbolic discourse). However, seeds were planted in the fertile soil of neocolonial and decolonization processes that through the realms of the aesthetic and the cultural would further support the growth of African-centered practices. The decades following the Black Power movement were critical to the emergence of Spiritual Baptists and Orisha into Trinidad's public spheres (both civic and religious) and would witness significant national and international recognitions. The emergent spiritual citizenship in Trinidad's Ifá/Orisha community is firmly grounded in diasporic manifestations of the black radical tradition. The shifts in consciousness propelled by Black Power were a critical moment that set the stage for African-based religions to enter the public sphere in Trinidad and navigate the politics of multiculturalism with both a critical gaze and an organized voice.

CHAPTER 2

Multicultural Movements

From Margins to Mainstream

The procession of Orisha folk had moved down the streets of Arouca to end at Trinidad's African Ancestral Site. A year before the new millennium they were gathered to celebrate their faith and their community. First were the praises to the ancestors, next the granting of awards and a brief calypso interlude before the children lined up, performing their rehearsed dance even as water libations were made to cool the earth (Iba se Onile). For a person of importance, a holder of political power, had arrived. Claps and the Trinidad Orisha call—a warble yell produced by beating the hand against the mouth—greeted the political leader of Trinidad, Prime Minister Basdeo Panday, as he stepped onto Orisha holy land, a welcome guest. On this day he would speak to the Orisha folk and promise the support of his party and the government. In Parliament just a few months later, his promises would materialize.[1]

As put by Eintou Pearl Springer,[2] then a member of the newly formed Council of Orisha Elders, "We want to say that it is the first time that a Prime Minister of this country has come to be part of Orisha people business" (Panday 1999). The next day Prime Minister Basdeo Panday's photo at the festival would be on the front page of both national newspapers under headlines that read "Shango Rising" and "PM Promises More Rights for Orishas" (Henry 2003, 129; Taitt 1999). Panday spoke as an invited guest at the Second Annual Orisha Family Day on March 21, 1999. In the thirty-seven years since independence, he was the nation's first Indo-Trinidadian political leader. His appearance at this Orisha festival to offer his public support, through both speech and actions, was remarkable in a country where the religion's adherents had long been marginalized even after emerging from a history of colonial criminalization. After his speech, Panday would pour libations of water, honey, and rum on land dedicated to the African ancestors. This public performance of respect to the African ancestors, and by extension to the members of the Orisha religion, was monumental.

Orisha in the Public Eye

In 1999, Orisha was on the rise while the first Indo-Trinidadian government was in power. The Orisha community had an increasingly public profile that included major media coverage, state concessions, and the hosting of an international conference. All of this built on energy generated by the 1996 granting of Spiritual Baptist Shouter Liberation Day as a national holiday and the earlier visit, in 1988, of the Yorùbá religion's highest official, the Ọ̀ọ̀ni Ọba Okùnadé Síjúwadé Olúbàse II of Ilé-Ifè, Nigeria.[3] In this chapter, I focus in part on the question of the United National Congress (UNC) government's sponsorship of Orisha in an environment of ethnic party politics and competing interests (shaped by constituencies of African and Indian descendants—each with 40 percent of the population). How can we locate the political efficacy of Trinidad's first Indian political leader and his decision to embrace and support African religious traditions?

To further consider Prime Minister Panday's political position, I focus on the rhetorical and performative aspects of his participation in a gathering of different Orisha shrines, leaders, practitioners, and supporters who celebrate the faith in Trinidad. The Orisha Family Day was in its second year in 1999 and was well on its way to establishing itself as "one of the most important public event[s] in the Orisha calendar" (Henry 2003, 126).[4] Held over three days, the festival included an opening march followed by prayers, speeches, musical performances, an awards ceremony, and an ancestor ritual featuring Egungun masquerade dancers (see plate 2).[5] This last element was organized by a recently established Egungun society (from the Orisha shrine, Ile Eniyan Wa, led by Iya Amoye in Princes Town, South Trinidad), whose presence, Henry notes, "confirmed the importance of bringing genuine Yoruba elements back into the faith" (129). The establishment of Orisha Family Day was important for bringing the Orisha religion into public view. The national newspapers would run major stories on the festival, with

Prime Minister Panday's presence in 1999 and President A. N. R. Robinson's the following year garnering front-page coverage. This positive attention reflected the organizing of the newly formed Council of Orisha Elders and marked a new era of cooperation in a historically decentralized religion. Through the organizing of individual shrines (religious congregations), the Orisha community was able to identify national leaders who could (and did) represent Orisha to the state. It was these changes in leadership that provided the environment for Panday's landmark visit to the Orisha Family Day festival.

Panday's presence was a "public affirmation of the religion [that] demonstrated political legitimation, providing evidence of the importance of the external forces effecting changes in the status of the religion in society" (Henry 2003, 129). However, his presence was greeted both warmly and critically by the Orisha devotees because many other politicians had made earlier promises that never bore fruit. Eintou Pearl Springer was quoted in a national newspaper as saying, in reference to promises of land, "It have plenty slip between cup and lip so we asking for we deed please" (*Trinidad Express*, March 22, 1999). With this Panday was put on notice that his presence and words were not enough; he would be judged by his actions.[6]

Panday's rhetoric clearly spelled out his support for the Orisha community and set a high bar for his administration. The theme of the festival, "Many Orishas, One Family," was chosen as the focus of his remarks. In strong terms he declared:

> If we fail to achieve the Orisha ideal of One Family, we shall all surely perish. In no way am I suggesting religious syncretism. We already have cultural syncretism in the creolisation of our culture. That is the most visible product of our diversity. Some say it is the most valuable dividend of our diversity. Leadership in this national mission to create one national family out of our unique diversity must come from our Orisha Elders, and from all of our country's religious leaders. That is the leadership to which we must look for the redemption and the restoration of the soul of our nation. (Panday 1999)

Panday's speech contains obvious allusions to creolization and syncretism as cultural (and not religious) models that address the diversity of the nation. He links this diversity to the challenge of nation building ("create one national family") while placing this project firmly in the hands of the national religious leadership and specifically, in this speech, into those of the Orisha elders. After the Orisha religion's long history of persecution and denigration, Panday's rhetoric was particularly noteworthy: in an unprecedented way it positioned the Orisha tradition and its elders on an equal level with other religions in Trinidad. In this same speech, he would pledge to introduce legislation granting entitlements that would be passed by Parliament later that year. This effectively moved Panday's support beyond the rhetorical, to active political sponsorship. In his project to realize "the harmony in diversity which is our nation's manifest destiny," he embraced the leadership of the Orisha movement in Trinidad and identified these leaders as key players in his particular vision of the multicultural nation-state (Panday 2000).

Panday's public support would help to solidify the entrance of the Spiritual Baptist and Orisha religions into Trinidad's public sphere. This support for African traditions could be considered an implementation of the multicultural rhetoric long heard in Trinidad's independence politics as voiced by the traditional Afro-Creole leadership.[7] Or it could be viewed as a strategy to create alliances in the postcolonial era across traditional ethnic divisions. In the 1960s, with independence came the consolidation of a largely Afro-Creole middle class in national and political leadership positions, building on an older entrenched black and Creole middle class that had roots going back to the mid-nineteenth century. The following decades witnessed the challenges to neocolonialism raised by 1970s Black Power and the subsequent decade's oil boom which countered the critical politics of the prior era with the increased circulation and distribution of wealth. New sectors of the working class moved into the middle class, including increasing numbers of Indo-Trinidadians. Shifting demographics between Indo-Trinidadians and Afro-Trinidadians culminated in the 1990s with changes in political leadership. This was simultaneous with the continued movement of Indo-Trinidadians from traditionally rural areas to urban areas alongside their expansion into the middle- and upper-class communities (Khan 2004a; Munasinghe 2001b). These divisions of race, ethnicity, class, and geography also extended to religion. Reflecting on Panday's sponsorship of Orisha entitlements, a middle-class shrine leader characterized him as "very savvy and smart" as he had "courted all the different religious communities, including both Orisha and the Pentecostals."

In other social and political arenas, Panday was widely held to be perpetuating the tradition of ethnic-based patronage by granting leadership positions, key appointments, and lucrative government contracts to Indo-Trinidadians (Meighoo 2003; Ryan 1999). These sentiments only served to fuel the Afro-Trinidadian unease and suspicion of an Indo-Trinidadian political leadership. Rather than allaying these fears, Panday's backing of the Orisha movement was dismissed by many Afro-Trinidadians as mere political posturing and thus gained him little favor. According to Meighoo, "[One] of the UNC government's main efforts was to 'celebrate' diversity, and attempt to turn it into a strength. However, such efforts were often greeted with hostility by those who suspected that though apparently promoting equality, the aim was to covertly usher in Indian hegemony, undermine the positions of Afro-Trinidadians, or both" (2003, 213). Any attempt to disrupt the dominance of Afro-Creole representation in national culture and politics has been met, over the decades since independence, with public outcry from Afro-Trinidadians.

The rhetoric of ethnic party politics has shaped the landscape of national culture to the extent that race and ethnicity (alongside color and class) are implicated in every political decision. Because Panday's long-standing political roots go back decades to his early 1970s leadership in the All Trinidad Sugar and General Workers Trade Union (followed by almost twenty years as leader of the opposition), he clearly had a keen grasp of the ramifications of his support of the Orisha religion. In negotiating this ethnic terrain, Panday drew heavily on a multicultural rhetoric not dissimilar from that of former prime minister Eric Williams.[8] Panday's active support for cultural traditions, both Indian and African, extended beyond rhetoric to state patronage in an attempt to expand the national imaginary beyond its Afro-Trinidadian boundaries to become inclusive of all ethnic identities. Given this, it may be worth considering that his position was more than posturing. It contained significant risks, indeed, alienating voting segments of the largely Afro-Trinidadian Pentecostals even as Panday courted them as well. With these factors in mind, it seems necessary to look beyond obvious political strategies for a solution to the question of what makes Panday's support of the Orisha movement politically efficacious.

How does the promotion of a particular political constituency rooted in the Orisha religion, whose members are characterized here under the rubric of an African or black cultural citizenship and an emerging spiritual citizenship, serve the interests of the state's multicultural discourse or those of Indo-Trinidadian leadership and their promotion of an "Indian" cultural citizenship? Munasinghe astutely identifies the form of multiculturalism currently promoted in Trinidad as one where difference is to be valorized and recognized as the basis for equality rather than a fictive equal distribution or blending, thus creating a new homogeneity out of particular culturally appropriated heterogeneous elements.[9] This shift in definition and focus of multicultural rhetoric reveals an ideological shift, one demonstrated by Panday, which has proved to be politically effective for both the Indo-Trinidadian political leadership and the burgeoning Indo-Trinidadian middle class. An emphasis on the equal place afforded to difference in the national project (in terms of particular cultural, ethnic, or religious groups) then creates a space for Indo-Trinidadians as culture bearers who contribute to the nation, shifting a position that had been foreclosed in the earlier multicultural rhetoric informed by a model of creolization based on a binary racial logic of black/African and white/European.

The Spirits in the Law

The process of politicization of African-based religions has roots that stretch from British colonialism to the present moment. The tying together of social position and political power to culture, religion, race, and class continues to shape relations of power and formations of identity in Trinidad while informing the dynamics of national politics. The cultural politics of identity and nationalism have their genesis in the Spanish and British colonial regimes and their attendant Christian religions. In the 1800s, the competition for social and spiritual dominance between French Catholic elites and British Protestants created a social and political opening for non-Christian practices in the colony. However, by the 1880s, "African" religions became subject to increasing persecution and control as the British emerged triumphant and asserted their social, political, and religious dominance. Colonialism's use of religion as a disciplining and "civilizing" practice has been documented in Africa and the Caribbean (Austin-Broos 1997; Jean Comaroff and John Comaroff 1997).

The institutional persecution of African religions culminated in the Shouters Prohibition Ordinance (SPO) of 1917, which outlawed gatherings after dark, drumming, bell ringing, and other cultural practices associated with the religions.[10] The SPO was "modeled" on St. Vincent's 1912 prohibition of Spiritual Baptists and banned "a person from holding flowers or a lighted candle in their hands at a public meeting, ringing bell or wearing a white head tie, and from any form of shaking of the body" (Henry 2003, 32; Herskovits and Herskovits 1947, 345).[11] Additional legislation, the Summary Conviction Offenses Ordinance of May 19, 1921, specifically targeted traditions including *obeah*,[12] Bongo, and drumming after 10:00 PM (and currently is still on the books).[13] The legally sanctioned persecution largely drove the practices of African religions underground (literally into the forest or, as described locally, "the bush"). Earlier legislation in the nineteenth century, such as the Drum Dances Ordinance, outlawed African forms of religion (1869) and drumming (1883) and informed the police harassment of both faiths in the latter half of that century (Glazier 1983; Henry 2003, 34; Trotman 2007, 234). However, the 1917 legislation put teeth behind the harassment and led to people losing their homes, livelihoods, and liberty. The SPO was used against perceived African practices in general and often specifically targeted Orisha worshippers, as well as those perceived to be practicing obeah as generally understood. The existence of these laws enabled landowners, managers, and other authorities to discriminate against members of Spiritual Baptist and Orisha congregations.[14] This resulted in an atmosphere of fear, secrecy, and concealment (prayer meetings often took place in the "bush" or deep forest) that has only shifted in recent decades. Thus, a history of persecution led to the development of decentralized and independent networks of practitioners, skilled not only in secrecy but also in resistance and political action.

Following successful attempts to overturn the SPO and "legalize" African-based religions in the 1940s and 1950s, the Black Power movement of the 1970s initiated a change in understanding of Africa and its cultural and religious heritage in Trinidad. In a remarkable departure from previous decades of persecution and denigration, this change developed in the 1980s and 1990s into a revalorization of Africa that contributed to a public resurgence of African diasporic traditions and religions marked by significant negotiations with, and concessions from, the state.[15] Prior to the 1990s, various administrations, from those of Williams to Manning, had different levels of association with the Orisha and Spiritual Baptist communities that remained rhetorical (with many promises broken). Only after Panday became prime minister in 1995 was legislation passed granting entitlements to the Orisha movement. One such example is the Orisha Marriage Act, Number 22 (1999), which granted state-registered Orisha priests the legal power to perform marriages.[16] Implementation of the act required mechanisms by which shrines and priests could register. While the legislation has been seen as a social and political boon it is only rarely utilized, with very few priests having registered.

However, this legislation did build on earlier state recognition, through legal incorporation of shrines, in the 1980s and early 1990s (Coker 1999).[17] In 1981, the Act for Incorporation of the Orisha Movement of Trinidad and Tobago Egbe Ile Wa was passed.[18] In the following decade, Opa Orisha Shango, another umbrella organization that was newly incorporated (1992), "flexed its political muscle—attending the inauguration of the new parliament and the spiritual leader, Baba Clarence Ford, offering Orisha prayers at the National Day of Prayer" (Houk 1995, 126). These incorporation acts would be followed by later inclusion of the Orisha religion within the nation's ecumenical advisory (nongovernmental) board, the Inter-Religious Organization (IRO). Activist, poet, and scholar Eintou Pearl Springer initiated an application to the IRO in 1995 on behalf of the Orisha religion. Over the next six years, a series of conflicts, both public and behind the scenes, would ultimately resolve in favor of the Orisha religion whose representatives "officially" joined the IRO in 2001 (Henry 2003, 86–89). This same period saw the campaign for a national holiday (Lord Shango Day), which laid the groundwork for the 1996 recognition of March 30 as Spiritual Baptist Liberation Day (Henry 2003, 65–74; McNeal, K. E. 2011, 275; Scher 1997, 317). While the holiday was intended for Spiritual Baptists, their overlapping membership with Orisha devotees (alongside public perception that conflates the two religions) effectively facilitated the government's attempt to address two faiths with one day. There are still sectors of the Orisha community advocating for a separate Orisha holiday.[19] Additionally, a twenty-five-acre land grant, deeds and all, was provided for the creation of an African Spiritual Heritage Park in 2000. Prime Minister Panday described the land grant as "another step in [my] drive to bring all faiths into the mainstream of Civil Society" (2000).

The extensive media coverage of these actions, and the debates that surrounded them, only served to raise the profile of the Orisha religion in Trinidad. Panday leveraged this in his campaign to expand the inclusiveness of the nation and disrupt the cultural, social, and formerly political dominance of Afro-Creole culture. Since before independence in 1962, the Afro-Creole middle-class leadership in Trinidad, drawing on a black/white binary that valorized European traditions, had laid claim not only to the development of the nation but also to the national imaginary. This had left out large sectors of the population, mainly non-Christians and Indo-Trinidadians, who drew on religious and cultural traditions largely informed by African and/or Indian (and not exclusively European) heritages.

Indians Arrive: Prime Minister Basdeo Panday

In 1995, Basdeo Panday, longtime political organizer and head of the Sugar Workers Trade Union, came to power as political leader of the UNC and prime minister. His success was largely brought about by a combination of charisma, shifting population demographics that brought Indians to an electoral parity with Afro-Trinidadians for the first time, and a key political alliance with a minority party, the National Alliance for Reconstruction (NAR; Meighoo 2003; Premdas 1996, 1999; Ryan 1999). The election resulted in a tie, with the People's National Movement (PNM) and the UNC each holding an equal number of seats in the Parliament. President A. N. R. Robinson, former prime minister under the NAR government from 1986 to 1991, held the key swing vote.[20] The NAR, which held the two pivotal seats, joined forces with the UNC, providing them with the necessary seats to control the government and thus elect the prime minister. Robinson's actions effectively appointed Panday as Trinidad's first Indian prime minister. In turn, Robinson was designated minister extraordinaire and then elected president in 1997 (a largely ceremonial role that he held until 2003).

In the face of rising racial tensions, Panday attempted to address Trinidad's deeply entrenched ethnic divisions through appeals to a multicultural vision of the nation. The view that Panday's ascension to national political leadership represented a generally feared East Indian takeover of the government led to great anxiety among Afro-Trinidadians (Meighoo 2003, 198–199, 216; Premdas 1999, 354). This was true especially of members of the Afro-Trinidadian middle class, who feared losing their traditional positions of economic and cultural power, which they perceived to be tenuous and dependent largely upon state patronage. Alternatively, Indo-Trinidadians celebrated their increased representation and leadership in national politics as long overdue. The increasing wealth and education of Indo-Trinidadians can be seen in their participation in middle-class and urban sectors traditionally reserved for Afro-Trinidadians and the small remaining French Creole elite. Panday's negotiation of this ethnic terrain has drawn heavily on a multicultural rhetoric not dissimilar from that of former prime minister Eric Williams.

Prime Minister Panday shared much of the rhetorical style of Dr. Williams, another charismatic leader who advocated unity. The main difference between them lies not in the outward form of their multicultural rhetoric. Panday heavily promoted national unity, with catchphrases such as "All we is one" and "Unity in diversity" and liberal use of the national motto, "Together we aspire, together we achieve"—all expressions very similar to Williams's own rhetorical style. The gap between rhetoric and policy was evidenced under Williams's leadership, where the Afro-Creole population, economically, socially, and especially culturally, became identified with nation building and the national culture in spite of a multicultural rhetoric.[21] As Selwyn Ryan writes of Williams, "Despite his genuine intellectual commitment to multiracialism, he refused to concede minority communities the right to elect their own kind, or to articulate their own version of the national community. The majoritarian thesis implicitly promised a homogeneous society, a non-racial rather than a multiracial society" (1972, 375). Panday pointedly used rhetoric similar in style to Williams's own and has faced similar charges of majoritarianism. Despite his frequent proclamations of "unity in diversity," the common perception is that the UNC government favored the Indo-Trinidadian community (at the expense of Afro-Trinidadians) with key positions, contracts, and other entitlements. Yet what distinguished Panday from Williams was the former's support of diverse ethnic cultures, not only in speech but also in political action. As discussed previously, Panday introduced and passed legislation that recognized and supported various cultural traditions not limited to the Indo-Trinidadian sphere.

The role of Trinidad's state in constructing a national community out of two equally large minority populations has involved both cultural politics and a discourse on multiculturalism. Panday's past support of particular cultural and religious (i.e., non-Christian) identities may have contributed to a perception of Indo-Trinidadians as active participants and contributors to the nation and the national imaginary. His inclusive formulation of multiculturalism attempts to expand the bounds of national culture. The public support by the state of the Spiritual Baptist and Orisha religions, with their particular claims to an African identity, reflects a shift in the basis for their multicultural rhetoric. Through moving away from a "creolization" model, as advocated by Williams and his party, the PNM, and the early (Afro-Trinidadian) nationalists, the national culture could be redefined to include particular cultures—each distinct, separate, and equal. In this instance, the national identity then becomes one of contributing a unique culture—and thus creates a space for particular cultures, especially the East Indian, to be active and dynamic contributors and members of the national culture.

Public Relations and African Spirits:
Reflections on the Multicultural Nation-State

Over the fifty years since the SPO of 1917 outlawing African religious practices was repealed, African religious communities continued to struggle for recognition and equality (and still do into the contemporary moment). In the 1980s and 1990s, national councils were organized to represent different sectors of the community, with the aim of increasing their political power, representation, and effectiveness (Scher 1997). However, the lobbying attempts of the Council of Orisha Elders had largely been unsuccessful before Panday took office in 1995 (Henry 2003). During the course of his administration, from 1995 to 2001, the council garnered greater state recognition and entitlements. As a result, the Orisha tradition acquired an increasingly high profile in the public sphere. This visibility was reflected and sustained by the extensive media coverage during a period in which many entitlements were received, including the previously mentioned designation of a Spiritual Baptist national holiday (Scher 1997, 317). In 1999, Panday's administration went further and passed legislation to officially sanction Orisha rites of passage (the Orisha Marriage Bill, 1999). In doing so, Parliament (the state) recognized more than two hundred shrines.

The political and social discourses surrounding the Orisha and Spiritual Baptist traditions are based largely on this multicultural rhetoric. In his essay "Unveiling the Orisha" (1997), Philip Scher provides an analysis of one such site of contestation, claims to authenticity and authority, in the moment of Orisha's movement into the mainstream. He maps out "attempts on the part of various Orisha groups to make themselves known and, if not accepted and understood, at least tolerated" and finds that they "have used as a strategy the national rhetoric of tolerance found in the national anthem ('where every creed and race finds an equal place')" (Scher 1997, 317). These religions have organized nationally and mobilized politically to ensure their place in the nation, building on both the valorization of Africa that was the legacy of the 1970s Black Power movement and Trinidad's historical claims of multicultural equality. Much of this was directed by new Orisha leaders who had risen to political prominence, in contrast to "traditional" leaders whose positions were based on religious knowledge and ancestral lineage. This new leadership is in large part composed of members of the long-established Afro-Creole middle class, which in itself both represents and promotes increased social acceptance for the tradition

(Henry 2003, 91–92; Houk 1995, 37). Henry has noted, "There is an entire new class of membership composed of middle-class professionals who are either devotees themselves or who publicly support and affirm the validity of these religions. Their very presence lends legitimation to these religions. The major change here is not only because of the eminence of these new members but also because of the public nature of their commitment. For some, adherence becomes a public celebration" (2003, 92). Among these newly public middle-class devotees were national, religious, cultural, and political leaders, including several members of Parliament who have affiliations within the Orisha and Spiritual Baptist communities. This included Spiritual Baptist archbishop Barbara Burke, who has been a longtime senator, first for the PNM and later for the UNC.[22] This new middle-class leadership, drawn from the Afro-Creole community, has been effective in providing a public voice for the Orisha faith and raising its status (and thus making it more respectable and acceptable) within the national culture (Aiyejina and Gibbons 1999; Henry 2003).

At the turn of the millennium, the shifting grounds of the state's multicultural discourse illuminate dynamics that have brought the Spiritual Baptist and Orisha traditions further into the mainstream, under the patronage of Indo-Trinidadian political leadership. The independence rhetoric of creolization, one that Panday referred to as "the most visible product of our diversity" (1999), put forth a homogeneous vision of the nation that marginalized the Indian experience and contributions to nation building while centering the role of an Afro-Creole elite in the nation (one whose values were defined against a projected European standard that was held comparatively high above that of denigrated African traditions). Subsequently, with its rise to political power, the Indian-dominated UNC faced fears and accusations of merely switching roles in the same mechanism of ethnic domination. Since independence, Trinidad's political history, with the brief exception of a five-year coalition-led government, has conditioned the population to both expect and accept ethnic-based party politics (Meighoo 2003; Premdas 1996, 1999; Ryan 1999).

Yet in trying to make sense of Panday's government and the sponsorship of African religious traditions, another possibility beyond posturing emerges. Though on the surface much of the multicultural rhetoric employed by Panday appears similar to that of the nation's founding political leader and intellectual Dr. Eric Williams, there is a marked distinction: an emphasis on difference that values the unique cultural and religious contributions of diverse people as a piece of the whole instead of the creation of a homogeneous society based on Afro-Creole sameness (this sameness itself was generated by the independence project of claiming and sanitizing the cultural production of the lower- and working-class, or grassroots, Afro-Trinidadians for consumption by the middle class in the name of "developing national culture"). This reading of the political support for the Orisha and Spiritual Baptist movements, as intended to expand the base of cultural and religious contributions to the national imaginary, is certainly more hopeful than theories of tokenism hiding ethnic party politics.

The challenge to understanding Panday's support of the Orisha movement in Trinidad is related deeply to the viability of multiculturalism. In supporting the entitlement claims of particular interests (identity politics), did the state, as led by Panday, provide the stage for ethnic party politics and patronage? It is possible that he truly meant to implement policies that respected and recognized difference while supporting all groups equally—in his mission to create "one national family." His reelection in 2000 highlights the success of his political rhetoric among the largely Indo-Trinidadian segments of the population. However, his victory was very close, with Panday having lost support of a critical bloc, the small sector of Afro-Trinidadians who broke away from the traditional ethnic-based affiliation of the PNM. (In the following year, Panday would lose his political office through key defections from his party.)[23] The Afro-Trinidadian perception of state patronage of Indo-Trinidadian interests during the UNC government was not successfully countered by Panday's support of the Orisha movement. Whether his support of particular cultural identities significantly contributed to a change in the perception of Indo-Trinidadians as active participants in and contributors to the nation (and the national imaginary), rather than as passive outsiders, remains questionable. In the end, Panday's support of one family branch did little for the recognition of his own "outside" branch.[24]

Panday's cultural strategies attempted to expand the basis of national identity and cultural citizenship. It was these logics that had him, a champion of Indo-Trinidadian culture, putting state resources toward the recognition and legitimation of African diasporic religious practices. Having displaced the postindependence hold on political leadership of Afro-Trinidadians, Panday made political decisions in regard to the Spiritual Baptist and Orisha communities, which were directed at challenging and disrupting the prevailing multicultural norm that privileged Afro-Trinidadian contributions to the culture of the nation. Ultimately, the entitlements and legislation "not only transformed public perceptions of Orisha but also changed the position of Orisha spiritual practices in the Afro-Caribbean diaspora," facilitating Trinidad Orisha's emerging engagement with the transnational spiritual networks of Yorùbá-based religions (Hucks 2006, 35). Nowhere was this more evident than in the international conference on Orisha that was hosted by Trinidad in 1999 and sponsored by the Panday administration.

It was here that I personally entered Trinidad's unfolding narrative of Orisha and Ifá, upon my long-deferred return. In a pivotal moment at the Sixth World Orisha Congress, a fieldwork conjuncture if you will, I would meet my primary interlocutors in the field. And in a manner that was at the time totally unexpected (only to become all too familiar in the not so distant future), these meetings were at the intersections of the personal and the professional, the unfamiliar and the familiar, the spiritual and the secular.

A significant portion of Trinidad's Orisha leadership today can trace their participation in the religion to the local 1970s Black Power movement, Pan-Africanism, and other forms of political activism (see chapter 1). Further, much of their rhetoric and political subjectivity can be tied directly to these formative social movements. One problem my research has identified is how a black cultural citizenship that is largely informed by Black Nationalism coexists with and negotiates the state rhetoric of multiculturalism. This became visible when I examined the relationship between Panday and the 1990s momentum of the Orisha religion. One critical element was the increase in visible membership, including many middle-class participants who had their roots in Black Power. Notably, many had returned from living abroad, bringing with them a broadened African diasporic frame of reference. I have identified Trinidadian black cultural citizenship grounded in Orisha as informed by a larger African diaspora cultural citizenship that both recognizes differences of blackness and African descent while insisting on a shared basis for belonging. This embrace of difference runs largely counter to the racial essentialism represented in much of the work on Black Power and Black Nationalism.

In working through this dynamic, I have found that the consideration of black cultural citizenship in Trinidad illuminates a different form of multiculturalism, one where there is not a singular majority, and specifically not a white majority. This is important because the academic literature and the circulating discourse on multiculturalism are largely based on the assumption of a white majority (as in the United States). Apparent contradictions between a black cultural citizenship that arises out of Black Nationalism and multiculturalism are not as defined in Trinidad as academic theories and circulating discourses would suggest (though of course tensions do exist). I have found this even as the black cultural citizenship in Trinidad clearly evidences hallmarks of Black Nationalism (self-sufficiency; self-definition; social, political, and religious organization; revaluation of Africa and black subjectivity).[25] However, it does so while also navigating different levels of social organization, including pluralism in the organization of society, multiculturalism in political discourse, and creolization on the level of national culture and Trinidadian identity (though contestation exists between two continua, Afro/Anglo and Afro/Indo).

Additionally, I locate the importance of a diasporic perspective that embraces the differentiation of blackness within the context of this African diasporic consciousness. Thus, "black" cultural citizenship has to be specific; we must ask, "whose blackness?" and tie the answer back to a broader conceptualization of African diaspora cultural citizenship. The tensions between "blackness" and the African diaspora come to the forefront when one thinks about cultural citizenship and the religious ethnic identities of "Yoruba" priests and devotees throughout Latin America who situate themselves within the framework of the African diaspora, though ethnically and racially they are marked as Hispanic and largely not marked as "black" or African descended socially, politically, or phenotypically (Castor, forthcoming). One outcome of this *spiritual ethnicity* is the decentering of U.S. racial systems. This creates space for difference among constructions of blackness and what this means for belonging—to a community, to the nation, and within the diaspora. Another outcome is the recognition of difference, which has the result in Trinidad of distinguishing within the Afro-Trinidadian community various religious, cultural, and political stances among identifications of black/ness and Africa/ness.

Ultimately, an examination of Basdeo Panday's sponsorship of the Orisha religion during his years as prime minister reveals a black cultural citizenship that, as informed by the Orisha religion, engages with locally informed multiculturalism (and creolization) and in doing so opens up a space for a differentiated blackness, one intimately tied to a larger transnational community of the African diaspora.

PART II

Emerging Spiritual Citizenship

CHAPTER 3

Around the Bend

Festive Practices in a Yorùbá-Centric Shrine

Iba Orun.
Iba Osupa.
Iba Aiye.
Iba Ile.
Iba Afefe (air),
Iba Ina (fire).
Iba Omi.
Iba Ile-Ife.
Iba Oke Itase.
Iba Trinidad and Tobago.
Iba Shrine Gardens.

We pay homage to the sun, the moon, the cosmic realm, the earthly realm.
We pay homage to Ile-Ife the home of our tradition.
And we pay homage here in Trinidad and Tobago to Sierra Del Aripo, the
  highest mountain,
and Caroni the longest river.

We pay homage to Shrine Gardens, IESOM here in Santa Cruz . . .
and we ask for blessings and guidance.

We pay homage and ask for blessings for this day.
We pay homage and ask for blessings for yesterday.
We pay homage and we ask for blessings for tomorrow.

The time would come when we would all be one and we ask for guidance.

In a rhythm not unlike the sound of rain on a galvanized tin roof, a steady cadence of prayers both gave thanks and asked for blessings. Baba Erinfolami, standing center stage in flowing whites, poured libations of water. His words of invocation opened the Twelfth Annual Rain Festival at Ile Eko Sango/Osun Mil'osa (IESOM), Santa Cruz Shrine Gardens.[1] I watched, listened, and felt as Baba Erinfolami invoked sacred energy after sacred energy, called the praise name of Orisha after Orisha, in a chant designed to both clear energy for the festival to come and bring blessings to us all. I present a small sample of the divine energies invoked to give an idea of the prayer's rhythm, which raised the energy (or ase) with each invocation,

> *We pay homage to our Oris, and we thank our Oris for bringing us here this morning.*
> *Ori it is you and only you who would guide this destiny of ours,*
> *And we ask you for blessings this morning.*

> *We pay homage to our mothers, those in the heavenly realm and those on the earthly realm, for it is they that brought us from the heavenly realm to this earthly realm and we ask to constantly bless them and we ask for their blessings.*
> *We pay homage to the fathers, all our fathers, our protectors, the strong ones who brought us to this level of understanding.*
> *We ask for your guidance this morning and we ask for your love.*
> *We ask for your protection.*

> *We pay homage and ask for blessings from Esu Odara the divine messenger, who opened the door from heaven to earth so that we, we could share this morning.*
> *Papa Esu it is you. . . . . The great one whose voice is heard throughout the universe,*
> *We ask for your blessings this morning and we ask for your guidance.*
> *Open the door for all goodness and close the door to all negativity as we celebrate this morning.*
> *We ask for love and we ask for protection.*

> *We pay homage and we ask for blessings from the mighty Ogun, the clearer of all pathways.*
> *We ask that Ogun in all his roads and all his manifestations will protect us on this journey.*
> *And that he would clear a mystical path for us,*

and he would clear a mystical path for us,
that he would clear a mystical path for us.

And we ask that the orphans may never go to sleep hungry,
that he would always prepare a meal for the orphans so that they may never
  go to sleep hungry.

We ask for blessings and guidance from the wise and powerful Oshosi who
  keeps us directly on the target.
Everything we do—bring us back into alignment Baba Oshosi, the one who
  shoots the arrow straight to the target.
Orisha of speech, communication, thought, light, sound, trajectory and
  mental telepathy.
We ask you for blessings this morning and over this three-day period,
and over the next year until we come back here next year at this time to
  celebrate.
We ask for your blessings.

To Osain, the owner of all leaves and herbs and all the forest, for your
  protection always, we ask for blessings.
To the blessed omiero that cleans and cleanses us, to the food, the herbal food
  that cleanses and purifies us.
To you Oshosi, we ask for blessings

To Oluorogbo, the scribe and educationist of the Yoruba people.
The Orisha of divine intellect, the one who draws our pictures so that
  Obatala could mold us, so that Olodumare could put life in us.
We ask for your blessings, and we ask for your guidance.

To the mighty Obatala, the one who makes eyes and makes nose.
We call on you today, father of the Orisha to bring us blessings of peace,
  harmony, balance, long-life, purity.
You the pure one with pure intentions.
We ask for your blessings this morning, we ask for your guidance this
  morning, we ask for your love, we ask for prosperity.
All the good things from you Baba, bring blessings.

We ask for blessings and guidance from the wise Mother Onile.
And we ask Onile, the mother of the Earth,
 we ask you to forgive us for being disrespectful, treating the earth in the
  manner that we treat it.

We ask you to forgive us.
And we ask that all good things would come to us this morning and in the
  future.
Please Momma, grant us peace, grant us balance.
We ask for guidance.

We ask for blessings and we ask for guidance from the great Mother Oshun,
the owner of all rivers, the mother of civilization,
The mother of arts, the mother of science, the mother of dance.
Cleanse us and purify us.
Eighty percent of our bodies are water.
You Momma, we ask you to always cleanse and purify us.
Mother of Charity, sophistication and elegance,
The mother of fertility, we ask that we would always be fertile, that we
  would always be fertile.
We ask for your blessings great mother.

We pay homage and ask for blessings from Yemoja, the mother who always
  walks.
The mother of initiation and birthing, the nurturer,
The mother of the womb,
We ask for your blessings.

We pay homage and ask for blessings from Mother Obba.
The great Mother Obba, the teacher.
The one who taught Shango and Oya how to use the long and the short sword.
First to protect the children and then to seal the community so that nothing,
  no harm would come to them.
We ask for your blessings mother.
We ask for your blessings as mother of commerce, the mother in the
  marketplace
That your children would always be successful in everything that they do.

We ask for blessings and guidance, and love and protection from Mother
  Oya, the mother of the ancestors. The great mother.
The mother of the wind and the mother of the thunder and the mother of the
  hurricane.
Bring us blessing great Mother Oya, bring us good fortune,
We ask that we would always have good fortune and we pay homage to you.

To the Egbe, our mates in heaven,
we ask for blessings this morning and we ask for guidance this morning.
We ask that all who would have come, all who wanted to come, all who heard
* about it, and all who wish us well, we ask for their blessings.*

As he continued on to invoke the shrine's patron Shango a wind blew through the valley, bringing coolness to an otherwise hot and still day. Twelve minutes into his prayers after the invocations of Orisha had passed (those mentioned here and many others) I began to hear other things that I was not expecting in his *iba* (prayer).[2] Baba was going beyond the bringing of sacred energy into our space, into the shrine deep in the Santa Cruz Valley. He was delving into the social and political, deftly weaving them into his sacred narrative.

I heard him sending prayers out to the national leadership:

We pay homage to the president of Trinidad and Tobago, and his wife, and all
* the people of Trinidad and Tobago.*
We ask that he may stand as a beacon to the people of Trinidad and Tobago
* in this world.*
We ask for blessings.
We pay homage to the prime minister, and we ask for blessings for her, that
* she may treat her job in the way that Orisha would want her to, in the way*
* that the people would want her to.*
That she would be successful.
We pray for her husband, who is not well at this time.
We ask for blessings. We ask for guidance.

We pay homage and we ask for blessings for all those people, who - from the
* diplomatic corps who are here and who represent the people here.*

And then his words would draw from (and on) an imagined space, beyond the national, invoking an African diasporic space:

We pay homage and we ask for blessings for the people in Cuba, Haiti, Santa
* Domingo, and Puerto Rico, Jamaica.*
We pay homage to those in America, Canada, Mexico, Guatemala, and
* Belize, and Nicaragua, Honduras, and Costa Rica.*
We pay homage and ask for their blessings.
For those in Panama, where many of our ancestors went to build the canal,
* we ask for blessings.*
We pay homage to those in Venezuela, Colombia, Peru, Bolivia, and Chile.

Those in Brazil who practice the Candomblé.
We ask that they come, the wise ones from there would come this morning
and spend time with us,
for those in Uruguay, Paraguay, and Chile,
for those in Suriname and Guyana, and Barbados, Grenada, St. Vincent,
St. Lucia, St. Kitts.
We ask for their blessings,
for those from the Virgin Islands, St. Croix we ask for those blessings.
We have family all about and we call on them.
We call on those in French Guyana, we call on those in Curaçao and Aruba.

The African diasporic space signaled by the litany of locations throughout the Americas included the Caribbean (which I half expected) but went beyond into Central and South America. The inclusion of Panama made sense to me, specifically referencing the history of West Indians who worked on the Panama Canal ("where many of our ancestors went to build the canal"). Other locations went farther afield in the diaspora than I expected, including Uruguay, Paraguay, and Chile. This spoke to an imagining of African diaspora that is wider than the conventional understanding, one that drew upon cultural and religious networks not always visible to everyday understandings of diaspora, or even academic ones.

As if he was listening to the conversation in my head, Baba then called:

And all those people who practice this tradition wherever in the world
from the Ooni of Ife, the Araba, the Agbongbon, the Oru Ojugbona
all the priests and priestesses.
We call on them this morning to make this ritual a success,
to make this Shango Rain Festival, Sango/Osun Mil'osa Rain Festival a
success.
We ask for blessings.
We ask for guidance and peace and love and protection and harmony and
balance and truth.
All the ancestors of our bloodline who sit at the feet of Olodumare.
All the generations that met generations in Orun.
We call on them this morning,
come and spend time with us so that we will never fail.
We pay honor and respect to you and we ask that you break the cycle of
negativity that stifles our spirituality as a people.
Bring blessings and bring guidance.

In his invocation of transnational spiritual networks, "all those people who practice this tradition," he folded time and space by calling on the ancestors, for this spiritual community spans not only space but also time. In going back through the generations ("All the generations that met generations"), the spatial connections become visible and tangible. As many have argued, historical subjectivity, historicity if you will, is a central component to the African diasporic imaginary and identity (D. Scott 1991, 1999; Trouillot 1995, 1998). This is clearly evident in Trinidad's African diasporic religions, specifically here in the cosmology of Ifá/Orisha. As Paul Christopher Johnson writes of African diasporic religions, they are dependent not only on having a family tree "elsewhere" but also on "having a double consciousness in relation to place . . . that awareness is central, even actively conjured in their lived experience" (2007, 31). I argue that for Trinidad Orisha, the double consciousness referred to by Johnson operates on the levels of both space and time.

As I pondered the spanning of space and time in Baba's litany, the conversation in my head, seemingly between us, continued as he directly invoked history:

> Those who died in Africa, who died in the Middle Passage, who died fighting
> injustice on the plantation,
> who were hung and quartered.
> We ask to uplift you. Come.
> We ask to uplift you so that you could uplift us.
> It is on your shoulders that we stand this morning and ask for blessings.

Here it was being said directly, it is through our work here to uplift the ancestors, "those that have gone before us," that we in turn are uplifted. And especially those who perished in the Middle Passage, who were lost far from home and never received the proper burial rites (I will return to this in the next chapter through a close look at Asewele, a ritual designed to fulfill this charge). This invocation speaks directly to the spiritual work of belonging in Ifá/Orisha community. I have found this work to be a form of spiritual citizenship, one that undertakes what M. Jacqui Alexander (2006 307) refers to as sacred praxis, where efforts and labors are organized to be in alignment with one's beliefs and principles, putting into action the more expressive and abstract parts of a religious system, of spiritual belief.

After paying respects to the elders of the shrine, Baba continued:

We ask for upliftment and we ask for guidance.
May Olodumare continue to bless us.
For Iya Sangowunmi, for Baba Wande Abimbola, for Baba Popoola, and for
*   Baba Kolade.*
And for all those who would come from time to time to spend time on this
*   beautiful shrine and to assist us in our spiritual development through*
*   Orisha, through Ifá, through the ancestors.*
We ask for their blessings.

Baba finished his prayers by dismissing negative energies (*ajogun*):

Shame and envy will be no more.
Negativity and loss will be no more.
Disrespect will be no more.
Court cases will be no more.
Sickness will be no more.
Disease will be no more.
To be overwhelmed will be no more.
Paralysis will be no more.

Then he invoked the blessing of long life and good character for all who had gathered and all who were called:

All we ask for is immortality,
all we ask for is immortality.
May we never fail,
may we never disrespect the ancestors.
We ask this in the name of Olodumare, great and powerful one.
Ase, ase, ase.

After finishing his extensive prayers, Baba performed divination to ensure that they had been accepted. He touched a bitter kola nut to Iya Sangowun-mi's head, as elder of the shrine.[3] He then bit the bitter kola into four sections, after which he offered the sections to the four directions, to heaven, and then finally to the earth. He threw the bitter kola and reading how it landed, he announced:

Oyeku Meji —the averter of death, the ancestors giving us protection over
*   the next 365 days.*

This was followed by throw number two:

Osa says we will have transformation and we have good fortune through the mothers, all the great mothers will bring good fortune.

And, again, throw number three:

And Iwori says that all good things will come to us.
And we should be patient, never rush to be in front,
but do what we have to do.
And we have work.

With this, Baba said his final words, passing the energy and space back to Iya Sangowunmi:

We give thanks and we ask for blessings.
Ase.
Thanks for the opportunity.

Iya's response of "*Adupe* [thanks], Baba" concluded the opening litany. Now another Rain Festival could begin, ritually renewing the annual cycle of the rainy season. Attending this Rain Festival felt like returning home as I had attended the festival every year for several years. This was a deep return to community that echoed my initial return home.

Homecoming

I had returned to Trinidad in 1999 as a graduate student, going there to present a paper based on my proposed master's thesis, "Orisha Online: Virtual Community in the Black Atlantic." I also planned to do some preliminary fieldwork because I was considering doing my doctoral research in Trinidad, specifically on the Orisha and/or Spiritual Baptist community. To complicate things further, I was staying with family on my father's side and getting reacquainted with relatives who had last seen me as a child.

The Sixth World Congress of Orisha Tradition and Culture was held at the Holiday Inn (now the Crowne Plaza) in downtown Port of Spain. As the car I was taking dropped me off from the nearby suburban middle-class neighborhood of Woodbrook, I was surprised to see a huge banner, reading, "Welcome to the Orisha Congress Delegates," across the multi-lane thoroughfare. I had thought that the Orisha religion in Trinidad was hidden. I had not expected to find a huge official banner crossing a major street welcoming the Orisha Congress. My surprise continued at the extensive media coverage of the congress, which included large newspaper headlines, live TV coverage of the opening, and numerous radio show discussions of Orisha.

I had been put on notice by my parents before coming to Trinidad: the Orisha religion (or Shango, as they called it) was a seldom-practiced, dying faith among "poor folks in the country." This sentiment was commonly held in mid-1960s Trinidad around the time that my parents emigrated to the States. This association is mirrored in the literature of the time, including Simpson's study that looked for Shango adherents among the "lower class people of African descent" (1962, 1204). Further, my parents assured me that at this conference I would mainly find foreigners talking among themselves about Orisha. In fact, they couldn't tell me why an international conference on Orisha was being held in Trinidad. That was one of the things that I intended to discover, namely, why was Trinidad the site for the Sixth World Congress? And quickly following this was another question: How could my parents be so unaware of the extensive Orisha tradition in Trinidad?

All of this was on my mind as I entered the Holiday Inn. My first view was of an unexpectedly bland though pleasant reception area. The only indication that there was an event being hosted at the hotel was the number of people, some sitting on benches and others milling about in the atrium and at the check-in counters, wearing "African cloth."[4] Following signs, I found my way down the hall and took a right into an open registration and book exhibit area. Faced with an explosion of color and noise, I stopped abruptly. There were dozens and dozens of people, almost all African or of African descent, all wearing African clothes or at least African prints. I was instantly self-conscious in my relatively plain purple skirt and cream sweater, which clearly marked me as American.[5] I, myself, made the error of categorizing people as African or American based on what they wore only to discover that they were actually Trinidadian, oftentimes based on hearing their accents.

I found my way through the press of people to the registration table. With some trepidation, I set out to locate the organizers (this was only my second academic conference as a graduate student). I wanted to record some of the conference sessions on cassette tapes (this was 1999!), especially those related to organizing the Orisha tradition, either in Trinidad or globally. I asked at an information desk for the organizers and was directed to two people standing at the top of a flight of stairs. Suddenly I wished that I had thought to wear a *gèlè* (headwrap), something I often did in the States along with Western clothes, or at least more formal clothes than the graduate student garb I was wearing.

"Excuse me, are you the conference organizers?" I asked, belatedly realizing that I was interrupting the couple's conversation. I received two sets of looks, slightly askance but acknowledging, and I rushed on: "My name is Nicole Castor, and I'm a graduate student at the University of Chicago. I'm here to give a paper, but I'm also interested in Orisha. Would you mind if I taped some of the sessions on a tape recorder?" All in one breath, the words tumbled out over each other while I stuck out my hand to shake theirs. (Only looking back on this later, after living in Trinidad for years, would I recognize how very American I must have appeared, in both my dress, my affect, and my rapid speech.)

The response I got in return was unexpected. Despite all my "American" markings, "Where you from? You have family here?" came the question. (I would be asked this repeatedly during my time in Trinidad—a foundational question as people sought to place me in a category. Although I sound American, I "look" like I could be Trinidadian.) "Yes," I said, "my family is from Woodbrook and Newtown." As introductions were made, I discovered that Charles Castle and Pat McLeod were indeed the organizers. They told me I could record the sessions as long as I was doing so for academic purposes. I prepared to withdraw and head to the welcoming anonymity of a conference room. I had accomplished my goals. And caught up in my own thoughts, I almost missed the question coming from Mr. Castle. Hand on his chin he asked, "Is your mother's name. . . .?"

I was taken aback—how could he know this? "Yes," I said. Before I could say anything else, he asked, "Did she use to live in Boston?"

"Why yes," I said again, now even more puzzled.

"Eh, eh, but I know you from when you were this high," he said holding his hand at hip height. This was followed with exclamations to me and Mrs. McLeod that Mr. Castle knew my mom in the 1980s. He was part of a group of Trinidadians that she knew. I was caught off guard, not only with no memory of him, but also trying to figure out how my mother, who claimed no knowledge of Orisha, knew the organizer of this Orisha conference.

Busy thinking about all of this, I almost missed—again—the next disturbing question. As Mr. Castle was explaining who I was to Mrs. McLeod, the question of my father's surname had come up.

"Did you say your father's family was Castor?" Mrs. McLeod asked as Mr. Castle added, "Yes, her dad is a Castor."

"Of the Castors in Woodbrook?" she asked. "Yes," I nodded. "Do you know a J. Castor?" came the next question.

"Yes, she's my aunt. She dropped me off here." After that, more questions and comments came fast and furious. Mrs. McLeod was a childhood friend of my aunt, having gone to primary (grammar) school with her. Hugs followed, and I was declared "family." My head was spinning as I tried to take it all in. Not ten minutes earlier, I had approached two conference organizers, two strangers, only to find out that one knew my mother and the other knew my father's family.

While I tried to get my bearings, the conversation continued without me. Mr. Castle was explaining to Mrs. McLeod my mother's maiden name. An "eh, eh" of recognition followed. Sure enough, Mrs. McLeod knew my mother's family as well, as became apparent when she started asking me about this aunt and that aunt. With promises to bring my Aunt to the conference (which I later did), I excused myself and walked away. Finding a seat tucked away in a corner, I tried to reorganize my universe. How was it that these Orisha conference organizers knew my family? The same family that disavowed all knowledge of Orisha, on issues of both race (that was the African/black thing) and class (that was that lower-class/grassroots thing). So how was I to understand what had just happened?

These formative moments of entry into "the field" informed foundational questions that shaped my research. The intersections of race, class, nation, and family that I witnessed in the conference dynamics, media coverage, and conversations with family and strangers all demanded an untangling, a translation. At that time, in 1999, I would have been shocked to know that the voyage I was embarking on would take more than fifteen years and lead me to an entanglement of performance, spiritual and cultural citizenship, and the Afro-Trinidadian (African in local terms) middle class. How I got from that one conference experience to this complex theoretical and analytical configuration is, I hope, evident in this study. Here I further locate my entry into the field as an ethnographer, an Orisha practitioner, a graduate student, and both a returning Trini and an American (echoing the section titled "Locating Myself, Locating the Ancestors" in the introduction to this book).

That initial meeting with Pat McLeod would turn into a decade-plus working relationship, initially largely with her leadership and spiritual role as Iya Sangowunmi. Slowly, over the years, this important relationship developed from one involving an informant and a researcher (if it was ever just that) to one of collaboration and familial mutual respect and admiration. This has greatly enriched my project and this study, but it also has complicated the process of ethnographic description and analysis. This chapter has been among the hardest to write because it remains among the most personal, even as the rich relationship has allowed me to bring together and illuminate key strands of class, race, and citizenship in the entanglements of Trinidad Orisha practices.

Sixth World Congress of Orisha Tradition and Culture

At the end of the twentieth century, Trinidad's hosting of the Sixth World Congress of Orisha Tradition and Culture increased the profile of the religion both at home and abroad. Rawle Gibbons (a lecturer at the University of the West Indies and an Orisha devotee) announced to the first Orisha Family Day in 1998 that Trinidad's hosting of the biennial conference "was a step towards the building of the pride and profile of Orisha internationally as well in Trinidad" (Henry 2003, 127). In the early days of the Internet the news of the Orisha Congress circulated via e-mail lists and was posted on Orisha-related websites. In fact, my own awareness in Chicago of the Orisha Congress was the reason for my first research trip to Trinidad to present my master's work on virtual Orisha communities. My experiences at the congress further motivated me and provided the seeds for my future research project.

The World Orisha Congress is a global conference of Orisha practitioners, priests, and scholars, which has also been held in San Francisco; Ilé-Ifè, Nigeria; Cuba; and Brazil.[6] Earlier attempts at hosting in Trinidad in the 1980s had failed due in no small part to the contentious and fragmented nature of national leadership. This fractured intracultural politic combined with public hostility to the Orisha tradition created an inhospitable environment for organizing, which resulted in the conference being located elsewhere. Subsequently, in less than twenty years, segments of the Orisha community were able to organize and sponsor this international conference with both public and governmental support. This 1999 moment was important to Trinidad's Orisha practitioners. Orisha in Trinidad was being granted recognition through the coming together of priests and scholars from Africa, Brazil, Cuba, the Americas, and Europe in full view of the global public.

In large part due to this, the international recognition of the Yorùbá-based religions, the local community gained additional status and legitimacy.

Though Trinidad successfully hosted in 1999, the conference was not without controversy. Even the invitation to host it was contested, as described by Henry: "According to some, it was a few positioned participants from Trinidad who secured the offer. To others, it was the purity and sincerity of their religious faith that convinced the international executive committee to select Trinidad" (2003, 147). With "ownership" of the conference contested, the location of the secretariat in the offices of I. T. McLeod (a local real estate developer and quantity surveyor; late husband to Patricia McLeod [aka Iya Sangowunmi]) in St. Clair, an upper-middle-class neighborhood west of Port of Spain, did not escape notice. As one of the principal organizers, Iya Sangowunmi leveraged the resources of their family business to provide phones, fax lines, photocopier access, computers, and staff. At the time, Iya was associated with Kenny Cyrus Alkebulan Ile Ijebu, one of the older established family shrines in Trinidad, going back several generations, and volunteers from the shrine staffed both the secretariat and the conference (147).[7] The conference was organized to include academic papers, cultural performances, a marketplace, an art exhibit, and country reports.

The king of Ilé-Ifẹ̀, the Ọ̀ọ̀ni, was the patron of the congress and the planned keynote speaker. This generated a flurry of government activity as preparations were made for formal high-level receptions. However, he was kept away by "pressures of state in his own country" and sent a representative, Chief Omótòsó Elúyemí, the Apènà of Ifẹ̀, Nigeria (Henry 2003, 149). Chief Elúyemí's presentation was well received at the opening ceremonies, where almost the entire government leadership was present, including Prime Minister Basdeo Panday and President A. N. R. Robinson, the leader of the opposition, cabinet ministers, and senators. The attendance by these individuals was a highly visible statement of the state's support for the Orisha faith. Adding to the public profile, this event was broadcast live on the national television station, TV6. President Robinson (holder of an honorary Yorùbá title, Chief Olókun Ìgbàrò) held an official state reception at his residence for representatives to the conference, contributing to the conference's formality and government presence.[8]

As part of an educational campaign, a series of articles appeared in leading newspapers in the months preceding the Sixth World Orisha Congress. These articles were printed under the auspices of the National Council of

Orisha Elders and aimed at educating the public, with titles such as "Orisha, Defining Our Caribbean Culture" (Sankeralli 1999d) and "Of Obeah and Sacrifice: The Demonizing of African Traditions" (Sankeralli 1999a). The weekly column that ran in the *Trinidad Guardian*, the establishment newspaper, was written by Burton Sankeralli, a cultural activist and scholar, who attempted to educate the populace while demystifying and valorizing the Orisha faith (or, as he calls it, "Orisha Work"). In addition to newspaper articles, there were TV and radio programs in the weeks before, during, and after the conference, all aimed at educating the public about the Orisha religion (e.g., members of the Council of Elders were interviewed on radio talk shows and accepted questions from callers). This high media profile was in stark contrast to the public persecution and degradation of African religious traditions that had existed only decades earlier.

Orisha Polarities: From Trini-Centric to Yorùbá-Centric

The World Orisha Congress was the culminating event in a series of momentous events in the 1990s, building on the energy from the previous decade's visit of the Ọ̀ọ̀ni of Ilé-Ifẹ̀, Nigeria. The conference was made possible, in no small part, by the sponsorship of Prime Minister Panday's United National Congress government, which provided TT$550,000 in funding and access to governmental resources in the planning and execution of the conference (Coker 1999).[9] The political complexity of multiculturalism that I explored in the previous chapter only becomes legible with an attention to the distinctions of difference, along lines of class and color, within the Afro-Trinidadian community.[10] Orisha political leaders, mainly Afro-Trinidadians, have traditionally been supporters of the "Afro-Creole party," the People's National Movement (PNM), and its leadership (i.e., ethnic party politics). In the middle to late 1990s, these same Orisha leaders found themselves working closely with Panday. The marvel is not only that Panday followed through on his promises of land, legal reform, and national recognition (as discussed in the previous chapter). The remarkable aspect is that those prosecuted for their perceived African practices by the colonial administration would be championed not by the political leadership of African descendants but by that of Indo-Trinidadians, those who were historically separated from, and politically opposed to, the Afro-Trinidadian community. However, it would be a mistake to reify the category of Afro-Trinidadian and not explore the differentiation within the community, especially evident in the contested performance of culture and religion where race and ethnicity (blackness and Africanness), color and class inform fault lines.

At the conference it was evident that the grassroots (i.e., working-class) Orisha practitioners were underrepresented. That is, the leaders who could afford to go to a conference during working hours for several weekdays were in a different position economically than the average working-class practitioner, and for that matter even most middle-class people.[11] This obvious class distinction struck me in my interactions with those at the conference, calling me to take a look beyond the economics of participation to the cultural economics of representation and identity. Among the Trinidad Orisha practitioners present at the conference, there was a clear tension between those who looked to "Africa," specifically the Yorùbá religion of Nigeria, for the source of knowledge, authority, and authenticity about the tradition and those who viewed the source for these same things as local to Trinidad. This dynamic, which I noticed in my first interactions with Trinidad's Orisha communities, manifested itself throughout the period of my intensive fieldwork from 2002 through 2005 and continues into the contemporary moment.

Research has established that this dynamic between different segments of the Orisha community has been apparent in Trinidad Orisha from at least the late 1980s (Houk 1993).[12] Observations of these trends have been made in numerous works on Trinidad Orisha since that period. As Hucks and Stewart have pointed out, "A significant trend within Trinidad's Orisha community involves an emergent internal movement among several practitioners to place 'Africa' at the center of its religious rites and practices" (2003, 179). Commonly agreed upon in the literature is the presence of separate foci for authority and authenticity, one focused on Trinidad and one on Yorùbá lineages based in Nigeria, though there are differences between authors in both language and understandings of the dynamics. The most commonly used term is "Africanization," which Houk defines as "a renewed emphasis on African 'roots,' which has mostly involved a tendency. . . to expurgate the Christian and Hindu elements from *orisha* worship and to return to a liturgy that is exclusively Yoruba" (1995, 42-43). In the work of Houk and others, Africanization is then juxtaposed to a local Trinidadian practice using several awkward phrases (e.g., adding "orthodox" or "traditional" to Trinidadian Orisha).

I intervene on two points, one being language and the other regarding the level of dynamics. I understand that there is an "imagined" Africa (see

Mbembe 2001; Mudimbe 1988, 1994) referenced as the source of Orisha religion in Trinidad and constructed variously as a "pure" or a "corrupted" forgotten source for the Orisha religion. Additionally, the imagined "Africa" is, by turns, the homeland, the land of the ancestors, a source of cultural or religious identity, a symbol of loss or shame tied to slavery and the slave trade, or, at its most extreme, a land of depraved cannibals. As such I find the term "Africanization," when referring to the trend to reorient Trinidad Orisha practices with those in Yorubaland (often an imagined ancestral pre-colonial Yorubaland), to be overburdened with more layers of meaning than can be effectively understood at either an analytic or a discursive level.

Another factor in my antipathy for this term is that it analytically re-inforces the conflation of specific cultures and religious practices into an over-generalized and imagined Africanness. For these reasons I propose the use of the term "Yorùbá-centric" to refer to that trend in Trinidad Orisha that looks to Yorùbá-based lineages to inform its practices.[13] I like the suffix "-centric" because it indicates a focus or center rather than a process with an implied teleology, as if there is a state of "pure" African tradition that could be realized (as opposed to the functional shift of Africa in Africanization). Analytically, I think that attention to language use is critical in constructing models of dynamic, plastic, and polyvalent practices. While the practice of ethnographic writing cannot but create narratives that are more static and simplified than the reality they represent, I hold that awareness of this tendency and attempts to ameliorate it remain important.

The View from Goat Island

When I arrived in Trinidad to start my fieldwork in the fall of 2002, I fol-lowed up on the initial contact I had made at the 1999 World Orisha Con-gress and reached out to Iya Sangowunmi with a phone call. This resulted in an invitation to come and visit with her. I planned to catch up on what was going on in Trinidad's Orisha community while also making some ini-tial plans for my research. Everything was falling into place! And then, of course, there was the catch.

"I'm going to the islands," Iya told me. "If you want to talk with me, you could come."

"Sure," I said, eager to start off on the right foot and not miss an oppor-tunity. "I can go to the island with you."

We made plans to take the ferry to Tobago. It was only later that I would look back and locate this as the initial moment of a misunderstanding. For when Iya said "the islands," I thought she meant Tobago. And it was a natural mistake to make. Typically, when people in Trinidad talk about going to an island for rest and recreation, it is almost always Tobago (only occasionally Barbados or Isle de Margarita, off the coast of Venezuela). There were also some small islands off the coast of Trinidad; these were referred to with the phrase "going down the islands." Unbeknownst to me, Iya was not referring to those islands at all.

The ferry trip was largely uneventful, though at six hours it took the same length of time as a direct flight to New York. I used the time to start getting to know the three men accompanying Iya, which included her son, her driver and handyman, and an electrician (making the journey to install a new generator). All of us talked on and off for much of the journey. Or, rather, I should say they engaged in the Trini practice of "ole talk" while I listened and tried to follow along (ole talk involves a combination of storytelling, jokes, posturing, and other discursive strategies of play; see Abrahams 1983 for forms of performative discourse throughout the Caribbean). Our arrival into Scarborough, Tobago's port and largest town, witnessed a family reunion of sorts. My godfather lived up the hill and came down to meet the boat and greet us. I mention this because his exchange with Iya Sangowunmi echoed my meeting of her at the Orisha Congress.

"How long has it been?"

"Have you seen so and so?"

"You hear about . . . ?"

What I heard situated Iya Sangowunmi within a map of local family and class relations. Despite her religious affiliation, Iya Sangowunmi, or rather Pat McLeod, was the inheritor of a middle-class lineage, one that could withstand her focus on African culture and Pan-African-informed politics. Even at the turn of the millennium, membership in the African religions of Orisha and Spiritual Baptist endangered one's social status. This positioning would come up again before the trip was over.

After hugs and promises to stay in touch, we left the port. It was not until we had been driving for a while on the dark, curving roads, deep into Tobago's countryside, that I asked where the house was. "On the island," came the reply, which confused me because I thought we already were on the island. After I explained my confusion, there was a moment's pause. "No, we're going to the island—that is where the house is, on the island."

"On another island?" I asked. "What island?!"

It turned out that the McLeods owned an island off the coast of Tobago, commonly called Goat Island.[14] After a long journey, including not only the car but also a small boat, we arrived on "the island" in the early hours of the morning. It was when I woke up later that morning that I saw the glorious view of the bay between the house and Tobago.

I could not help but feel that this was an excellent place to catch up on Orisha in Trinidad and start to strategize my research plans. Over the next three days, easy conversation flowed with Iya Sangowunmi on Orisha, Trinidad, race, culture, politics, family, and many other topics (even, or perhaps especially, without the electricity that the new generator had been brought for but failed to provide). Years later, I look back at those days as some of the best times of my research. It was here that I got my initial glimpse at how deeply a worldview could be structured by the Orisha religion and yet, on the surface, also be so engaged in the normal day-to-day routines of life.

In those conversations we discussed how we had each come to be where we were in relation to Orisha. Iya Sangowunmi came to the religion through Pan-Africanism and the political consciousness that grew out of that. In the 1970s, her exposure to Black Power in Trinidad and London had sparked a consciousness that led her to found the African Women's Association of Trinidad and Tobago. As Iya Sangowunmi remarked in an interview, one of the stated purposes of the organization was to change the consciousness of Afro-Trinidadians, especially around the concept of Africa and things African:

> Why I did that is that most people even though they would say they were pan-Africanist they were afraid to associate themselves with African, the word African and if you had an association that means first you would be honouring your roots as African to be able to identify with the philosophy of the association. So as we came along, there was no spiritual base to this at all, it was just a pure pan-African base with lectures and programmes we try to organize and so. (quoted in Henry 2003, 99)

Speaking on these issues of Pan-Africanism and reflecting on her return to Trinidad in the early 1970s, she would say to me, "One of the things that always bothered me was a lack of African base to worship." In subsequent years it would be the bringing together of her Pan-African politics with religion that would propel her to explore the Orisha faith. From those days, and through the next forty years, African culture and religion would be central to her expressions of cultural and national identity. One of her primary goals has been to recast negative associations with all things African in Trinidad.

In later years, Iya Sangowunmi would say in one of our conversations on the local complexities of identity, especially in relation to African culture and religion, "The very things that make people Trinidadian are African." African heritage and culture are fundamental to Iya's sense of national identity. Her statement reflects an Afrocentric perspective that African culture is central to Trinidad's culture. This perspective is in tension with the contemporary rhetoric on creolization and multiculturalism. These narratives privilege the creation of the "new" from either a Creole mix (African/European) or an Indian/African mix, reflecting new discourses of multiculturalism (see chapter 2 for the latter). Beyond these tensions, the Afrocentric perspective espoused in Iya's statement is a direct contradiction of the colonialism she grew up under, which privileged all things European over the non-European denigrated "Other." Iya's political consciousness is reinforced by her spiritual work. Combined, they inform her path of spiritual citizenship; one grounded in a vision of a decolonized world that recognizes the cultural contributions of people long dismissed and devalued.

Years later, in a meeting to go over my notes and double-check my representation of her in this study (i.e., details of her biography and her positions on different issues), I would revisit our conversation on Goat Island. Though we were generally in agreement on most of my understandings, I would be corrected on one subject. I had recorded that Iya Sangowunmi had come to Orisha through Black Power. "Not so," she gently responded. "I was Pan-African, I never felt the term 'Black Power.'" She continued, explaining that she did not like the emphasis on "black" as it seemed narrow and exclusionary. For her, then, the focus was on culture rather than race, though in recent years her position has modified. She now sees "black" as a global attribute applying to people around the world, including aborigines and other indigenous people.

Over the next decade, I would return again and again to these foundational conversations. My experiences with Iya Sangowunmi and other elders in the Orisha religion, together with participation in festivals and rituals, would both challenge and bring greater clarity to these initial understandings. Ultimately, the core of Iya's story was conveyed in those early days of my research. She has focused on growing various businesses and organizations for many years, in directions informed by a Pan-African consciousness, until ultimately she came to the Orisha religion. Her passion became a joining of Pan-Africanism with the spiritual principles of Ifá and Orisha. Together, these two influences inform Iya Sangowunmi's practice of African middle-class spiritual citizenship.

Orisha Plays Mas'

The focus of this section is a particular shrine in Trinidad, Ile Eko Sango/ Osun Mil'osa and its contribution through the development of festivals to national and transnational cultural politics. When I arrived in Trinidad in 1999 for the Sixth World Congress of Orisha Tradition and Culture Orisha was in the newspapers, on TV, and on radio talk shows. The national profile of Orisha was on the rise, as could be seen in the huge banner traversing Wrightson Road, a major commuter and industrial thoroughfare, across from the hotel that was hosting the conference. Even as that banner flew, the profile of Iya Sangowunmi, a primary organizer of the conference, in the national Orisha community was on the rise. Her national spiritual work would continue to build as she formed a shrine in the hills of Santa Cruz and established a calendar of public and private festivals that celebrated the Orisha, the change of the seasons, and the contribution of individuals to local, national, and regional spiritual culture.

Within religious communities, including Orisha, political leadership is often a site of contestation that can reveal the intersection of ritual and political fields where issues of ethnicity, class, and status and their relation to national identity and citizenship are foregrounded. Iya Sangowunmi, a highly public Afro-Trinidadian middle-class figure, was until recently a member of the Orisha Council of Elders. Her membership on the council had been facilitated by her leadership role in the Sixth World Congress. As discussed previously, she played a prominent role in organizing the congress, with her family business providing a large number of the resources such as office space and access to phone and computer networks. Subsequently, she left the council over a dispute about the public representation of Orisha in Carnival.[15]

In 2002, Iya Sangowunmi launched a masquerade band, *Faces of Osun*, though the previous year the Orisha Council had ruled unfavorably on the representations of Orisha in Carnival. This contestation over mas' and the representation of Orisha was one of the defining moments that positioned Iya Sangowunmi and her shrine publicly in sympathy with a Yorùbá-centric perspective. When I arrived in Trinidad in the fall of 2002, the last part of the Carnival saga was unfolding. Thus, I experienced only part of the story in real time. In 2000, two shrines in Trinidad independently organized to launch Carnival mas' bands the following year that featured Orisha. Egbe Onisan Eledumare, headed by Baba Oludari Massetungi, "sponsored a Carnival band featuring major Orisha personalities such as Shango, Yemoja, Oshun and Ogun in February 2001" (Hucks and Stewart 2003, 181). This band, along with Iya Sangowunmi's offering, were the subject of a Council of Elders meeting and recipients of a subsequent letter outlining the council's position, which was "that the sacred Orisha [sh]ould not be polluted by the profanity and bacchanal channeled through the national Carnival" (182). This position was a point of public debate and contestation "regarding the role of the Orisha religion in the formation and preservation of Trinidad and Tobago's national culture" (181).[16] In part, the debate here was over the role of religion in Trinidad Carnival and the right of minority cultures to contribute to national culture. On another level, one internal to the Orisha community, were concerns about the sacred being corrupted by the profane. This latter concern became further refracted into contention over the approach to Orisha in Trinidad and ultimately centered on the issue of authority, elucidating some of the issues at stake in the dynamic between the Trini-centric and Yorùbá-centric trends.

For Iya Sangowunmi, her path to presenting an Orisha-themed mas' band was clear. She was approached by a priest of Oshun, Iya Osunyemi, with a message from a dream, which was confirmed through Ifá divination where Ọ̀ṣẹ́ Méjì (the fifteenth of sixteen major odu Ifá; see Appendix III) was cast. The Orisha Oshun speaks in this odu Ifá, and this casting was interpreted as a clear message of blessing and benediction (personal communication). "She [Oshun speaking through Ifá] said the Ancestors and Orisa are with us and we have their blessings for the band" (Sangowunmi, quoted in Hucks and Stewart 2003, 183). Iya Sangowunmi conveyed this information to the council in a letter responding to its decision. Her concern in conveying the "birth of the band" and the support of Ifá was to establish spiritual authority: "I immediately want to make it clear that I always act in accordance with the tenets of the tradition and the sixteen laws of Ifá. *Ifá and only Ifá is my source of authority, guidance, and direction*" (180; emphasis added). The choice was clear when it came down to a conflict between the Council of Elders (backed by the authority of Mother Rodney, spiritual head of Trinidad Orisha and signatory to the original letter) and direct communication from Orisha and through Ifá divination. It is this stance toward Ifá that informs the position of Iya Sangowunmi, and her shrine IESOM as Yorùbá-centric. This shows that for spiritual citizenship the ultimate authority is Spirit, even over the authority of a council of spiritual elders.

The decision to launch an Orisha band had other aspects for Iya Sangowunmi, one of which was educational, while another was both political and polemic. On the one hand was a desire to educate the larger public about the beauty of Orisha (personal communication). Through mas' performance, different aspects of Orisha could be represented.[17] Thus, the Carnival mas' band would expose the average Trinidadian to the Orisha religion both on the streets and through the media. Carnival offered a medium that people understood and an exceptional stage for the dissemination of information to the national community—information that could dispel lingering negative images by displacing ignorance. The polemic involved an argument, both historical and national, about the origins of Carnival: European or African. One outcome of the postindependence Afro-Creole middle class claiming and sanitizing lower-class cultural practices (i.e., Carnival and steel band) involved highlighting European influences and downplaying African ones. Informed by a Pan-African perspective, Iya Sangowunmi's involvement in Carnival was "in part an attempt to reclaim the African roots of Carnival masquerades. . . . She views Carnival as one of many traditions with roots in the Yoruba religious-cultural heritage of ancestral masquerading societies. Carnival stands as a living testimony to the dynamic power of the Orisha religion as it evolved in the local Trinidadian context" (Hucks and Stewart 2003, 183). The motivation behind the Carnival mas' band again returns to the voice of Oshun in the Ifá Odu Ose Meji that speaks of the blessings of ancestors alongside those of Orisha. The "secular" Carnival (as the Catholic pre-Lenten festival is understood and experienced by many) becomes reframed as a spiritual festival when viewed as an ancestral practice that links Trinidad with Africa.

In 2003, Iya Sangowunmi brought out a Carnival band that followed the historical (late nineteenth-century) Carnival route in east Port of Spain, that went "behind the bridge" and down Picton Street. This was done explicitly to evoke the ancestors (as was the case with similar decisions in the annual Emancipation Kambule; personal communication). Ironically, while asserting the authority of Ifá over that of local spiritual authority (i.e., Mother Rodney and the Council of Elders), Iya was also honoring ancestors, both locally in Trinidad and abroad in West Africa. Honoring and contributing to national culture through appeal to a transnational authority, located in Yorubaland, Nigeria, remains a central dynamic of Iya Sangowunmi and IESOM.

Iya Sangowunmi's participation in Carnival had the declared goal of educating the public and displaying Orisha in a positive light. Her decision to portray Orisha not only in a public festival but as a symbol of national culture in Trinidad may have as much to do with accruing cultural capital and the preservation of status as with educating the public. Her attempts at raising the cultural capital of the Spiritual Baptist and Orisha religions can also be read as an attempt to preserve her own status and social capital. Iya Sangowunmi has had considerable access to state resources that she mobilized to bring attention to the Spiritual Baptist and Orisha religions. Rituals at her shrine are often well publicized in the national media and regularly attended by cabinet-level government officials. Her highly public profile calls attention to the diversity of religious identities and representations and the complexity of their relationships to citizenship and national identity, state, and nation.

Festive Circuits/Festive Connections

Yorùbá-centric shrines organize their activities around a series of annual festivals (rather than an ebo, or feast). This festival-centered approach has become a hallmark of the Yorùbá-centric shrines (Henry 2003, 119–25). Two overlapping circuits of Orisha ritual have developed nationally, with one set going regularly to feasts and the other going to festivals. (I do not want to overemphasize the separation between the two as a number of priests and practitioners attend both types of ritual practice.) In this section, I focus on these ritual changes as reflective of the shifting terrain of Ifá/Orisha and what I believe are two major factors in these changes. As an example, I focus on IESOM, where within the last fifteen years the Iya Sangowunmi shrine in Trinidad has been involved in producing a series of festivals that have become part of the national cultural calendar (as evidenced by their inclusion in the calendar of events on the VisitTnT website, run by the Trinidad and Tobago Tourism Development Company).[18]

Every year in June, Iya Sangowunmi's shrine celebrates the end of the dry season in Trinidad with a large public festival, the IESOM Rain Festival at the Santa Cruz Shrine Gardens (see plates 1, 2, 6 and 7 for scenes from various Rain Festivals).[19] Over the past fifteen years, the Rain Festival has become a fixture on the national festive calendar with attendance by devotees, shrine neighbors, cabinet-level officials and babaláwos (international, from Nigeria, Canada, and New York and a growing number of local Ifá initiates). In addition to prayers and divination marking the beginning of the rainy season, the festival has developed a translocal focus, bringing together exemplars from Trinidad, the Caribbean, and beyond in several days of events, including a formal ritual opening and closing; cultural performances by guest artists and youth groups; an annual award ceremony; art exhibits; keynote addresses by notable politicians, artists, and priests; workshops; storytelling; tree planting; ancestor rituals; a marketplace; and one year, on the last day, a Maypole dance by the Maracas Youth Group.

In its own way the Rain Festival replicates every year (and embellishes on) the diversity of the 1999 World Congress, with a focus on bringing together different strands of Orisha in the diaspora that share a Yorùbá-centric approach. Both award recipients and visiting Ifá priests engage in a performance of transnational spiritual networks through various public and private rituals. Several international Ifá priests have attended the festival repeatedly over the years, serving as visible reminders of both the African roots and the diasporic branches of the Orisha tradition.[20] As part of this educational performance, they may also conduct separate workshops, give interviews in the media, and even appear on local TV talk shows. The programming is in part chosen to realize one of the stated goals of the festival, namely, "to make our Nations' understanding of the concept of Harmony in Diversity an example in the world" (IESOM 2005). Award recipients have included Dr. Molly Ahye (an Orisha leader, dancer, and cultural activist from Trinidad) and Iya Osunide L'Antoinette Stines (a Jamaican choreographer and Oshun priest; see figure 3.1). In specific years, other activities are associated with the Rain Festival, including in 2005 the bestowing of a chieftaincy title to Trinidadian artiste LeRoy Clarke and a two-day youth conference, "Children: A Product of Our Environment."[21] As stated in the festival's brochure: "The Rain Festival brings people together to celebrate, rebirth commitment, understanding and responsibility in a physical and spiritual sense. The Rain Cycle serves to sensitise the entire nation of the importance and sacredness of the rain. It is a period for reflection, thanksgiving, cleansing and preparation. . . . The earth's resources contribute immensely to our National well-being and that of the Universe as a whole" (IESOM 2005).

The important work that the Rain Festival is charged with performing annually was invoked by LeRoy Clarke days before his chieftaincy where

FIGURE 3.1 Baba Ogunkeye, on behalf of Ile Eko Sango/Osun Mil'osa, presents an award to Iya Osunide L'Antoinette Stines, Jamaican choreographer and Oshun priest, for her contribution to the Orisha community as part of the shrine's Fifth Annual Rain Festival. Santa Cruz, Trinidad, 2006. Photo by N. Fadeke Castor.

he was given the title Chief Ifa Oje Won Yomi Abiodun of Trinidad and Tobago (plate 6 and 7). In his opening address to the IESOM Sixth Annual Rain Festival in 2005, Clarke performed (rather than just stated) with his poet hat on, "Festivals arrive with us as unusual mirrors of our conscience, reflecting the motion and the grading of achievement in o[u]r ongoing experiences. They are also the means by which we are launched to higher flight in demonstrations of faith, offering-up ourselves to imaginary gifts of God's esteem transported to us by the graciousness of Ancestor worship!" He also called for a "meditation" on the "dwellings and cultures that are now the thrones upon which our ancestors sit" and stressed that this will lead to "vistas of a vast matrix of ideas that spawned our Africa." For Clarke, as for many of the festival participants, it is through the communal ritual that the self is reimagined and recreated, informed by the wisdom of the ancestors and through them an imagined Africa. Or as put poetically by Clarke, "Festivals . . . stands out as a celebration of homecoming to the best gathering of what we are; . . . we are inspired to boundless self-refinement that the possibility of creating a completely new world view; . . . we are calling, as we must, on our innermost selves to re-chart ruins, in order to re-create ourselves" (2005). This homecoming and recreation of self that is grounded in a "new world view" informed by the wisdom of African ancestors reflects the stated goal of the shrine, the enriching of Trinidad culture and people through reestablishing and strengthening the link with their ancestral African heritage. Their primary method for doing this is through festivals that have been developed by Iya Sangowunmi in fulfillment of her *ita* (divination reading received during initiation).

These festivals also serve as public sites on both a local and a transnational level. The media attention and the presence of visiting babalawo and cabinet-level speakers have attracted a large group of attendees, mostly middle-class, from outside the religion. The majority of activities can be experienced (passively) as "culture" and involve very little ritual outside of prayers in Yoruba and libations. Largely absent from the public face of festivals are activities such as sacrifice or possession that might challenge the sensibilities of nonpractitioners (and trigger prejudices rooted in stereotypes). The effect of this is twofold: a large number of people have become increasingly comfortable attending Orisha festivals, and the more public shrine festivals have taken on a more secular and celebratory character.[22] I consider this an example of the philosophical and spiritual focus of IESOM, where the underlying principles of Ifá and Orisha are embodied in all spheres of life activity, for example, informing the celebration of children and community elders (reflected in the Rain Festival programming). For Iya Sangowunmi, this perspective is expressed when she says the following, "we have come to a point where we have to [work] for continuity, for the understanding of our own children and to save our own children[.] We have to put some structures in place and this is the point where I am at because when I was initiated, my Eta [*sic*] was about . . . putting Shango as a priestess of Shango on the ground" (quoted in Henry 2003, 105). As evidenced by Iya's reliance on her ita Ifá informs and structures how festivals are organized in the IESOM shrine and beyond into the wider Yorùbá-centric community. The organization of festivals are informed by Ifá divination, from the details of when they are scheduled to the content of programming.

The turn to Ifá in Orisha communities has shifted the focus of dynamics beyond Trinidad's local and national community to a larger global frame. Ultimately, Iya Sangowunmi's projects are not embedded primarily within a national network but rather within the wider frame of global Orisha practices, a transnational spiritual network that is visible through the movements of devotees for migration, pilgrimage, and initiations and especially in festival moments. It is within these gatherings, whether of the World Orisha Congress or the Rain Festival, that a form of spiritual kinship and lineage (well documented) and spiritual citizenship (less documented) are performed, engaged, and negotiated. These identities that are grounded in transnational spiritual networks ultimately inform both local ritual kinship and lineages, and national citizenship. Iya Sangowunmi's transnational roles and links have reinforced and reinscribed her national identity and informed a spiritual work that is aimed at healing the nation and building a decolonized national culture.

CHAPTER 4

Trini Travels

Spiritual Citizenship as Transnational

"The old people say you're not doing the work." These words from Baba Er-infolami, an Ifá/Orisha elder seemed to hang in the air. I was sitting across from Baba and talking about Orisha and Ifá in Trinidad on a warm night in St. James, Trinidad's urban neighborhood that never sleeps. *Thwack, thwack, thwack*! The fan, missing the front protective grille, kept hitting something as it went around. I was struggling to hear Baba speak about his path in Yorùbá religion over the sound of the fan (which was needed to keep the mosquitoes off). As my focus returned, I realized that he was describing one of his visits to New York. His path in Orisha had pivotal moments in many countries, as seen by his answer to my question about Ifá in Trinidad. It was there in the late 1990s that he had discovered Ifá in a book of odù Ifá verses (ẹsẹ) from a street seller outside Brooklyn's Slave Theater.

Fadeke: When did you first learn of Ifá? At some point, it was just Orisha, right?

Baba E.: Mm-hm. Yes.

Fadeke: And when did Ifá come into it?

Baba E.: [motioning with his hand] Open that book.

Fadeke: Epega? [I leaned over and grabbed a dog-eared, well-worn version of Epega's book *The Sacred Ifá Oracle*.]

Baba E.: I went New York and bought this book, I bought this book outside the Slave Theater in New York at night in the snow. What's the dates in it? I went, I come back here, and they tell me, "The old people say you're not doing the work." I started to read Ifá every day.

A discussion of dates followed that put his earliest Ifá studies in 1999 based on his copious handwritten notes marking the different Odù verses. Within a couple of years, Baba would take major steps toward Ifá initiation. "It come like, it like food. . . . this is how I feel about Ifá, it come like food" was his response to my question about the impact of Ifá on the Orisha practice in Trinidad. His equating of Ifá with food, something necessary for survival, for life, shows its importance for him. Ifá for Baba is an essential form of sustenance. *Thwack, thwack* went the fan. Baba raised his voice over the sound to explain:

> The history of the tradition in Trinidad is something that I keep meh focus on, and I understood that we couldn't go any further with the way we organized the tradition here.
>
> Because you're gone by Ford, you start with Christian ting, he gone to the Orisha, and by six o'clock in the morning he down in the back doing some Kabala ting.[1] You understand that kind of thing? And that's what was happening all about. So I say I am not going to be a party to that.
>
> That don't make no sense.
>
> We go by a man, say he an Orisha priest. You know? And he had some Christian saints here. And I personally take all [saints] and throw all out by Mother Rodney. See the grandchildren gone pick [saints] up in the rubbish, up in the back. So I say well [shrugs].
>
> Some have Hindu stuff in place, some have some Christian stuff. Some have some all kind of stuff and say they practicing Orisha. I say but they couldn't know anything about the Yorùbá people. You know?
>
> So my situation was hop on a plane. So 2001, 2002, I hop on planes and went to Nigeria. 2004, they came here to make me the Alaagba. 2006, I head back to Nigeria for Ifá.

Baba's situation was the inherited legacy of Trinidad Orisha, a tradition marked by layers of syncretism and creolization. These layers can be read as a palimpsest of colonialism, settlement—both forced and free—followed by independence, Black Power, and the historical conjunctures traced earlier (see chapter 1). His movement to Ifá pushed him to seek beyond this.

To connect to the "original" Yorùbá culture and religion that had largely informed Trinidad Orisha.[2] He was not alone.

At the turn of the millennium, an emergent spiritual citizenship was visibly grounded in the transnational spiritual networks of the Yorùbá religion evident in the 1999 Orisha World Congress. Changes in Trinidad would further manifest in the following year, when the Council of Orisha Elders would host the Third Orisha Family Day at the ancestral site (held at a slave burial ground) in Lopinot, Arouca. The honored guest was President A. N. R. Robinson, whose presence followed on the previous year's substantial political presence from Prime Minister Basdeo Panday. Also in 2000, Mother Melvina Rodney, a venerated Orisha elder and former head of the Council of Orisha Elders, received a National Independence Day Award that on its face value indicated recognition of the Orisha religion and its leadership by the state. However, the lack of a proper biography and introduction, including her leadership role in Orisha, revealed that despite Orisha's many inroads, the "public," including sectors of the government, did not understand or know how to represent the religion in a public way (see McNeal, K.E. 2011, 285, for more on this controversy).

The turn of the millennium continued to witness institution and network building that created the fertile ground in which to plant Ifá. After Trinidad's Orisha World Congress in 1999, organizer Iya Sangowunmi would continue to offer classes on Orisha and Ifá at the secondary school she ran. Additionally, under the guidance of her ita and Orisha, she inaugurated an annual Rain Festival (see chapter 3 for more on this) that marked the transition from the dry season to the rainy season at the beginning of what those in northern climates call summer. As she built her shrine, Ile Eko Sango/Osun Mil'osa (IESOM), Iya Sangowunmi drew on networks that she had established when studying under Awiṣe Wándé Abímbọ́lá, a senior Nigerian babaláwo, and Ifá ambassador to the world. Her studies of Ifá took her to Boston, Massachusetts, to work with him. There she met other initiates and accessed knowledge on Ifá and Orisha from a West African perspective. Through these networks, she met Awo Ifakunle, the self-named "Ifá priest of Harlem" babalawo, and invited him to work with her shrine in the Santa Cruz Valley of eastern Trinidad.[3] Awo Ifakunle's extensive research and ritual experience throughout both the diaspora and Yorubaland were rich resources that he drew on to connect with various communities in Trinidad, including both Spiritual Baptists and Orisha. Those connections would also expand the network available to Iya Sangowunmi and IESOM.

A reminder is useful here that the documentation of movements and changes within Trinidad's Orisha and emerging Ifá community represents one partial view of a subset of the national community. As with any field of networks, there are points of convergence, overlaps between circuits and outliers. This is certainly true of the community in Trinidad. The convergence that I focus on is largely, but not exclusively, Yorùbá-centric (see previous discussion of this term in chapter 3) and made up of a network of individuals and connected shrines that are largely informed by a Pan-African and Afrocentric worldview with political roots in the 1970s Black Power movement. The local hosting of the Sixth World Orisha Congress in 1999 had brought together various sectors of the local and international Orisha and Ifá communities, while leaving others out. A legacy of this was the organization of the Council of Orisha Elders, which facilitated the receiving of government resources (see chapter 2 for more on this). Another legacy from this conference was the exposure of local Orisha priests to presentations on Ifá, to numerous Ifá priests, and to opportunities for networking. The latter would bear fruit in years to come as elders and shrines in Trinidad aligned and affiliated with notable Ifá elders and shrines in Yorubaland (as in the previous example of Iya Sangowunmi and Awo Ifakunle). An initial step toward these closer connections would be evident during the subsequent 2001 Orisha Congress in Ilé-Ifẹ̀, Nigeria.[4]

Exploring how these deeper connections developed raises the issue of economic resources and class. People need access to resources to do the kinds of traveling that I document in this section, which often is far beyond their means. The number of people who would like to go to Nigeria, Brasil, Cuba, and other important locations for Ifá/Orisha is much greater than those select few who are able to mobilize the substantial resources needed to make such trips. Historically, in the 1970s and 1980s, the individuals who were able to travel to the continent were often academics, who, like me, accessed institutional and grant funding sources to support their research. Included on this list are the notable Dr. J. D. Elder, Dr. Molly Ahye, and Dr. Maureen Warner-Lewis, who would be joined in later decades by people who had come of age during the time of Black Power. Over the decades between the 1970s and the new millennium, even as Orisha became more mainstream in Trinidad, larger numbers of Orisha practitioners would come from the middle class or would become middle class. This shift in class demographics both contributed to and benefited from a sea change, where public association with African religion no longer hindered a successful business, professional, or even political career. Access to more economic resources supported increasing international travel, including travel to West Africa. This in part explains the larger numbers of the Trinidad Orisha community that were reaching the continent in the twenty-first century (with many of them making multiple trips between 2000 and 2015).[5]

Much of the travel documented here was facilitated by the resources of "middle-class" Ifá/Orisha devotees, along with some state subvention and collectives pooling resources. I want to complicate the label of middle class.[6] In Trinidad, as in most places, class is a complex label of background, locality, family, culture, presentation, and various other factors in addition to the availability of and proximity to economic resources. The status of middle class is positional and shifts depending on perspective. The same could be said for the local label "grassroots," which often refers to people who are viewed to be working class or lower-working-class. (Depending on the context, "grassroots" may also refer to people perceived as poor and disenfranchised. And in another context, "grassroots" could refer to people who are thought of as culture bearers and culture creators.) Of course, these varying definitions are not exclusionary. They can, and do, exist in multiple and overlapping combinations. When a religious dimension is added to this complex of characteristics, things are further complicated.

Part of the heritage from colonialism is a well-documented politics of respectability and reputation in the Caribbean (for more on this see discussions in Burton 1997; D. Thomas 2004) that privileges Christian religions, whether Catholic or Protestant, at the expense of any and all indigenous religions ("indigenous" here referencing both First American, West African, Asian, and South Asian religions, as well as those mixtures of the aforementioned groups, often with Judeo-Christian religions). Up until the present moment in the twenty-first century, class status in Trinidad has been highly plastic. One's class status can be altered by being linked to a non-Christian religion, and specifically within certain Afro-Creole communities by being linked to African diasporic religious traditions (including Ifá/Orisha and Spiritual Baptists). Thus, many folks who from the grassroots perspective appear to be middle class due to their educational attainment, regularity of employment, or location of residence can also become less than middle class when viewed through a "social" or "status" lens by elements of what might be called the "established" or "mainstream" middle class. Alternatively, styles of dress or other performatives can be markers that will shift with one's class based on how they are read (and who is doing the reading).

An example from my own experience in Trinidad speaks to this fluidity of status. One day, after paying respects to my family grave in the St. James cemetery, I asked my uncle if we could go by the mall. I was taking advantage of having access to a car to run an errand, as I needed to pick up a DVR cassette for my video camera. These tapes were difficult to find in Port of Spain, so I was headed to a store in the upscale West Mall that I knew carried them. What I forgot was that as a form of both respect and spiritual protection I had put on a gèlè (head wrap) while paying respects at the cemetery. And because I forgot I went into the mall with the head wrap on. As they say in Trinidad, "Who tell she to do that?" Though I had been to the mall many times before, and since, I never experienced the level of rudeness there that I did on that day. I was dismissed, disregarded, and disrespected at the counter, from the scornful gazes that I received to the service that I did not get. (Trinis are not known for their stellar service, but this was beyond the pale.) In order to get waited on, I had to raise my voice and highlight my American accent. All of this due to a head wrap!

As an important part of what makes this story intelligible, I should mention that I am relatively light-skinned, with freckles and other features that mark me racially as "red" in contemporary Trinidad.[7] This further illustrates the truth that throughout the Caribbean, class and color are closely intertwined.[8] Because my appearance is read as red, I am usually classified as middle class in Trinidad. This is bolstered in no small part by my American accent, which can be a double-edged sword that garners both favor and resentment depending on the context and the audience. Generally, though, being perceived as red, American or not, affords me niceties of access and service. The feeling evoked from having a simple piece of cloth alter how I was treated, powerfully illustrating the fluidity and contingency of class categorization, has remained with me to this day. (Of course, I went back to the shop at a later date without a head wrap and received my "normal" level of service.)

Many of the people I interviewed and spent time with grew up within that same established middle-class community. In converting to Ifá/Orisha, they found their status and identity to be at risk, though the extent of that risk has changed greatly over time. Others grew up on the borderline of working/middle class and gained both economic resources and social capital while getting involved in Ifá/Orisha. In other words, attempting to draw a fixed line of class positionality and placing people on that social barometer is a project mired in futility; doing so would do violence to the complexities of lived day-to-day identities in Trinidad.

Notably, however, spiritual knowledge and its pursuit provide their own kind of alternative status, one of spiritual capital (Bourdieu 1984). The early years of the new millennium, from 2001 to 2005, marked a contemporary watershed in travels to gain knowledge of the Yorùbá religion and its culture. Specifically, the Orisha World Congress that followed the one hosted in Trinidad was held in Ilé-Ifè, Nigeria (the sacred center of the Yorùbá religion), in 2001. A sizable contingent from Trinidad attended the conference and used the opportunity to develop relationships that originated in 1999, visit sacred sites, receive Ifá readings, and go through initiation ceremonies to Ifá and various Orisha. As discussed earlier, the Sixth World Orisha Congress included a number of Ifá initiates from Nigeria, London, the United States, and other locations, with the majority being male Ifá priests (babalawo). The connections made at that conference formed the foundation for the transnational relationships that would develop. Awo Eniola says that his initial meeting of Chief Adelekan at the 1999 Orisha Congress began a relationship that laid the groundwork for his visit to Ilé-Ifè in later years.[9] In interviews, others mentioned this conference as being a foundational or pivotal moment in their relationship with Orisha, Ifá, and the larger transnational community. An increasing flow of experienced babalawo, including Àwíṣe Wándé Abímbọ́la, Awo Ifakunle, and others, came to Trinidad in 2000 and 2001. All of this laid the groundwork for folks going to Ilé-Ifè in 2001 and encountering the prominence of Ifá. (These first five years of the millennium are an important precursor to the explosion of Ifá in Trinidad that will be discussed later in this chapter). These transnational travels, and others along similar networks, would inform increased status for African religions on both sides of the Atlantic.

Travels to Ilé-Ifè, Nigeria

The Orisha World Congress that followed the one held in Trinidad was critical for key people's awareness of Ifá and the continental practice of the Yorùbá religion. This 2001 conference was an important conjuncture, which became apparent from my interviews. The Seventh World Orisha Congress was held in Ilé-Ifè, Nigeria, on August 5 through 12, 2001. The invitation, posted on the World Wide Web and distributed via e-mail, announced the conference theme, "Time Is Ripe. The Orisha Tradition in the Twenty-First Century," and provided this further description: "The conference seeks to celebrate the Orisha traditions, culture and spiritual experience; demonstrate unity, coherence and inter-connectedness of Orisha traditions world-wide; work on organization, propagation and re-orientation of notions about Orisha traditions in the 21st century." Activities were planned to spread over several key sites in Yorubaland, including Ilé-Ifẹ̀, Osogbo, and Oyo. After numerous previous conferences held in locations throughout the diaspora (Brazil, 1990; United States, 1997; and Trinidad, 1999), it had been more than a decade since a conference had been held in Nigeria (1986). The Orisha World Congress was returning home to the continent at the turn of the millennium.

Following the conference in Trinidad, this continental congress provided a landmark opportunity for members of Trinidad's Orisha community to travel to Yorubaland. In fact, there was specific outreach to then Orisha leaders to come to the 2001 meetings; among those who received a personal invitation was Mother Melvina Rodney (whom the Ọọni, the king of Ilé-Ifẹ̀ and regarded by many as the head of the Yorùbá religion, had declared a head of the Orisha religion in Trinidad during his 1988 visit). These invitations contributed to the large contingent of priests and practitioners from Trinidad who attended the conference. Besides Mother Rodney, notable participants from Trinidad included Eintou Pearl Springer, Baba Jeffrey Biddeau, Mother Joan Cyrus, Aina Olukayode, and Baba Erinfolami, among others. Many of the visitors from Trinidad used the opportunity to meet local elders, visit Orisha shrines, and receive Ifá readings. Several elders had unique opportunities to receive recognition of their work in Trinidad and meet with spiritual leaders in Ilé-Ifẹ̀.

One examples is Mother Joan Cyrus who came to the attention of the Ifá leadership during the 2001 Orisha Congress. In a 2011 interview, one of her shrine members recollected: "Sixteen babalawos went up to Oke 'Tase and divined to find out if that was the person to bestow. And we were waiting, we couldn't understand what was happening. Then they came down. And they spoke." When the Ifá priests emerged, they declared that Ifá had decided Mother Joan was to receive the chieftaincy title Ìyálóde Awo Àgbáyé, literally meaning Mother of the Mysteries Worldwide (figure 4.1). A ceremony would be held later in the Ọọni's palace to officially bestow the honor. Holding this title would mark Mother Joan as one of the early holders of a Yorùbá chieftaincy in Trinidad, especially notable as a woman in an internationally recognized leadership position.

FIGURE 4.1 Iyalode Awo Agbaye Ifakorede Oyayemi Aworeni,
Mother Joan Cyrus, sits in the palais at her shrine, Kenny
Cyrus Alkebulan Ile Ijebu, in Enterprise Village, Chaguanas,
Trinidad with the badges of her chieftaincy title that she
received in Ilé-Ifẹ̀, Nigeria: a beaded necklace (ileke) and
crown, 2012. Photo by N. Fadeke Castor.

Mother Joan's gender may have been a factor in the reaction of disbelief that she received when she returned to Trinidad. As Agba Ifagbola (née Charles Castle) recounted, "Most people didn't believe that she had an authentic chieftaincy from the Araba of Ife." In fact, he received calls in the States (where he was living at the time) asking him to confirm her title. "I remember I was in Boston and I got a call. 'Charles, weren't you there?'" to which he responded, "But I'm saying I was there!" Despite Mother Joan's impeccable credentials in Trinidad as a decades-long leader of one of the oldest continuously operating Orisha shrines, her chieftaincy title garnered incredulity and required confirmation. Another reason for the disbelief, besides her gender, was the novelty of the event. While fifteen years later there would be enough holders of chieftaincy titles in Trinidad to make up an organization (the Council of Traditional Afrikan Chiefs of Trinidad and Tobago), at the time, Mother Joan's was among the first titles held by an Orisha elder resident in Trinidad. The recognition of her leadership by the Ifá priests of Òkè Ìtasè (who are collectively known as the Awomérìndín-lógún) was also recognition of the Orisha religion in Trinidad. This served to reinforce the burgeoning connection between the two religious communities and laid the groundwork for future encounters and exchanges.

It was at this multiday conference and its surrounding events that people from Trinidad were exposed to the Yorùbá religion in its "home" context. The chieftaincy of Mother Joan speaks to one of the reasons that the 2001 Orisha Congress was so important to Ifá/Orisha in Trinidad. In this home context, chieftaincy becomes visible as an institution of recognition and patronage that recognizes community leaders. When referencing Yorubaland, I do not use the term "original" as that would imply a static and artificial authenticity that cannot be found in today's postcolonial Yorubaland, predominantly situated in Nigeria. Certainly, in the "imagined community" of Yorubaland it would be hard to think of day-to-day Nigerian life in the contemporary moment as the "original" context of the Yorùbá religion.[10]

The 2001 trip to Ilé-Ifè would affect both how people moved forward with their Orisha practice and how they moved forward with regard to Ifá. Other people who had not made the trip would become inspired by (or curious about) the stories that attendees brought back and organize their own subsequent trips to Yorubaland. The pairing of 1999 and 2001 conferences in Trinidad and Ilé-Ifè marked a pivotal conjuncture in making Trinidad visible and situating its Orisha religion within the larger transnational community of the Orisha and Ifá religions.

Looking for Orisha, Not Seeing Ifá

[Ifá] started to become mainstream after some time, and Trinidadian nationals
started traveling to the United States and to Nigeria and to Cuba and to Brazil
and to other places and receiving initiations and returning to Trinidad with their
experience—and encouraging and inviting others to do the same. As relationships
grew, Nigerians started coming here and eventually started performing initiations
here in Trinidad. The numbers of people therefore being exposed to Ifá was . . .
growing—there was a time when you knew all of the people who initiated; you could
have counted them on your fingers and toes. But now that's off the chain.
—Awo Eniola

In 2003, the connections engendered through the two conferences, travels, and initiations began to bear fruit, as the exchanges that had begun in
the previous five years gathered momentum. Increasing numbers of people
went through the many steps required to journey from Trinidad to Nigeria, including obtaining a visa, locating the finances to purchase a plane
ticket, and securing a host or accommodations. There were also increasing
numbers of initiations on these trips. Many of the journeys for festivals,
spiritual instruction, and initiations emerged from a chance encounter or
Ifá reading at one of the Orisha congresses (in 1999 or 2001). In this same
period, there was an increase in activity in Trinidad among the Yorùbá-
centric shrines that coincided with the visits of several babalawo, including
Awo Ifakunle (United States), Awo Somorin (Nigeria), and Awo Faloju (Canada). The ritual activities and travels during this period laid the groundwork
for the establishment of Ifá lineages in Trinidad (explored further in the
next chapter).

   In the new millennium, the first cluster of people from Trinidad were initiated to Ifá. These historic journeys began with Awo Ifá Korade, a longtime
Orisha priest from South Trinidad who had studied Ifá under Awo Ifáyomi
during the previous decade. Korade would travel to Ogun State in Nigeria in
January 2003 for Ifá initiation into the Epega lineage. Also in 2003, Charles
Castle followed up his 2001 trip and stayed with the Àràbà of Ilé-Ifè, where
he received Ìtefá (i.e., initiation to Ifá) and received the name Ifagbola. That
same year Awo Amosun (Baba Sangodele) was the third Trini to travel to Nigeria for Ifá initiation. This increased focus on Ifá knowledge and spiritual
energy built on earlier Orisha and Ifá international conferences (1999 and
2001), initiations into Ifá in Nigeria, and the visits of babalawo from the

diaspora (Toronto, Canada; Harlem, in New York City) and the continent (Ode Remo, Ogun State, Nigeria). This local buildup in Trinidad continued to be fed by circulations of priests and practitioners along the transnational spiritual networks that secure the continent's position as a foundational component of the diaspora. One example of movements along this circuit would be the "Sacred Journey to Ilé-Ifẹ̀" in 2004, organized by Trinidad's Egbe Onisin Eledumare, which brought together people from Trinidad, the United States, and the United Kingdom.

Even as these Ifá circulations and encounters were increasing in number, I experienced this time through the lens of Orisha activities, events, and rituals. This was one of the central years of my ethnographic research in Trinidad. If I go back into my archive for notable "Orisha" events for 2003, they include festivals across Trinidad, from north to south and east to west: the raising of the twenty-four-foot Oṣe Sango (double-headed ax wood sculpture) at Ile Eko Sango/Osun Mil'osa; the Orisha Family Day; the Gelede (masquerade ritual dance to appease the mothers) in Princes Town; the Oshun sailout in Toco;[11] the Oshun festival in Salybia (plate 4); Odun Ojo Orisha (the Festival of Light) at IESOM; and Egungun at Eniyan Wa in Princes Town. All these events can be read through a lens of ancestral Trinidad Orisha practices, which I largely did at the time. I argue here that reading them solely in this way provides an incomplete picture that reflects the partial nature of ethnography, even at its best. The reasoning for this argument comes from the dividend of longitudinal research and the hindsight that it provides. Ten years later (or more), the archive can be read, alongside more contemporary ethnographic inquiries, to reveal the emergence of Ifá. When viewed through this different lens, the events listed here reveal levels of meaning, becoming important moments in a new story.

Let me emphasize that just because the Ifá lens adds a layer of meaning, that does not invalidate other meanings or experiences. And by no means do I want to imply that there are separate levels that can be cleanly demarcated. They are mutually imbricated, messy, and at best organized from the outside as a continuum for heuristic purposes. The everyday lived reality of the Ifá/Orisha devotee is intersectional. These lineages that I have pulled apart for the purposes of analysis are in fact overlapping communities of practice. This remains one of the central challenges that face ethnographers— how to process, organize, and communicate an experience without doing unavoidable damage to that experience. And how to relate one's own experience to those of the people they work with, that they claim (even in a limited way) to represent. My representations here seeks to go beyond the "thin" surface reporting ("just the facts, ma'am") while negotiating the "hubris" of thick description where as anthropologists we run the risk of providing an "imagined ethnographic thickness to be far thicker than it actually is" (Jackson 2013, 13–14; see also Geertz 1973). There are many views and approaches to the story of Orisha and Ifá in Trinidad, all of them partial and contingent, and the anthropologist's pathway of experience is not necessarily more authoritative or insightful than any others.

Despite Ifá becoming increasingly dominant (the story I principally tell here), the ancestral tradition, teachings, and ase of Trinidad Orisha remain vital and central. In exploring the context and meaning of Trinidad Orisha songs, the collaboration of a local ritual expert (Phills), a scholar (Gibbons), and a Trini-based Nigerian scholar (Aiyejina) provides a nuanced and sophisticated perspective:

> Against the background of the signifying potentials of these songs, we find it disturbing that some Trinidad Orisa devotees often feel that until they go to Nigeria for their ase (spiritual authority), they are not true devotees. What our interrogation of Trinidad Orisa is establishing is that what exists in Trinidad has its own integrity and its own internal logic, which, more often than not, parallels or complements the Yoruba practice of the tradition. Orisa in Trinidad is therefore a unique recreation of one version of what Africa means for the New World African. The ideal situation therefore is one in which global Yoruba cultures enter into dialogue with each other not as authentic or inauthentic "others," but as rivers with the same fountainhead. Such a relationship will go a long way to formulate a template for the global relationship between Africa and its diaspora. (Aiyejina, Gibbons, and Phills 2009, 135)

It is remarkable that these authors, all local residents, feel the need to defend the coherence of the Trini-centric (my term) faith. The Orisha religion in Trinidad has a history going back well over a hundred years and includes rich practices that have been passed down from generation to generation. These authors situate the "ideal" relationship as one that moves away from a politics of authenticity. My own focus on Yorùbá-centric shrines and the introduction of the Ifá lineage to Trinidad is not an attempt to engage in these moribund politics. Rather, I am interested in the emergence of new practices, ones that in many instances endeavor to respect ancestral traditions while integrating new rituals and bodies of knowledge.

Examining the Orisha events that I attended in 2003 and 2004 through the lens of Ifá reveals interesting layers, dynamics, and nuances. Starting with the raising of the Ose Shango, a carving of the deity's iconic double-headed ax that in its base stands four stories tall, at IESOM, the Ifá aspect is visible in the directives given to the shrine's leader, Iya Sangowunmi (plate 9). In erecting the statue to Shango, and in building the shrine in Santa Cruz, she was following Ifá's directive from her initiation to plant Orisha and Ifá in the ground in Trinidad. I have touched upon this theme throughout this volume because it is these directives that have guided the establishment of IESOM and the construction of its rituals and festivals. Without the benefit of Ifá's perspective, the direction of IESOM and the nature of its activities can be confusing or unclear, especially when viewed from the perspective of Trini-centric Orisha. When I look at the other events held at IESOM during this time, I find glimpses of the central place Ifá would come to occupy in the subsequent years. For example, in photos from the Odun Ojo Orisha at IESOM, I can now take note of banners hanging from the ceiling marked with odu Ifá. At the time I took the photo, I had no idea of the meaning being conveyed behind me (figure 4.2). According to Ifá the Odu are cosmographic representations of the sixteen principal energies of the universe. When asked about the banners, Iya Sangowunmi said she was directed to place them there by the ancestors in order to bring the energy of the Odu into the shrine. More immediately apparent in my memory was the presence of an Ifá priest, Awo Faloju, at the ritual. He had also held a series of classes at IESOM on Orisha and Ifá from the perspective of his training in Nigeria (augmented by travels to Cuba and Brazil). In fact, as I look back, I realize that even though I sat in on a class and took notes, the information on Ifá literally went over my head, both as an academic and as a spiritual person. Thus, at the time I did not understand the import and potential impact of this class on IESOM and its members. It is only in retrospect that this has come into focus.

So what does this mean now? It means that to choose a fixed point in time and declare that this is when Ifá arrived in Trinidad would artificially disrupt the complex unfolding of interrelated and interdependent events. As much as I would like to be able to pinpoint one event or nexus of relationships as *the* moment, that would be an overly simplistic fiction. If at this juncture there are communities in which many of the practices of ancestral Trinidad Orisha have been displaced and taken over by "traditional" Yorùbá Ifá, this point may be more important to the ethnographer and the process of ethnographic writing than it is to the practitioners of African diasporic

FIGURE 4.2 The author at Ile Eko Sango/Osun Mil'osa in Santa Cruz, Trinidad with two red banners behind her on the wall that are marked with odu Ifá; Ọ̀bàrà Meji on the left and Ọ̀yẹ̀kú Méjì on the right, 2004. Photo by N. Fadeke Castor.

religions in Trinidad. For people in Trinidad, their practices remain in flux, mapped out more by lines of efficacy (does it work? does it make my life better?) than by issues of authenticity, status, or alignment with imagined transnational communities (even as the latter issues also inform their ritual practices). I do insist (as do many ethnographic theorists) that it is possible to track and map changes in an ethnographic "field" (Jean Comaroff and John Comaroff 1992, 2003a; Gupta and Ferguson 1992). As is often said, the one constant in life is change. This is certainly true in ethnography, in our lives as researchers and the lives of the people we share time with; it is quite exceptional when we can locate the precise moment in the stream of everyday life when categories change.

In charting the flows of African diasporic ritual and spiritual practice in Trinidad, I cannot select an arbitrary moment in time as being the one point at which Ifá came to Trinidad. Looking back on my experiences and research (my "ethnographic data") over a decade, I can track a propensity to compartmentalize and organize events into a neat temporal flow so that clear markers become visible. I continue to resist this tendency because I think it can produce a false, if palatable, picture of what has happened (see Trouillot's *Silencing the Past* [1995]). The "hubris" of ethnographic thickness that John Jackson (2013) warned us against lies in wait amid these heuristic categories. And yet organization is needed to tell a story, one that follows a seemingly linear narrative, where one event occurs after another. Even as I lay the tiles of such a tale, I present a challenge and disruption of such a "neat" offering. While the journey of emergent spiritual citizenship becomes visible in Ifá's development, it is important to remain aware of the less visible underlying rhizomatic roots made from the myriad spiritual and material moments and connections of ancestral Trinidad Orisha.

Bridging Diasporic Geographies

In the five years that followed the World Orisha Congress in Ilé-Ifè, Nigeria, the groundwork was laid for the establishment of a local Ifá lineage in 2007. This truly remarkable moment, establishing a new ritual lineage in the diaspora with all its esoteric spiritual technology and ase, will be explored further in the next chapter. Here, I take a closer look at the circuits and connections that paved the way. And in doing so, I map out the emergence of a spiritual citizenship grounded in both a radical black politics and an African consciousness. This history, together with a commitment to building a liberatory community guided by spiritual praxis, informs the core of a spiritual citizenship that would be further nurtured and energized by the establishment of Ifá. The knowledge base and access to new forms of spiritual technology, new sources of ase available through Ifá, and newly expressed commitments to generations past, present, and future all contribute to spiritual citizenship's building of institutions and community.

As discussed previously, this included the incremental integration of Ifá, from prayers to divination, into ancestral Trinidad Orisha rituals and practices. Increasingly, rituals would begin with expansive invocations in the Trini dialect of Yorùbá as seen in the iba or prayer that opened the previous chapter. These opening prayers, central to ritual in Yorubaland and throughout the diaspora, serve as genealogical maps that locate the reader, and those who witness, in space and place. The location of the invocation, let us say the IESOM shrine, now gets placed into a specific diasporic reading of history that spans time going back several generations as the ancestors are invoked.

In the African diaspora there are often historical figures (say Haiti's Toussaint L'Ouverture) whose name when called is a form of ancestral invocation, that places the assembled people into a "fictive" lineage of notables, oftentimes freedom fighters and revolutionaries. The construction of this historical memory through positioning these historical personages creates a geography of the Black Atlantic, locating the present locality (Santa Cruz, Trinidad) within a diasporic field. An important facet is that this Black Atlantic religious landscape is inclusive of, and often centered on, "Africa"; this includes the "imagined" Africa and the historical Africa and the contemporary Africa (Mbembe 2001; Mudimbe 1988, 1994). This "Africa" in all three constructions is usually centered on the geographic region often designated as "West Africa" and commonly focused on the Yorubaland area (including roughly southwest Nigeria, Benin, and Togo). In the diasporic iba this is often done by invocations to place-names (Ilé-Ifè), notable Ifá leaders (e.g., the Àràbà and the Ọòni of Ilé-Ifè), and notables (e.g., Dr. Ìdòwú Odéyẹ mí). This sacred geography locates Trinidad (at its most general) and the shrine and the priest doing the invocation (at its most specific) within the space/place of African diasporic religions that are in turn: ancestral (going back over time, passed from generation to generation), historical (tied to key ancestors and events such as the Haitian Revolution), geographical (mapping relative locations across the Atlantic), and radical (privileging a historical narrative or, rather, counternarrative, that foregrounds African diasporic and alternative spiritual knowledge systems and challenges imperialistic power relations).

"Ifá Was Always Here"

While conducting a series of oral histories, I was taken aback when I heard repeatedly, "Ifá was always here"—an unexpected assertion that came from people of different lineages and diverse organizations. As put eloquently by Trinidadian Awo Eniola, "In a sense Ifá was always here—but not necessarily in a form that everybody would recognize and acknowledge, except in the case of exceptional individuals." Note the nuance that he brings to the statement, with the phrase "not necessarily in a form that everybody would recognize." This raises the question of what forms of Ifá were in Trinidad—and how could they be recognized?[12]

In 2011, I sat down with a number of Ifá priests and practitioners I knew to hear how they had come to Orisha and Ifá (the latter almost always following the former in Trinidad at that time). I interviewed sixteen initiates and practitioners in open-ended conversations that lasted from two to six hours. From these sessions arose a complex picture of the spiritual journey that brought people to African diasporic religions (many started as Christians), often passing through other faiths such as Spiritual Baptist before arriving at the Orisha religion. This rich material supplied many of the stories and direct quotes that inform the upcoming sections, adding a valuable facet to my existing longitudinal ethnographic data gathered from rituals, festivals, and ceremonies over fifteen years.

The older Ifá that people referenced was different from the transnational Ifá lineages and practices of the new millennium. A picture of the "form" of Ifá that may have been present in conjunction with widely known and recognized Orisha practices emerged from these interviews. Rawle Gibbons commented, "Saint Anthony [in Trinidad] is Orunmila. . . . in our system . . . he's the prophet. He's the teacher." This locates the energy of wisdom and teaching associated with Orunmila within Trinidad's cosmology of Orisha, associated with a saint known for locating lost items (often associated with Esu/Legba in Lucumi). In his book *The Lost Orisha* (1996) Conrad Maugé, known by his Yorùbá name Awo Ifayomi Epega-Agbede, discusses the impetus to "re-Africanize the religion" in relation to the Catholic elements in Trinidad Orisha: "The older age set was more Catholic orientated than African. What added to my confusion was that the name of one saint may be given to the orisha by one house and the name of another saint given by another house. One orisha therefore, could have syncretized names of saints depending on the particular association of a house and their order of worship" (190). In his own accounting, Orunmila, the prophet of Ifá, was associated with Saint Joseph, while Saint Anthony was linked with the Orisha Dada. A quick survey of the texts on Trinidad Orisha would support Ifayomi's observations of the multiplicity of associations between Orisha and saints in Trinidad (in contrast to a greater level of standardization, for example, in Cuban Lucumi/Santería).

Another perspective comes from the observations of Babalawo Ifakunle (who is based in Harlem in New York City) on his visits to Trinidad that led him to conclude, "I believe that Ifá was still there." He went further to add to the complexity of associations with Ifá/Orunmila and identify Ifá with Saint Francis in Trinidad Orisha, finding that:

> they had sometime, somehow integrated Ifá and who Ifá was with who they call Francis. And I thought it was a combination of Ifá and Osayin

that I thought they were calling on. They saw the relationship between Osayin and Francis. And saw it that way. They always had to light a big fire for Francis to appear. That is something very similar that needs to be done to be able to call Ifá. So I thought at that point in time that it was definitely that there were similarities.

Having been there and seen some of the things that went on during some of the festivals, I know for sure that there was a close association with Saint Francis and Orunmila. The same association that the Cubans found. The Cubans had associated Saint Francis of Assisi with Orunmila, and this is the same way that they would do the association.

This perspective of a trained Ifá priest from outside of Trinidad's Orisha system and culture demonstrates the visibility of Ifá practices. Interestingly, Ifakunle's perception of Ifá/Orunmila draws on his knowledge of how the cosmology is structured in Cuban Santería. His comparative and diasporic gaze "reads" into Trinidad Orisha associations that augment other perspectives (mentioned earlier) that understand Saint Anthony to be Òrúnmìlà. Though different associations between Orunmila and saints have been observed in Trinidad, one constant is that the energy associated with Ifá/Orunmila had found a place within Trinidad Orisha—a place that then became open to expansion with the new influx of information. Though, of course, this was—and is—not without tensions and conflicts (more on this in the next chapter).

Divination practices are other places where Ifá can be found in Trinidad Orisha. The practice of divining with *obi* (kola nut) is well documented in Trinidad (cf. Henry 2003; Herskovits and Herskovits 1947; Lum 2000; K. E. McNeal 2011; Simpson 1965). This practice goes back generations as became clear in a discussion with a couple of Ifá priests in Trinidad:

Baba M.: So I think Olodumare in his divine wisdom gave particular energies to us as a people. But there was one common thing—divination. Throughout the diaspora, to divine to find out if this decision that I am making, if it's correct.

Fadeke: What was the predominant mode of divination before there was so much Ifá in Trinidad?

Baba M.: Obi.

Fadeke: Obi is grown locally?

Baba M.: We have local trees, yes, and they're from Grenada long ago. . . . I remember a story about Maracas [village on Trinidad's north coast]. They were saying it was a lot of Yoruba people who used to live across there, and they were the ones who used to plant obi.

Another person joined in:

Baba A.: They have obi all over Trinidad, they have in Chaguaramas, Toco, Manzanilla, along the [east] coast. It is the two-lobe, not the four-lobe. Not the abata.

Here these speakers are referencing the difference between the obì used for divination throughout West Africa and the one that was commonly used in Trinidad, the distinction being the number of lobes. With four-lobe obi (*obì àbàtà* as used in Yorubaland; figure 4.3), the number of ways the lobes can be read is multiplied versus the two-lobe obi that were historically available in Trinidad and the eastern Caribbean. Obi is both a sacred and central tool of Ifá divination and a food offering for the Orisha and Ifá. As described by Baba M.:

It was the basic form of divination. That is what we used to use long time ago. The obi seed. Right? Again we are told that it was just a yes or no answer. That's not true. That is so far from true. That so far from the truth.

Obi used to tell us if somebody going to die. Obi would tell you that somebody going to die. I remember when they would stop the drums and ask if anybody had someone sick or in the hospital. Or if anyone here is sick. And they would give them the message.

This story speaks to the complexity of information that was read from obi, going well beyond the binary "yes" or "no" that is more commonly read now. It also hints at the more esoteric levels of obi, where it is both a food offering and a spiritual one that can turn *ibi* (imbalance) into *ire* (balance). A common Yorùbá saying, "He who gives a person obì gives a person life," speaks to its importance in the culture and religion.

As well as the sacred use of the obi itself, the language associated with obi divination has been transformed over time. An illustration is a change in the terminology associated with obi divination that was brought to my attention in a couple of my interviews with Ifá/Orisha elders.[13] Some of this is clearly illustrated in the following story:

FIGURE 4.3 The four-lobed variety of obì àbàtà (kola nut) is shown here with two sides up, two sides down. All four lobes can be read according to how they fall when thrown to reveal answers to yes or no questions. Lagos, Nigeria, 2014. Photo by N. Fadeke Castor.

Mother Joan: A case in point, long ago when the old people, they would say, used to say when they going to the oracle, they would say they going to da the obi. This what Papa Neezer used to do, "Da the obi." And when they da the obi, they would say oh, the obi laughing. Right, and I know about laughing. And this is before I heard it is *alaafia*. [everybody laughs] So when the obi was laughing . . .

Agba M.: And that is how we have progress. Because when we first came here, we knew the obi was laughing. Now we know it's alaafia.

Ifagbola: So you see the connection?

Mother Joan: It's alaafia.

Fadeke: They were throwing—they were daing two-lobe obi or four-lobe obi?

Mother Joan: They were daing what they could have gotten here in Trinidad, which was the two lobes.

This description shows the inheritance and transformation of Yorùbá language,[14] where the word alaafia (which references all lobes of the obì falling up and indicates a positive answer or resolution) is an onomatopoeic sound for "laughing."[15] Thus, the term in Orisha practice shifted from "alaafia" to "laughing" far enough in the past that the link between the two terms had been forgotten—that is, until the influx of Yorùbá-speaking Ifá priests in the new millennium helped to make the connection, as illustrated in the preceding story. This also points to a historical practice of "throwing" obi or divination that has clear links to the part of the Yorùbá religions that is recognized as Ifá. This is an important link in the story of Ifá's new initiatory lineage in Trinidad because it shows that Ifá was not entirely absent, that is, the new lineages are extending and deepening a preexistent knowledge base.

There is another metaphysical level beyond the two levels of Ifá's presence in Trinidad—in cosmology with Saint Anthony or Saint Francis, and in divination with obi. Another level was expressed again by Awo Eniola, who reflected, "There are those who on a more personal basis were able to encounter Ifá esoterically through their mystical experiences." The esoteric level referred to by Eniola includes information conveyed through dreams, manifestations, visions, and other forms of divine communication. Eniola depicts one such form, in which he "had the exposure to elders who serve as Spiritual Baptists, and in the Trinidad Orisha context who describe going through a Spiritual Baptist mourning ceremony and receiving *ikin* [Ifá's sacred palm nuts that are the voice of Orunmila]. Telling that to their elders, but nobody knew what is was, and then fifteen, twenty years later, then getting to know that is what it is." The Spiritual Baptist practice that he describes is a vision quest (rooted in a biblical verse, Daniel 1:10) in which seekers/devotees lie on earthen ground for days, wrapped in fabric bands holding in place sacred texts and symbols (whose colors also carry sacred significance).[16] There on the ground they fast while praying under the supervision of church elders and travel in the spiritual realms. Upon their return, the visions are decoded by the church leader, who can then inform the seekers of their role in the church. This mourning practice, as Eniola indicates, also takes place in "the Trinidad Orisha context" because the two religions have overlapping ritual practices and constituencies/congregations (though they remain separate religions). Receiving ikin Ifá signifies that the person receiving this instrument of Ifá is being placed under Ifá's protection or marked for initiation to Ifá.[17] Up until 2007, in the latter case this could only

PLATE 1 While holding the sacred obi abata (kola nut) to her forehead, Iya Sangowunmi says a prayer to the Orisha Shango. This preceded her throw of the obi to find out whether the three-day Rain Festival was successfully completed and could be ritually closed. Ile Eko Sango/Osun Mil'osa, Santa Cruz, Trinidad, 2006. Photo by N. Fadeke Castor.

PLATE 2 Iya Sangowunmi and her Shango give a blessing to Iya Osunide L'Antoinette Stines at the closing ceremony of Ile Eko Sango/Osun Mil'osa's Seventh Annual Rain Festival, Santa Cruz, Trinidad, 2006. Photo by N. Fadeke Castor.

PLATE 3 Babalorisa Olakela Massetungi (affectionately known by his former title "Oludari") is the founder and leader of the Egbe Eledumare Onisin shrine in Petit Valley, Trinidad, and a longtime Black Power activist, Pan-Africanist, Orisha priest, and Ifá advocate, 2011. Photo by N. Fadeke Castor.

PLATE 4 Candles, flowers, fruits and other foods are gathered as offerings in a communal shrine at the Oshun Festival on the beach at Salybia Bay, Trinidad. Visible between the bamboo flagpoles is Orisha Elder, Baba Clarence Forde (deceased, iba), with devotees dressed in pink in honor of Oshun visible to the right, 2004. Photo by N. Fadeke Castor.

PLATE 5 An Egungun masquerade sits next to drums and in front of a basket containing alcohol (oti) and palm oil (epo) that are used in offerings to Orisha shrines. Ile Eko Sango/ Osun Mil'osa, Santa Cruz, Trinidad, 2012. Photo by N. Fadeke Castor.

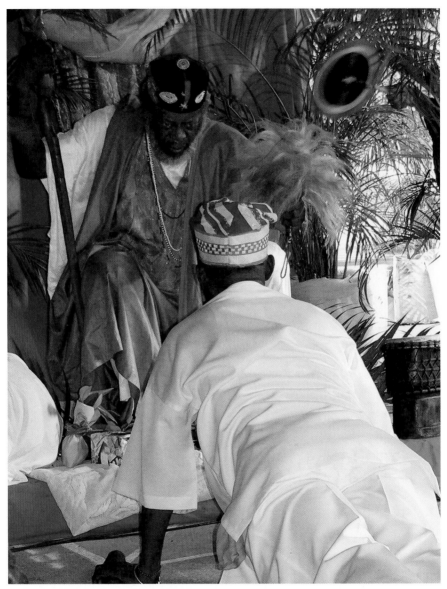

PLATE 6 During the Ile Eko Sango/Osun Mil'osa's Sixth Annual Rain Festival, the newly installed Chief Abiodun bestows blessings on Baba Erinfolami as he performs a dobale in a sign of respect. Santa Cruz, Trinidad, 2005. Photo by N. Fadeke Castor.

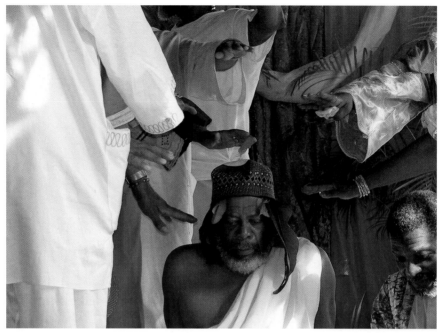

PLATE 7 The hands of Orisha elders extend in benediction over LeRoy Clarke's head as he receives the chieftaincy title, Chief Ifa Oje Won Yomi Abiodun of Trinidad and Tobago, during Ile Eko Sango/Osun Mil'osa's Sixth Annual Rain Festival, Santa Cruz, Trinidad, 2005. Photo by N. Fadeke Castor.

PLATE 8 This sign on the grounds of Ile Eko Sango/Osun Mil'osa marks the space both as "sacred ground" and as an extension of the historical Oyo kingdom of a shared Yorubaland imaginary ("Little Oyo"), while also clearly marking the national space ("Trinidad"), 2012. Photo by N. Fadeke Castor.

PLATE 9 Shango's double-headed ax (ose) was carved for Ile Eko Sango/Osun Mil'osa by Yorùbá artist Hassan Olanipekun, and is shown here painted by Makemba Kunle for the Seventh Annual Rain Festival, Santa Cruz, Trinidad, 2006. Photo by N. Fadeke Castor.

PLATE 10 Baba Erinfolami (front right) holds palm oil that he has recently poured as an offering in the creation of a new Asewele shrine at Ile Eko Sango/Osun Mil'osa dedicated to the spirits of lost travelers, especially those Africans enslaved who died far from home without access to proper burial rites. Santa Cruz, Trinidad, 2015. Photo by N. Fadeke Castor.

have been undertaken by travel abroad, to locations ranging from Nigeria to Cuba or even the United States.

The visions received through mourning are one example of the transmission of sacred technology through esoteric means that were brought to my attention. Iya Sangowunmi recounted to me how the ancestors had appeared to her and communicated the exact wording for the motto of her temple. Years later, a visiting Ifá priest from Nigeria would see the saying and compliment her knowledge of odu Ifá, the collected sacred verses of Ifá. What she had been told by the ancestors proved to come from the odu Ifá corpus. In telling me this story, Iya Sangowunmi was making the point that the knowledge of Ifá comes through in one way or another. Her claim is one made by many of the priests in Trinidad with whom I spoke. They recounted their own stories of how esoteric knowledge of Ifá had been communicated by sacred intelligences (the Irunmole), and though much of Ifá's knowledge has been "lost," certainly not all was lost. There was still an open avenue of communication.

As Orisha devotees in Trinidad became aware of the Ifá corpus, priesthood, and its practices, they were able to connect Ifá with these existing practices, even as they increasingly got a sense of the knowledge gaps. This has informed a curiosity (what is the practice like in its homeland?) and knowledge seeking (what can I learn and bring back to my practice here?). In 2001, these two dominant motivations, among others, had led folks to go to Ilé-Ifè, Nigeria, the heart of Yorubaland, for the Seventh Orisha World Congress. Building on this experience, more Trinidadians would continue to travel to Nigeria to attend festivals, undertake different trainings, receive divinations, and undergo initiations.

Sacred Journey to Ilé-Ifè

In 2004, a large number of Orisha devotees with roots in Trinidad gathered in Ilé-Ifè, Nigeria (for many the ancestral source of the Yorùbá religion). Over a period of weeks, they would tour the sacred sites and shrines of Ilé-Ifè, the town where Yorùbá mythology locates the beginnings of humanity. Additionally, they had the opportunity for spiritual initiation. The large group (more than twenty people) included Trinidadians from the United Kingdom and the United States, as well as from Trinidad, who came together for the trip timed to coincide with the annual Ifá festival in Òkè Itaṣe.

The group was led by Oludari Olakela Massetungi, the head priest and founder of Egbe Onisin Eledumare (EOE).[18] The trip was arranged through his organization and made up of members and affiliates of EOE. This religious pilgrimage was foundational for many individuals in establishing their relationship (both positive and negative) to Ifá, through their experiences, connections, and ritual initiations. In Ilé-Ifẹ̀ they were hosted by members of the local leadership, including Chief Adélékàn. Some members of the group stayed at his home, and others stayed on the nearby Obáfẹ́mi Awólowọ̀ University campus or at a facility of Olóyè Abiódún Agboolá, Baàlà Awo Àgbáyé. Oludari reflected on the people he carried to Nigeria, "They are now the core of the Council of Chiefs, and those who are not chiefs are now leaders of shrines, or next in command to leaders of shrines in the Republic of Trinidad and Tobago." The implication in his statement was that it was the exposure to Ifá and the knowledge gained there, or later through connections made there, that contributed to these individuals' subsequent rise to positions of leadership and prominence.

Among the important themes that emerged from the ethnographic narratives in my interviews were the tensions of spiritual economies and spiritual knowledge systems between Trinidad and Yorubaland. The tensions fall along lines of divination, ritual authority, and economics (specifically money and value). I bring into focus here the diasporic entanglements that occur when the local politics (of Trinidad) travels and interacts with/becomes embedded in the local politics (of Ilé-Ifẹ̀) of the destination. What, then, would lead one member of the group to the position, which they described as follows: "When I returned from that trip, my inclination was to leave the group EOE and to leave Ifá practice as a whole, because what I had seen in Nigeria so turned me off of African traditional religion."[19] Such was the impact of traveling to Yorubaland that after this trip some people wanted to leave the religion, even as others went on to leadership positions, and still others began intensive studies in the religion (and some individuals certainly held more than one of these positions simultaneously).

One of my interviewees spoke on the trip to Ilé-Ifẹ̀ at length due to the impact of fraught dynamics experienced during the trip, especially with regard to the spiritual economies encountered. By spiritual economies, in this section I am referring to the transfer and exchange of value—whether goods, services, labor, or money—for spiritual labor, including (but not limited to) prayers, divination, initiations, trainings, and other exchanges of information and/or ase. During the trip to Ilé-Ifẹ̀, some members of the group alternatively underwent initiation, for example, to Ifá, Ọbàtálá, or Ògún, had divination sessions with a babaláwo, or received chieftaincy titles. These all came at a cost in addition to exchanges of time and investment of the financial resources needed to travel to Nigeria, which are considerable when coming from the United States or the United Kingdom and comparatively more for those coming from the Caribbean or South America, with a plane ticket easily costing one to two months' salary (approximately US$3,000 to US$4,000 in 2004)—and a middle-class salary at that! In addition, each prayer or initiation requires cash payment for the priest's expertise, time, and any necessary supplies.

In my own travels to Nigeria, I encountered the seemingly unending request for money in both secular and spiritual contexts. Every visit to a temple and every request for a prayer required a monetary contribution for the prayer to be recited on kola nut (obi) and alcoholic spirits (ọti), offerings that were routinely provided by the supplicant. These requirements are for all people seeking prayers, making offerings, or receiving divinations. (There is always some form of exchange, materially symbolized by money, whether the petitioner is foreign or local; the scale of expectations differs, however, depending on where the person is from.) The foreign traveler (òyìnbó) is perceived as being rich(er) and as such is expected to make generous offerings, almost to the point of obligation. One site of further confusion is the lack of consideration of the relative economic position among persons from the "West." This failure to distinguish differing economic positionalities through an overgeneralization based on national origin obscures more nuanced distinctions of class. To be clear, everyone, from priests and shrine leaders to market women, is astute at reading cues, say of dress and comportment, that are perceived as indicators of wealth. It is in their economic interest to do so. What is often missing is an apperception of the possibility that there may be a lack of wealth in spite of signs that signify (in this context) the contrary, such as electronic devices or Western clothes.

Note that in the spiritual economy dynamics, largely surrounding initiation, the devotees from Trinidad (and not the Trinis from the United Kingdom or the United States) were part of the group deemed "poor." That is, some of its members were perceived as being from a less developed/postcolonial group with access to fewer resources. Members of the group were charged only for materials, with nominal fees going to the elders. An aspiring initiate was able to get an itemized list of the charges and calculate the total; ultimately they were charged mainly for materials. That amount was then given to someone who went to the market for those items. This is very different from the "plight" of people from the United States and the United Kingdom who were charged US$3,000 each for the same, or ostensibly comparable, ritual. This contrast, with some paying more than seven times as much as others, troubled them so much that they wanted to leave the religion. The new Ifá initiate wanted to leave Ifá. The inconsistencies that they witnessed revealed to them the relative nature of spiritual economies and led them to view the ritual work being done as part of a "racket."

Another layer to consider is that exchanges are not only about money but also about relationships and often are policed by perceptions of who is an outsider and who is an insider. While these boundaries correlate directly with how much is charged for what (not only in Yorubaland but certainly in the diaspora as well), they also are at play in other levels of valuation. Among the most prized and valued aspects of Ifá/Orisha religion is esoteric knowledge. A recurring theme that I heard in my discussions about interactions between Trinidadians and specifically Nigerians centered on a politics of knowledge dissemination. That is, there was the perception that often Ifá priests from Yorubaland would share only a small portion of their knowledge and only at a high price. Not all things are given to all people.

The rituals they witnessed were compared to similar experiences in Trinidad and found wanting. They stated that for them rituals in Trinidad "were more esoterically profound, more ritually correct, more psychologically moving, than what I have experienced in Ife." This is quite a claim because it runs counter to the narrative trope of authenticity that privileges the "source" of the religion. That is, Ilé-Ifẹ̀ specifically is viewed from many sectors of the diaspora as the source of the Yorùbá religion. In the absence of extensive interaction with Yorùbá peoples and cultures, the circulation of priests across the Atlantic notwithstanding (see Matory 2005), there has developed a large body of myth that valorizes and upholds the Yorùbá as being above reproach and as holders of esoteric knowledge and a privileged access to àṣẹ (understood here as spiritual power). This imagined community of the Yorùbá is well known and widely documented in the academic literature (see K. Clarke 2004; Hucks 2012; Matory 2005; Simpson 1978). As well, priests and practitioners of the Yorùbá religion are aware of this trope and take different positions with regard to it, from champion and defender to critic (Palmié 2013).

Surely, with this trope in mind, this initiate's reaction is surprising. Or, then again, maybe not so much. The level of expectation held by those in the diaspora of the Yorùbá people, their culture, and their religion is hard to meet. Yet, I do not think that their critique and disappointment arose from this level of disillusionment. Our prior conversations revealed that they were critically aware of the distance between the places, the people, and their representation. Rather, this outrage appeared to focus on two levels: one, perception of an economic racket, and two, assessment of a ritual as lacking key esoteric aspects. Both of these findings were reflected in an interview I conducted with another Ifá initiate. This second initiate had gone to Nigeria for initiation the following year and had a similar reaction, evident in their recollection, "Receiving Ifá made me want to throw away my spiritual practice." When I asked them to explain, they answered: "Because now I'm even more lost than before. Now, gathering my—um, getting Ifá, I thought I would have really strong elders at my side. I thought I would have my Oluwo guiding me. I thought I was with these great people that represent the tradition in its highest esteem. And no. All I had people that saw me as an American that had a lot of money, and my Ifá just meant money." The subject of money came up again later in that same conversation: "I got so disappointed. I felt robbed and cheated. I felt as if my spirituality was just about money, money, money." Note how this second voice remarked that "these great people . . . represent the tradition in its highest esteem." Here can be heard the echo of authenticity and the value placed on the imagined community of Yorubaland.

In this person's story of initiation, they recounted being taken into a room, being put in a chair, and having people start to shave their head. All the while, they were unclear about what was going on, or why, and could not understand what was being said because the people surrounding them spoke only in Yorùbá. Ultimately, after demanding answers to these questions, they were told only that "Ifá's been waiting for you." Even more upsetting than the perfunctory explanation was the lack of clear guidance from elders in Ilé-Ifẹ̀ or later in Trinidad. Rather than exchange of money for tangible and intangible services (the holy ikin of Ifá being an example of the former and the ase of Ifá being an example of the latter), this person found the exchange to be empty of meaning. In fact, they found the exchange so empty that they felt betrayed and wanted to "throw away [their] spiritual practice." It was only through the intervention of another initiate, who had had a similar experience, that they received a reminder of their worth: "You have too much of a gift to throw it away." The initiate took this comment as a message from Spirit confirming the importance of their spiritual insights and visions. They indeed had something significant to contribute. Following this conversation, Spirit came to this person in dreams, providing guidance and leading them to recognize that "I have never been left alone. I just never recognized it. I did not have an elder to show me in physical form." So, in the end, it is the esoteric resolution that brings value back to Ifá. In the absence of physical elders to guide them (an absence linked to a lack of funds), Spirit stepped in and provided guidance, training, and knowledge on a spiritual level. This goes back to the earlier section "Ifá Was Always Here," where I discussed that in the absence of Ifá knowledge—both ritual and doctrinal—information was conveyed on an esoteric level through dreams, manifestations, and other means.

"This Is How I Feel about Ifá, It Come Like Food"

The travels documented here, and the encounters they engendered, were pivotal moments in creating a hospitable environment for the establishment of a new Ifá lineage in Trinidad. The meeting of the old with the new was not without challenges and pitfalls. Whether in Trinidad or Nigeria, the friction points between different cultures, languages, economic realities, and knowledge levels require negotiation. In some cases this has led to momentary disillusionment, whereas in other cases it inspired further commitments to learning the different paths of Ifá/Orisha. And in yet other cases both emerged from the same encounter. Even as one priest whom I talked with had said, "Receiving Ifá made me want to throw away my spiritual practice," that same person also came to the place where they felt that "Ifá . . . is such a beautiful world. . . . I praise the ancestors for carrying me on this path. I praise them." This personal and spiritual journey was also accompanied with some concerns about the adoption of Nigerian Ifá in Trinidad, with the observation that "they throwing away all that the ancestors have laid and sweat as if it's rubbish." This concern is certainly a valid perspective, and it reflects a promising valuation for the legacy of Trinidad Orisha practices, one reflected in numerous interviews.

When talking about incorporating the new knowledge with the old systems, many people such as Mother Joan were clear that one could do both—adopt the new and hold on to the old:

> You know what I always tell my spiritual children, the country where you live is going to dictate your rituals. We cannot do everything that they doing in Africa. We cannot. We are not imitating. But we are doing, you

know things. There are a lot of things that I have learned now. I am not letting go of what my grandfather and them used to do, you know. But I incorporate other things that I've learned now. I didn't know anything about ikin, right?

The balance in doing this has not been reached in a homogenous way across the country. Another way to say this is that the alchemy in the mix of old and new is very localized from shrine to shrine. The differing perspectives are still being negotiated, oftentimes publicly visible only in the larger festivals and rituals that draw an audience from across different shrines. One thing is clear, though; Ifá is in Trinidad to stay. The religion historically known by so many names (from obeah to Shango to Trini Orisha, to name just a few) has undergone another major shift. As Baba Erinfolami said of Ifá, "It come like, it like food. . . . this is how I feel about Ifá, it come like food."

CHAPTER 5

Ifá in Trinidad's Ground

"Unity is strength, strength is power." The words rang out like a bell. Oshun's bell! For it was Oshun herself who had manifested, gathered us, and then insisted that we repeat the words over and over until we were in unison. She had gathered folks from all over the shrine—from the local Trini workers and volunteers erecting tents, refreshing shrines, and clearing the kitchen to the newly arrived Venezuelans and Colombians and the VIP guest, the *oba* (king) of Oyotunji Village (outside Sheldon, South Carolina).[1] All these people were at the Ile Eko Sango/Osun Mil'osa (IESOM) shrine for the upcoming Alásùwadà Ifá conference. All were Ifá devotees, if not initiates, priests in training, or working priests. Shrine members and visitors united for a moment. In 2012, Trinidad had become an international destination for the study of Ifá. And those gathered were exploring the intricacies of Ifá cosmology and teachings to figure out how to make their lives better, make their communities better, and make the world better. This moment of spiritual citizenship, which encompassed both transnational community and concerns with social change and justice, had roots going back several years.

When and how did Ifá become firmly established in Trinidad? Initially, while doing the research on the rise of Ifá, I had thought that it could be tied to the separate visits of two highly visible and important Ifá priests, the Àràbà Agbáye Awoyemi Awóreni Adisa Mokoranwale of Ilé-Ifẹ̀ and Olóyè Sọlágbadé Pópóọlá, in early 2007. They had both gone to shrines, given lectures, conducted rituals, and performed divinations and initiations to Ifá, and their visits were still being talked about when I arrived in Trinidad later that year. For me those trips in 2007 were a pivotal moment—I started to see Ifá being performed wherever I looked. At events, individuals I had known for several years strictly as Orisha priests and devotees were now talking about Ifá, making public references to odu Ifá, the holy scripture of Ifá, or even wearing chieftaincy hats.

However, more research revealed a deeper and more complex system of roots below the immediately observable surface. Indeed, Ifá did become more visible in the years following the visits of these esteemed Nigerian babaláwo. Like a tree, these visible branches drew from an extensive system of roots that were below ground and not apparent to the eye. These roots go back—way back—into the sparsely documented past of the religion in the 1800s. For example, there is documentation of the arrival of Papa Nannee (as he was called locally), a diviner from the Kingdom of Dahomey (now the Republic of Benin). Papa Nannee arrived in 1855 and settled in the hills of Port of Spain, where he established a Rada compound, which has held ceremonies off and on for more than 150 years, up to the contemporary moment (Carr 1989; Lum 2000, 209; Sankeralli 2002). Historian Bridget Brereton provides greater detail on Papa Nannee's Belmont compound, in the foothills between Port of Spain and Laventille: "He was not a priest, but a seer and a diviner, credited with an extraordinary knowledge of the supernatural" (2002, 153). If he was not a full initiate at the time of his arrival in Ifá (or Fa, as it was more likely called in Dahomey), his status in the community and oral remembrances passed down from generation to generation would indicate that he was most certainly a trained diviner. In the early twentieth century, there is also evidence of a tradition of "lookmen," who performed divination through water gazing and other geomantic techniques (Herskovits and Herskovits 1947, 224–55). As discussed in chapter 4, there has been a long tradition of divination in Trinidad's African diasporic religions, with much of it connecting to Ifá. The new growth that I document draws both from these historical roots and from renewed routes or transnational connections with the traditionalist Yorùbá Ifá lineages.

These transnational roots and routes of the contemporary resurgence of Ifá have their own history on both sides of the Atlantic, spanning a time frame from the 1970s to the present moment. I have been able to locate and document references to Ifá playing a role in Trinidad, through various notable individuals and influential texts, going back as far as the 1970s. Certainly, in the 1980s and 1990s, references to Ifá become increasingly visible, though still few and far between. However, it was in the new millennium that a tipping point was reached, and the roots that had been growing strengthened to the point that the visible growth of shoots and stalks had become trunks and branches. Not to push the analogy too far, but now, in the twenty-first century, there is a healthy growth of Ifá in Trinidad, with well over two hundred initiates (and growing) from several local lineages informed by communities that are struggling to serve, support, and train a new generation of Ifá priests. And in Trinidad, Ifá has made significant contributions to an emerging spiritual citizenship that is becoming firmly embedded both locally and globally.

In the Ground

Ifá in Trinidad had a watershed year in 2007, which was when the first documented Ifá initiations were conducted on Trinidad soil. Over the following five years, the number of Ifá initiates in Trinidad would explode, from single digits before 2007 to being counted in the hundreds. Ifá initiations are continually being conducted at various shrines. This is an important and notable event as Trinidad's Ifá lineages are the only ones among the English-speaking countries of the Caribbean and join Cuba, Brazil, Venezuela, Mexico, and North America where one can receive initiation to Ifá.

How did this all come to be? Previous chapters have presented some of the history and context for these more recent changes. From the shifts of consciousness in 1970s Black Power to the shift into the public culture of the 1980s and 1990s, there were many moments that laid the groundwork for the blossoming of Ifá in the new millennium. As has been well established here, a critical component has been the circulation of priests, initiates, and practitioners across the diaspora, particularly between West Africa, Latin America, and the Caribbean. It should come as no surprise that it was the specific travels across Latin American and Caribbean pathways that led to the events of 2007.

I traveled to Venezuela in 1999 to map the connections between the two Orisha communities prior to starting my research in Trinidad. I did this because Venezuela is a very close neighbor with a significant Orisha religious presence. At that time I did not find any connections with Orisha in Trinidad, but I did document that the Orisha practitioners in Venezuela were closely tied to Cuban Orisha lineages. In the late 1990s, the religious connections between Trinidad and Venezuela that I found were West Indian laborers who actively venerated Maria Lionza, Venezuela's local deified ancestor and mythic historical figure, who is closely associated with El Sorte Mountain.[2]

By 2005, changes were evident in connections that were being forged between the Orisha communities in Trinidad and Venezuela centered on the continental practice of the Yorùbá religion. Iya Sangowunmi, chief priest of IESOM, was invited to be part of a Trinidad delegation to the International Festival of African Tradition and Culture, known in Spanish as the Festival Internacional de Tradiciones Afroamericanas (FITA), organized and hosted by Baba Santos, an Ifá priest from Caracas with spiritual links to West Africa.[3] The delegation included Orisha priest and singer extraordinaire Iya Ella Andall, among other people from Trinidad. The festival had an important place in the unfolding of Ifá's twenty-first-century emergence in Trinidad. It provided the context for African-conscious people, performers, and followers of African diasporic religions (including Ifá priests and practitioners) from throughout the diaspora and the continent to connect. This proved to be another perfect opportunity for diaspora and continental Ifá priests and devotees to connect, specifically Iya Sangowunmi of Trinidad and Olóyè Ṣọlágbade Pópóolá of Nigeria. In fact, it was at FITA that Iya Sangowunmi received her first Ifá reading from Olóyè Pópóolá, beginning a relationship that would continue over the next decade.

From that first Ifá reading would come Olóyè Pópóọlá's words to Iya Sangowunmi, "You could do this at home" regarding Ifá's guidance that she needed to receive *itefa* (Ifá initiation). These words from her divination session in Venezuela resulted in her inviting Olóyè Pópóolá to conduct her itefa in Trinidad, a major ritual that had never been done in that country. Within a few years of their meeting at FITA, Olóyè Pópóolá was addressing a crowd of Orisha priests, initiates, and practitioners at Iya Sangowunmi's shrine in the hills of Santa Cruz, Trinidad. There he reflected on this earlier divination session with her, recalling how impressed he was by her passion and commitment when they talked of Ifá and Orisha in Trinidad. It was from this divination session with Olóyè Pópóọla in Venezuela that doors were opened, leading not only to his subsequent visit to Trinidad in 2007 and Iya's initiation into Ifá at that time but also to the beginning of a new Ifá lineage in the Anglophone Caribbean.

Those early Ifá initiations at IESOM occurred in the wider context of several high-profile visits of Nigerians. In January 2007, the Àràbà Agbáyé visited Trinidad for several weeks at the invitation of Mother Joan Cyrus, leader of the Kenny Cyrus Alkebulan Ile Ijebu shrine. Àràbà is the highest chieftaincy title of an Ifá priest, and many towns in Yorubaland have their own Àràbà. However, the Àràbà who visited Trinidad was the Àràbà Agbáyé, which translates to the Àràbà of the whole world because his title is from Ilé-Ifè (held by many to be the mythical and mystical source of the Yorùbá people).[4] Chieftaincy titles of Ilé-Ifè are rendered as "from the source," and thus Agbáyé (meaning "of the whole world"), so the Àràbà Agbáyé Awóreni is viewed by most as the chief Àràbà of all the Àràbà in Yorubaland. To-gether, he and the Ọòni of Ilé-Ifè (who visited Trinidad in 1988) represent the most visible leadership of the Ifá religion, especially as seen from the diaspora.

While he was in Trinidad, the Àràbà was received by government officials and Orisha leadership. He visited the Nigerian high commissioner and sev-eral Orisha shrines. He was also available to receive visitors who came to pay their respects. When discussing the Àràbà Agbáyé, it is best to think in terms of multiple people rather than one person. A community supports the title and its holder. In this case, the Àràbà traveled with his son Asíwájú Awótúndé Awóreni, also an Ifá priest, who provided logistical support and, importantly, translation services. In my interviews, people often reported what the Àràbà said during his visit, yet due to his very limited knowl-edge of English, I understood that his pronouncements were largely made through his son, acting as translator.

The Àràbà and his son Awótúndé also conducted several rituals, including naming ceremonies, ọwọ́ kan Ifá, or hand of Ifá (the initial ritual introduc-tion to Ifá), and Ifá initiations. These contributed to the significant impact of his visit, especially on his hosts at the Cyrus shrine. "Since the Araba came we have a temple to Orunmila in this yard." Pointing to the back of the shrine, Agba Makanjuola says, "In there. We keep all of our hands of Ifá in there. And those are things that we never did before. It's the Araba who would have . . . well he gave us—" Mother Joan interjects, "He initiated that spot there." Agba Makanjuola continues, "He initiated that spot. Then we built it up. And we keep our hands of Ifá in the temple. And when we ready to do whatever we do with them, we go in there, and we pray with them and we feed them." What this tells us is that there were Ifá rituals done by the Àràbà and his group that consecrated an area of the shrine, which is now dedicated as an Ifá temple. They store their consecrated ikin, the sacred palm nuts that constitute the "hand of Ifá," in vessels there that can be prayed over and fed. The Àràbà's consecration of both ikin and land is an example of adding new àṣẹ, from Yorubaland, to the existing Trini ase that has gathered and grown generation upon generation, for over 150 years. Alongside the initiations done by the Àràbà, this served as a complementary context for the Ifá rituals that would occur at IESOM under the direction of Olóyè Ṣọlágbadé Pópóọla in the following month.

The spiritual technology required for Ifá ritual has been one source of confusion and controversy due to the many variations across lineages and geographic locations within Yorubaland. This is a complex dynamic, with roots in the mythos of Orunmila, where the sacred ẹsẹ odu Ifá (the verses of the 256 signs of Ifá) speak of his travels and how he gave different knowledge to different parts of Yorubaland. The myth reflects the history, where social and political conflicts led to warfare and migrations among the many subgroups that later formed "the Yorùbá."[5] The religious and ritual inheritances of these conflicts have led to a diversity of practices that are largely decentralized (despite the best efforts of various coalitions and power centers). One of the consequences of Ifá's diasporic movements out of its historical and cultural context is the loss of this knowledge built in the continental system, much of it coded in the Yorùbá language (even as the system has proved to still be effective).[6] Variation is built into the very foundation of the Yorùbá religion in general and Ifá in particular. As Omi Oshun Joni L. Jones notes in her richly performative text on the annual Òṣun Òṣogbo Festival in Òṣun State, Nigeria, speaking on the multiple narratives of Òṣun/Oshun as diviner with various tools, these differences "exist as collective realities reflecting the Yoruba ability to incorporate diversity rather than exclude philosophies and perspectives" (1997, 79).

This has led to much confusion across the diaspora as students of different Yorùbá lineages receive different teachings. One person will be told that for a certain ritual to be effectively done, tools A, B, and C are required. Another student will be taught that X, Y, and Z are required. Even with this oversimplification, the possibilities for confusion and even conflict are clear. Both student one and student two have claims to authentic knowledge from Yorubaland. And both can be right! Unless they are taught by their teachers that there is more than one approach to a ritual (a fact left out by many), when they come together to do ritual in the absence of their Yorùbá elders, there will be a problem of conflicting ritual practices. At this stage, the issues of authenticity around ritual knowledge can inform a conflict that would appear to be out of proportion to the problem at hand.

Such has been the case in Trinidad with the post-millennial introduction of Ifá ritual practices, and specifically with regard to initiations. At this point, let me quote Asíwájú Awótúndé Awóreni, the Àràbà Agbaye's son who was with him in 2007. "Tunde," as he is called, followed up on that initial trip with subsequent stays in Trinidad, where he further developed ritual and personal connections. In 2014, while I was in Nigeria I met with him in his hometown of Ilé-Ifẹ̀ to talk about Ifá generally and Ifá in Trinidad specifically.

> **Awótúndé**: What really happened in that aspect is that our system is more different to others. Even in Ilé-Ifẹ̀ we have five zone with five different practice.

> **Fadeke**: Aaaah. That is good information, thank you. So what does that mean?

> **Awótúndé**: For example, now, we have five zone. When I make ẹbọ we have five different processes, even in Ilé-Ifẹ̀. After five we have Òkè Ìtaṣè,[7] that of Òkè Ìtaṣè is now different from other five. So now, for example now, let me say I want to make ẹbọ. Some zone throw the obì before Òkanràn'sá, some zone throw the obì after Òkanràn'sá, some zone throw the obì on *Èjì Ogbè*[8]—and all are in Ifẹ. So it depend on what you belongs to. So, some—if you learn very well within Ilé-Ifẹ̀ people may demand that I want this system, you do this system for me, you do this system for me. . . . So the way one zone in fact is different from the other zone, even within Ilé-Ifẹ̀. And our system of initiation is also different. There are five zone with different practice. And after that five, that of Òkè Ìtaṣè is different.

After a brief discussion of how there are ritual differences throughout Yorubaland, even when it came to initiation, I turned the discussion to Trinidad:

> **Fadeke**: Did you have what you needed in Trinidad for Itefa?

> **Awótúndé**: Yes, we had it there.

> **Fadeke**: So what did you need in your system to do Itefa?

> **Awótúndé**: You want me to tell you everything?

> **Fadeke**: Yes, please. [laughter]

There was a pause, and then Tunde offered a tidbit of ritual information from his lineage: "In Ilé-Ifẹ̀ if you don't have Òsun [staff], you have the corner of your house." This last point is an important clarification regarding the sacred icon or icons that many lineages insist are a necessary presence in the Ìtefá initiation. Tunde's intervention here is that in some Ilé-Ifẹ̀ lineages based in Ifẹ there exists a spiritual technology that can transform the space where two walls and the floor meet ("the corner") into a spiritual force equivalent to the icon of Òsun, which can then be used instead. Tunde continued on to point out that what is compulsory in one system may not be compulsory in another system:

> One man's food is another man's poison. Báàyi laa ńse ní ilé wa, èèwò ni ni ilé elòmiràn, translated straight like that is, "This how we do in our house is taboo in your house." I'm not condemning anybody's system. But what I'm saying is that the way Orunmila do it here is different from the way he did it in Adó, it is different from the way he did it in in Ọ̀yọ̀, is different from the way he did it in Ìjèbú, and so on. Even within Ilé-Ifẹ̀, the way he did it there - a bit bit different.

This clearly illustrates that differences exist much more locally in Yoruba-land than is commonly understood in the diaspora. The existence of five zones of ritual distinctions within the single town of Ilé-Ifẹ alone speaks to the multiplicity of methodologies at the heart of Ifá. This adds much needed illumination to the question of which icon or invocation or offering is required for an initiation. What is required by one lineage may be optional or not important for another lineage. This is not to say that there is an absence of conflict in Yorubaland between members of different lineages over what they believe is universally required. Certainly this type of disagreement exists. However, in the Yorùbá religious tradition(s), there are many paths to one end.

The multiplicity of lineages and ritual conventions within the continental Yorùbá religion has been largely lost in the diaspora in general, and in Trinidad specifically. This has resulted in numerous misunderstandings, which came up in many of the conversations I had about Ifá. In Trinidad I kept hearing that people were dissatisfied with their initiations and that some had chosen to get "reinitiated." According to Orunmila, a person can get initiated to Ifá only once, as stated in a verse of Ogbè Ate (Ogbè Ìrẹtẹ̀). This idea of being "reinitiated" was a very delicate subject and involved controversial assertions, so I trod lightly when discussing it. In one interview, we did establish that this practice of "reinitiation" was occurring:

Iya O.: Yes, a lot of people in Trinidad who comes and has it done over.

Fadeke: Over? How you can get initiated over?

Iya O.: You don't know that happening in Trinidad?

Fadeke: No. Who? Tell me.

Iya O.: I ain't calling no names.

Fadeke: No names, but tell me about it just happening.

Iya O.: Well, they had initiation done, and because they say didn't have Odu present, and whatever, whatever, whatever, they said that how, that not Ifa. So they did it over for the people, charged them all the money in the world and do it over.

Further investigation revealed that the source of conflict was mostly about whether the sacred (and secret) icon of Odù was present at the initiation and to a lesser extent about Òsun, the holy staff of Odù (not to be confused with the deity Oshun, whose name can also be spelled Osun" in diasporic Yoruba and "Òṣun" in continental Yorùbá, where the dot under the s indicates a "sh" sound). There have been other conflicts about components of the initiation to Ifá that were done in some lineages and not in others. To understand these conflicts, the most important point to consider is, as Tunde said, that there are many approaches and understandings to the same thing.

An illustration elaborates on Yorùbá multiplicity, especially in spiritual praxis with regard to Ifá. There are known to be a couple of major different approaches to Ifá initiation. One method is called Ìtènífá and involves the presence of Odù. The other version, called Ẹlégán, does not require the presence of Odù. Over time, the differences between these two methods of Ifá initiation have become known in Trinidad. In fact, I first heard of these two terms in the week leading up to my own Ifá initiation. I had just met two priests who lived near to where I was staying. During our car ride home, in a state of excitement I mentioned to them that I was going to initiate to Ifá (each had been initiated to Ifá in recent years) and received a question in response, "Will it be Itenifa or Elegan?" I was stumped and thought, "What was this?" Though I had been a practitioner since 1993 and an academic researcher of Yorùbá culture and religion since 1998, I was not familiar with these terms. And I had no idea which category applied to me! I offer this to illustrate the complexity and depth of knowledge that one encounters with Ifá. And this is just a drop in a flood (more than a bucket) of knowledge, much of it embedded in specificities of the Yorùbá language. Thus, given the partial and often out-of-context knowledge available in the diaspora, confusion and conflicts occur frequently (even in Yorubaland) regarding the "right" or "proper" way to do something.[9]

Establishing an Ifá Lineage in Trinidad

On a Friday afternoon, deep in the Santa Cruz Valley of Trinidad, a visiting Nigerian babaláwo gave a lecture to a specially assembled group whose members were gathered together from different shrines across the country under the auspices of the Elders of the Ifá Yoruba Tradition. This diverse gathering contained youths and elders, initiates and noninitiates. Certainly, as has been established, there was a growing level of Ifá activity in Trinidad. That afternoon's lecture promised to be different from lectures given by visiting Ifá priests over the previous ten years.

These earlier public lectures had ranged from those of the New York–based babalawo of Trinidadian heritage, Awo Fayomi, in the mid-1990s to the more recent ones of Olóyè Abiodun Agboola's "The Essence of Ifá" in 2004. What, then, makes Olóyè Ṣọlágbadé Pópóọlá's 2007 lecture notable? His lecture stood out on three levels—one, his straightforward and clear delivery that drew an intimate connection with the people he addressed; two, the radical message that everyone should be initiated to Ifá; and, three, the sacred tools of Ifá (Odù and Òsun) that he brought with him specifically made for Trinidad. These three factors converged to make Ṣọlágbadé Pópóọlá's visit, his lecture, and ritual activity major contributions to making the year 2007 a watershed moment for Ifá in Trinidad. Through these events, taken together with the visit of the Àràbà, long-held visions of placing "Ifá in the ground" were fulfilled.

On that day, Baba Erinfolami opened with greetings to all and then introduced Awo Eniola Adelekan to perform the opening invocation. In a quiet voice, Awo Eniola poured water on the ground a few drops at a time while invoking the Irúnmọlè: "Iba Esu Odara . . . Iba Orunmila . . . Iba Sango . . . Iba Obatala . . . Iba Olokun." After each greeting, he would recite in Yorùbá an *oríkì* (praise poem) or call the praise names for each Orisha. The energy built as, in turn, Baba Erinfolami invoked the ancestors, calling on "all those who kept the tradition in this country so that we could continue to do here what we do today." He then called the names of local Trinidadian ancestors (Iya Louise Catherine Toussaint, Iya Pearl Primus, Ma Eudora Thomas, Papa Neezer, Kenny Cyrus—to name just a few past spiritual leaders), with the crowd responding to each name with "*kin kan mashe*" (a phrase used in the diaspora, as a "protective verse, incantation prior to calling and giving praise to living lineage of priests").[10] Following the names, Baba Folami invoked specific blessings, from the personal ("May shame and envy be no more . . . sickness be no more") to the political ("We ask for political stability as a people in Trinidad and Tobago"). The ritual opening ended with the calling and honoring of all the energies and ancestral spirits. Baba Folami then introduced Olóyè Ṣọlágbadé Pópóọlá with a short biography that emphasized his scholarship and global reputation.

"Everything about Trinidad and Tobago was like I was in Nigeria," Olóyè said as his opening remark. He continued on to share how the landscape on his way from the airport evoked a deep sense of familiarity: "It may not be in life, but I know that I have once been here. . . . I do not see myself as a visitor coming to visit you. I see myself as part of you who had once been here. I had gone and I am coming back home. That's the way I see it." He recounted how these were places that he had been dreaming about since he was young. Pópóọlá's rhetoric effectively located him not as a foreign outsider but as someone "coming back home" (a poignant refrain for an island culture with a large number of citizens living abroad). With this important positioning accomplished, he dived directly into talking about initiation to Ifá: "You do not need to travel to Nigeria to be initiated into Ifá again. You have all the ingredients here." Cries of affirmation ("*Ase o*") and cheering came in strong response from the crowd.[11] For many people, the primary obstacle to Ifá initiation was the cost of travel to Nigeria. In his talk, Pópóọlá continued to emphasize the empowerment of the local environment (with all the necessary plants being available) and the importance of local knowledge. His straightforward approach avoided mystification and proved to be very effective.

Olóyè Pópóọla framed the production of spiritual knowledge as a process of mutual engagement and sharing:

Whatever we are trying to teach you now is what you have already known before. It has been one way or another, but you must regain it. And I have a feeling that you have so many things that you have to teach us too. When all of us sit down together and we cross-fertilize ideas, we will be able to get all this information together, and we'll move forward. If I know five things and you know seven things, the moment I'm ready to share my five and you're able to share [your] seven with me, together we will know twelve things. And that is the way we can learn. Education is the only gift you share and retain. . . . At our level we need to share.

This rhetorical engagement is an important shift from the more common discourse of "we have sacred knowledge for you." He put people at ease by moving from a top-down model that privileges Nigerian/Yorùbá knowledge to one of sharing across a table where "all of us sit down together." This addressed several concerns that had already arisen by 2007, including the fear that foreign Ifá priests were targeting Trinidad as an opportunity to make money in a place desperate for knowledge. This fear grew out of the experiences of many who were dissatisfied with the level of information and training that they received after initiatory rituals. Another source of dissatisfaction included the prices charged for ritual, divination, initiations, and especially ẹbọ.[12]

Ẹbọ, the sacred offering specified in Ifá divination, is the critical step of ritual exchange that can turn bad favor (àyèwò; to search, used instead of a specific word for negativity to avoid calling the negative energy into being) to a blessing of good or balanced, positive energy (ire), or to ensure that the ire manifests. This critical element of Ifá is often costly depending on the needed materials. Offerings may include a combination of various elements, from the basics of the pap or cornstarch pudding, palm oil (epo), kola nut (obì), and gin (otí) to special medicinal preparations (depending on who is receiving the offerings) to blood (èjè from hens, roosters, or goats among other possible sources). All of these elements are offered by a combination of specific ritual incantations and movements. This spiritual technology is a hard-earned part of an Ifá priest's repertoire. There are monetary charges for both the materials and the ritual labor. The amount of these charges is usually determined by divination. One critical part is left to the discretion of the priest—how much can one charge to divine that will satisfy Ifá? Some priests start low, and some priests start high. In many instances, people in Trinidad experienced sticker shock at the price of ẹbọ. Certainly, traditional Trini Orisha practices were never so expensive. This comparison, joined with the Trinidadian penchant for valuing proven methods of spiritual efficacy, created popular debate around the value of ẹbọ. Many folks told me they didn't go for divination to that Nigerian priest or the other because "He gonna charge me an arm and ah leg."

In this environment, Pópóọlá's strategy of sharing was effective in laying the groundwork in the first thirty minutes of his talk for his upcoming radical pronouncement. He built his argument by stressing the importance of Ifá, linking initiation to the Orisha: "All of the 801 [Irúnmolè] were initiated into Ifá except for Òsanyìn." This explicit linkage between Orisha and Ifá is very important. In much of the diaspora, Orisha and Ifá have become separated, with distinct rituals and priesthoods. Certainly in Trinidad the Yorùbá-based religious practices have largely favored and focused on the energy of the Orisha. This reflects the pattern of the Yorùbá-based religions from Cuba to Brazil, where Ifá lineages were late additions to the well-established Orisha priesthood (D. H. Brown 2003; Harding 2003). The changes that I document here for Trinidad that reintegrate Yorùbá Ifá with Orisha practices have been (or are being) reflected to lesser or greater extents throughout the diaspora, in part through the same mechanisms of an increased post-1980s exchange of people across the Atlantic between West Africa and the Americas.

Olóyè Pópóọlá's delivery made clear his awareness of the history and the local context of Trini Orisha. His argument for the centrality of Ifá was strategically crafted to not alienate people whose religious worldview and identity have been grounded in Orisha. Trinidadians' relationship with specific individual Orisha—their propitiation, offerings, and manifestations— have contributed to a spiritual intimacy that informs a core spiritual identity. For an outsider to show up, dismiss all this history as having less meaning or value than what they offer, is an approach that, understandably, had led to resistance and resentment in the past. This was not the approach that Pópóọlá took in his speech. As we have seen, he positioned himself as "coming back home" and ready to "sit down together and share" while offering that Orisha "all know the energy of Ifá because they are part of the process." Building the foundation of his argument further, he continued, "Ifá is the religion of women, not men," effectively addressing two things at once: (1) that the Orisha leadership in Trinidad has historically been dominated by women, and (2) that in the diaspora the majority of Ifá initiates have been men, especially because their primary source, Cubans, until very recently initiated only men.[13] Surely for an approach to be successful in Trinidad, it needed to recognize the leadership role of women in ritual lineages and shrines, from Mother Toussaint to Iya Rodney, Mother Joan Cyrus, Iya Osunyemi, and Iya Sangowunmi—just a few of the women leaders in Trinidad Orisha.

The Power of Ìtefá, Ifá Initiation

All these rhetorical strategies laid the foundation and set the framework for Olóyè Pópóọlá's central message. Looking out at the audience while talking about the responsibilities of coronation to Orisha, he spoke clearly and slowly:

> It is compulsory, for everybody in this world to be initiated into Ifá. It is compulsory in the sense that it will give you your guide. Because when you are initiated into Ifá you will not pursue other people's destinies. It is very important. If Ifá tells you that you are going to become a millionaire in life, Ifá will tell you how you are going to become that millionaire, through what source you are going to become a millionaire. [Or] Ifá will tell you that, no, you will not starve in this world, but too much riches will not be yours. The minute you know that, you don't pursue riches a lot. You will think of other things that you will pursue. You will only know it if you are initiated to Ifá, because Ifá will let you know this is where you start.

He then moved on to introduce the Ifá initiates, whom he had initiated just that week, including Iya Sangowunmi, the leader of the shrine hosting his talk. Speaking of their Ìtefá, he drove his points home, declaring, "This is your soil" and "All the leaves, all the herbs that I wanted to use were here on the compound." The Ifá initiations that he was referencing were the first Ìtènífá done on Trinidad soil with the presence of Odù and Òsun. That is, as he described to the audience, he had brought from Nigeria the spiritual icons needed (according to his lineage) to conduct Ifá initiations, and his intention was for them to stay in Trinidad at the IESOM shrine. This began a new Ifá initiation lineage in the West alongside other Ifá temples and initiatory lineages that he had started in Venezuela, Colombia, Mexico, and Los Angeles, California—all part of his larger mission, which he shared with me many years later when I visited his compound in Nigeria, to "establish as many temples as possible so that we will change Ifá from becoming a very expensive religion to a religion that everybody can easily approach."

What is the importance of initiation to Ifá in the Yorùbá religion? According to Pópóọlá, it is through Ifá initiation that one will come to know one's destiny. In this way, all the decisions of an initiate can be made in alignment with the goal of fulfilling his or her destiny and avoiding things that detract from that destiny. As has been discussed previously, ita is the central vehicle that details one's destiny; what will support it (admonitions) and what will detract from it (taboos) are outlined in an Ifá divination on the third day of the Ifá initiation. This divination elaborates on the odù Ifá (one of 256 sacred geomantic binary signs of Ifá) that was cast for the individual. From that point forward, Ifá initiates have a road map to their life. Following this road map will ensure that they are on the right road to fulfilling their destiny and receiving the three things guaranteed by Ifá: long life, children, and patience. For Pópóọlá, then, and others of his spiritual lineage, Ifá initiation becomes fundamental for everyone to realize their destiny. As he said, "It is compulsory for everybody in this world to be initiated into Ifá."

This position of compulsory Ifá initiations tied together with the exhortation to perform them locally was new and sounded radical to the gathered Orisha priests and practitioners. As one attendee, Burton Sankeralli, remarked, "You said everyone should be initiated into Ifá. That is receive Itefa. . . . That is quite a revolutionary thing that you are saying." In response to Sankeralli's request for elaboration, Pópóọlá drew on a comparative example of Ifá:

> In Cuba, because there is no argument of the fact that but for the Cubans Ifá religion wouldn't have spread to on this level. The Cubans made it possible. They have a way of looking at it. They will say that those who have coronated with Èṣù cannot be initiated into Ifá. They will say that women cannot be initiated into Ifá. That is what they say. But I am telling you now that it is not so. The reason is this. If we are initiated into Ifá, what we want to know is our destiny. What we want to know is our direction in life. Is that one the exclusive right of men?
>
> There are some women who make more decisions in their life than men. So if we don't know the direction of such a person, how do we know where the person will take us to? Sometimes when we talk about babaláwo, the first thing you ask is what is his odù, when they tell you, you know what kind of person and you know how to deal with that kind of person. If you are going to blend, you will know. If not, you know how to give the person social distance. Immediately based on the odù. . . . That is the reason that all of us need to know where we are going and where we are coming from. It is our destiny, it is our right. It is not a privilege; nobody is giving it to us. It is our right to know. We don't need to be groping in the dark.
>
> Because if you consult Ifá every day you are still scratching it—on the

surface. You are not yet there. Ifá is like the onion. It is only through Ìtefá that you can get to the core of the onion. When you open one layer, you find another layer, when you open, you find another layer. When you open, you find another layer. But when you are initiated, you get to the core, to the very core of that thing. That is what Ìtefá is all about. So it is for everybody.

Here he is directly addressing gender bias in many Ifá lineages where initiation is reserved exclusively for men. Certainly, there are other positions on Ifá initiation, a fact he touched upon in his talk. Pópóọlá had firsthand experience with this, having done ritual work and initiated women into Ifá in Cuba, where until very recently only men were initiated into Ifá (and only "perceived" heterosexual men). These Ifá initiations provide membership into a select and elite priesthood that has largely been separate from the Orisha priesthood in Lucumi, even as the two lineages work closely in certain rituals. In America, many of the Ifá lineages are of Cuban descent and follow similar conventions. Other Ifá lineages, tied more directly to West Africa, follow the practices of their lineages. Throughout Yorubaland, and north to the Afa traditions of Benin and Togo, whether or not women are initiated depends on the local lineage. So while in one town both men and women can become Ifá initiates, in another town, say twenty miles away, it is men only. Historically, in Yorubaland there have been significant numbers of women Ifá initiates. This is counter to a common discourse circulating in diasporic Ifá/Orisha communities that including women in Ifá is a recent innovation brought about by interaction with the West. This is certainly not the case (though the increasing numbers of women in Ifá may reflect the current historical moment and shifts in gender roles, a more cynical reading offered to me by a Trini initiate focused on the economic motives for broadening the base of potential initiates). Elder Ifá priests with whom I have raised this gendered issue decidedly point out historical examples of women Ifá priests going back generations. They also quote from ẹsẹ odu Ifá that mention women performing the tasks of an Ifá priest or having that knowledge. When I recently asked Pópóọlá about this issue, he responded, "Shouldn't all people have access to their destiny?," echoing his words from a decade earlier in Trinidad.

Upon Initiation, or What Happens Next?

There have been challenges to Trinidad in establishing a new priesthood, and these challenges have consequences for the idea of spiritual citizenship. The building of community, if it is to be liberatory, must be done with integrity, while the spiritual praxis informing spiritual citizenship must also be sound. Leadership and initiation constitute a major issue that illuminates the challenge for the new directions of Trinidad Orisha. As more and more people, both men and women, are being initiated to Ifá, there is an urgent need to clarify the distinction between an initiate and a priest.

This distinction has not always been clear to me in my roles as both a cultural anthropologist and an Orisha devotee. I have seen this confusion mirrored within the diasporic Ifá/Orisha community as well, by initiates and noninitiates alike. A simplified definition of an initiate is a person who has been "crowned" or consecrated. Across all the diasporic traditions, these individuals will have, in one manner or another, undergone the process where the ase of Orisha or Ifá has been settled on their head. Under the tutelage of elders, they may then begin learning the rites and responsibilities available to them as initiates in training to become a priest. Thus, becoming an initiate is the beginning of a process of learning on a new level. I stress the difference between initiate and priest because confusion over these two categories has led many new initiates to take on roles and responsibilities beyond their status, experience, and knowledge as new initiates.

The importance of this is tied to the nature of these roles and responsibilities. Without exaggerating, the consequences can literally be on the level of life or death. When offering assistance to others, a misdiagnosis of a problem or a misunderstanding of an individual's spiritual pathway and destiny can compound existing problems or create new ones. For example, when leading a devotee to his or her own initiation, the supervising elder is responsible for ascertaining which Orisha will sit on that person's head. Getting this wrong can lead to disorientation, confusion, headaches, and other mental and physical problems for that person. A second example would be a client coming to get help with issues of fertility and conceiving a child. Before spiritual medicine or ẹbọ can be prescribed, the source of the problem must be correctly identified. If the person seeking counsel has a medical issue that cannot be resolved by the priest's available resources, including herbal and spiritual resources, he or she could need a referral to a Western medical practitioner. If that is not given in a timely way, there could be serious consequences that otherwise could have been avoided. In the community, stories of such mistakes circulate and often undermine an initiate's reputation.

Another kind of confusion occurs when the community is not clear about the distinction between initiate and priest. A new initiate may take on non-ritual roles, positions of leadership that are beyond his or her experience and accumulated ase. Hypothetically, how does a new Ifá initiate head an organization that dictates rules, procedures, and priorities to Trinidad Orisha practitioners and priests with decades of spiritual experience? Without pointing fingers, situations like this have certainly occurred and are constantly being negotiated. Receiving a Yorùbá name through Ifá initiation, or another ritual, does not by itself confer knowledge or *awo* (access to the inner mysteries of Ifá). Problems like these can be hard to address, especially when the multiple levels of Ifá eldership that exist in Yorubaland are absent, as they are in many locations in the diaspora.[14] This has been a special challenge in Trinidad, with the beginning of a new Ifá lineage. There have been awkward attempts to negotiate the status positions of the new Ifá initiates alongside the existing priesthood of Trini Orisha. A further complication has arisen from the varied level of experience among new Ifá initiates, ranging from Orisha elders to those who are new to the religion. Opportunities for training continue to be a challenge. The traditional model of apprenticing under an elder Ifá priest and (literally) sitting at his or her feet on the mat is difficult to follow when most senior priests with decades of experience are short-term visitors in Trinidad. The homes where they spend the majority of the time remain far away in Nigeria or other locations in the "metropole," such as New York, Toronto, or London.

Ifá/Orisha Worldview Practitioners Conference

"Our purpose over the next few days is reflecting on the past, sharing what we have as family and designing—not even projecting but designing the future. And we know that in Ifá, what we design comes into being. That is our purpose." These words from Rawle Gibbons, the day's master of ceremonies, opened the Ifá/Orisha Worldview Practitioners Conference, framing the meetings as drawing on historical memory while also creating ("designing") the future, through Ifá. In 2010, Iya Sangowunmi, members of her shrine, Ile Eko Sango/Osun Mil'Osa, and others in Trinidad's Ifá/Orisha community organized the first Ifá/Orisha Worldview Practitioners

Conference, scheduled to be held in conjunction with IESOM's annual Rain Festival. The conference lasted several days and was cohosted by the University of Trinidad and Tobago (UTT), with Àwíṣẹ Agbáyé Wándé Abímbólá as the keynote speaker and attendees from the Caribbean, Latin and South America, West Africa, and North America. A day of presentations was held at the new National Academy for the Performing Arts, followed by more presentations and ritual events held at the IESOM shrine in Santa Cruz. The conference, held a decade after the 1999 Sixth World Orisha Congress, served as an interesting bookend, further establishing Trinidad's presence on the global map of Yorùbá and other African diasporic religions.

After opening remarks, Gibbons introduced the individuals seated on the stage, providing brief biographies and details that situated them within the landscape of Trinidad and Tobago's Ifá and Orisha religious community. These notable people, heads of the Ifá family, were introduced in order, from left to right: Baba Erinfolami, the Alagba of IESOM; Yeye Iyewa, priestess of Ile Osun Obatala; Iyanifa Afideramo of IESOM; the collective ancestors (Egúngún), represented by an empty chair; Chief Ṣọlágbadé Pópóọlá; Àwíṣẹ Agbáyé Baba Wándé Abímbólá; Iya Sangowunmi of IESOM; Winston Peters (aka calypsonian Gypsy), the minister of arts and multiculturalism; Oluwo Ifá Korode; Chief Baba Mokum Awo, the Àràbà of IESOM; Dr. Hollis Liverpool, president of the Academy of Arts, Letters and Sciences at UTT (aka calypsonian the Mighty Chalkdust); and Olóyè Awo Oluwole Ifakunle, described in part as the babalawo of Harlem. In helping us to read this arrayed group of distinguished people, Gibbons's introductions provided a window into each person's contribution to the conference, to Ifá/Orisha, and to the "diasporic horizon" of the community (P. C. Johnson 2007, 2012). By mapping out a spiritual geography for the gathering, the biographies ranged from noting international accomplishments and impact to more intimate stories that engagingly conveyed important relationships.

"Iya doesn't recognize time." Gibbons's opening words about Iya Sangowunmi elicited laughter. "So when this idea of the conference came to her, I think it was maybe six o'clock or five o'clock in the morning. Or whatever time that she felt moved, she called, and I'm sure that she called all of her children and associates, and commandeered us to begin the work. That was about two years ago. And so it began to today's fruition." In this quick and amusing introduction, he located Iya Sangowunmi as the "visionary who conceived this conference," effectively positioning her at the center of the event. He continued to specify Àwíṣẹ Abímbólá as her Olúwo, or "spiritual father," which also placed Iya Sangowunmi at the center of a transnational Ifá/Orisha network with "bona fide" roots in Yorubaland, thus highlighting her local and foreign networks that brought together their energies to manifest her vision.

Next came the introductions of the Nigerian Ifá priests, the Àwíṣẹ Wándé Abímbólá and Olóyè Ṣọlágbadé Pópóọlá, in which Gibbons emphasized their respective roles in promoting Ifá. He situated Pópóọlá as the "person primarily responsible for the promulgation of the practice in the Americas." This was followed by lauding Abímbólá as "primarily responsible for the acceptance and the recognition of this Ifá tradition as a masterpiece of human heritage by UNESCO." At this point Gibbons was interrupted by widespread applause, punctuated by drumming, after which he continued, "And through that recognition he founded the Ifá Heritage Studies College [on the] tertiary level in Oyo." These statements located Abimbola and Pópóọlá as two central figures who had been critical to spreading and bringing value to Ifá. This rhetorically positioned the conference, and by extension the Ifá community in Trinidad, at the heart of the "promulgation" and "recognition" of Ifá.

This recognition was underscored as Gibbons continued his introductions, moving to audience members in the large auditorium afer he was done with the people on the stage. As his gaze swept over the auditorium, he acknowledged and introduced many of the priests and practitioners in attendance by name, providing an interesting perspective on Trinidad's spiritual landscape for foreign visitors and visiting anthropologist alike. In reproducing parts of his introduction here, I hope to offer a glimpse into the reordered landscape in the new era of Trinidad Ifá/Orisha, circa 2010. Part of the performativity of the conference, and the morning session of welcome speeches, was a display of the local version of Ifá/Orisha to an international audience, the state, and local dignitaries (i.e., especially the diplomats). Most important, the conference was staging the Ifá/Orisha religion in Trinidad to itself. Almost all the local priests and practitioners who attended the conference, whether as organizers, participants, or observers, had decades of experience in an earlier version of Trinidad Orisha, one that predated the events outlined in the opening section of this chapter— indeed, a history that for many went back as far as thirty, forty, or more years. From this foundation in Trinidad Orisha, they were exploring the new teachings and lineages of Ifá. In a sense, this conference was a "coming-out" event to the global spiritual networks of Yorùbá-based religions to the

Ifá/Orisha community in Trinidad (as opposed to the introductory nature of the 1999 World Orisha Congress).

The introductions highlighted another important theme: the link between the Ifá/Orisha tradition and the arts in Trinidad. This narrative started with the introduction of the minister of arts and multiculturalism, Winston Peters. In explaining that the minister was also a well-known calypsonian named Gypsy, Gibbons emphasized, "This is important. There is a deep connection between the tradition that we speak of and that we practice and the popular arts. And one of the sources is this tradition. So honorable Mr. Winston Peters, welcome home." This theme was picked up again when Gibbons introduced Dr. Hollis Liverpool, president of the Academy of Arts, Letters and Sciences at UTT (a sponsor of the conference), who was also known by his calypso sobriquet, Chalkdust (due both to his early career as a teacher and to his all-white goatee). Gibbons mentioned the eight times that Chalkdust won the annual Calypso Monarch competition, making him one of Trinidad's top calypsonians. In his remarks, Chalkdust linked his mission at UTT of reclaiming lost and marginalized cultures to the university's sponsorship of the Ifá/Orisha Worldview Practitioners Conference. This connection between Ifá/Orisha and culture and the arts was reinforced again and again as several calypsonians were identified in the audience, including Composer, Penguin, and Iya Omilade (aka Shanaqua).[15] It was emphasized again when Gibbons introduced Chief Abiodun LeRoy Clarke: "The tradition finds itself represented in all different ways. It is there in the popular arts. If there is one person that expresses the African tradition in art, it is of course LeRoy Clarke. It is not only in his art, his work, it is in his life." LeRoy Clarke is a master artist (a title conferred on him in 1998 by the National Museum and Art Gallery of Trinidad and Tobago) who describes his work as "His Calling" and views himself as a "Pointerman, pointing the way to O-be-ah-man-ness!" (www.leroyclarke.com). Known to many simply as "Chief," Clarke was awarded a "Staff of Eldership" and chieftaincy title in the Orisha community by IESOM during the Sixth Annual Sango/Osun Rain Festival in 2005. Among the many accomplishments detailed on his website, he refers to the granting of that award as "the crowning event."

The other significant theme that Rawle Gibbons touched on during his introductions situated Ifá/Orisha at an equitable level with Trinidad's other major non-Christian religions. He did this through remarks that recognized His Excellency, High Commissioner Malay Mishra by saying, "We walk hand in hand with India." He then acknowledged Trinidad's participation in the body of world traditions "in which the native peoples sit, as well as the Hindu and the Orisha people." Additionally, he singled out notable Indo-Trinidadian religious leaders who were present, representing the Hindu and Muslim communities respectively: Brother Ravi Ji, founding president of Prachar Kendra, a Hindu temple, and Brother Noble Khan, of the Trinidad Muslim League and former president of Trinidad's Inter-Religious Organization (IRO). Importantly, in referring to Noble Khan, Gibbons highlighted his role as the former president of the IRO, who "helped to usher Orisha onto the council."

To explain the importance of this to foreign visitors, Gibbons began, "You may not know [that] the Orisha religion in Trinidad," and then continued in an aside specifically to the diplomatic representative from Cuba, "Maybe not in Cuba, Your Excellency, but in Trinidad was highly stigmatized." This last comment invoked a comparative diasporic frame, one within the Caribbean, of relative religious histories. Gibbons went on to elaborate in a lowered voice, "If you talking about Orisha, you talking Devil business," to the amusement of the crowd. "You understand? So the business about public recognition, official recognition was extremely important to the growth of the religion. . . . And our participation at the level of the IRO, sitting among other religions equally, was specifically due to Brother Noble Khan." This public recognition did several things in presenting a narrative of Ifá/Orisha. Importantly, it recognized the role of Indo-Trinidadians and non-Christian religions in supporting African diasporic religions. This echoes the cultural citizenship examined in chapter 2 and links it to the emerging spiritual citizenship evident in the conference.

The remarks of Gypsy (Minister Peters) followed the introductions by Gibbons and were notable for his explicit weaving of national culture, multiculturalism, and Ifá into a singular narrative. After offering apologies for the absence of the prime minister due to "duties of state" (Parliament was opening officially that morning), Gypsy gave a "holistic definition" of culture that he used as a foundation to assert, "We in Trinidad are no strangers to the multiplicity of cultural manifestations. We all know our collective story of multiple migrations from all over the world so as to provide labor for the colonial empire. We can now boast of an Independent Republic of Trinidad and Tobago that's heir to the spiritual traditions of almost all the major societies in the world." Having established the multicultural legacy of Trinidad's colonial history by echoing the national rhetoric, he positioned Ifá within that diverse religious inheritance: "Ifá is one of these customs and one of the oldest spiritual traditions known to man. It anchors the life of the devotees via the conceptual, ethical, and moral codes, which are reinforced by its complex series of rituals. It is an intriguing discipline that facilitates direct communication with its deities via divination and manifestation."

Gypsy's definition of Ifá reflects an accurate and astute understanding of this complex religious system. I read this as reflecting either his personal knowledge of Ifá or, perhaps more likely, the knowledge of someone working for him in the Ministry of Arts and Multiculturalism. This explicit description of Ifá and linking to the nation's heritage of multiplicity is a direct inheritance of the Orisha community's negotiations of multiculturalism in the previous decades. At the 2010 Ifá conference, an emerging spiritual citizenship was evident, one premised on a previously developed cultural citizenship and informed by both ancestral and newly sourced streams of knowledge.

Following the Friday morning opening ceremony were several ritual events and presentations that stretched over the weekend. The ritual events included an Egungun festival held on Saturday morning at the IESOM Santa Cruz Shrine Gardens (plate 5). The presentations included topics ranging from herbalism and divination to Trinidad mas' in the Ifá/Orisha tradition. Highlights included an hour-long lecture by Olóyè Ṣọlágbadé Pópóọlá on the importance of Ifá divination and ẹbọ (prescribed ritual offerings), with recitations of ẹsẹ odù Ifá in Yorùbá followed by English explanations. The lecture's overall message was that Ifá was always aware of everything we did, and our lives would be better if (and when) we listened to Ifá and performed the required ẹbọ. Saturday evening finished with a formal sit-down dinner for conference participants.

The third day of the conference opened with the Nangare Sun Festival, followed by a lecture on the importance of initiations and rites of passage. After lunch the final presentation focused on next steps for the religion and the community. The end of the conference and festival was marked with a closing ceremony. Even after this, however, there were more events, a kind of postconference that took advantage of the presence of all the visiting Ifá priests. Among these events was the establishment of a shrine dedicated to those Africans who died during the Atlantic slave trade, especially those who died at sea and never returned home, fulfilling in part an important rite of passage as discussed on the previous day. This was followed by a different type of rite of passage, a set of Ifá initiations (Ìtefá) with a cross section of local Trinidadians and visitors from the United States undergoing initiation.

Aṣẹ́wẹ̀lẹ̀

"The souls of all these departed ones will continue to haunt these lands." The charge to address this and the spiritual impact of the losses of the Atlantic slave trade is one site of social action for the Ifá community and one expression of emerging spiritual citizenship. The disruption caused by the human trafficking from West Africa to the Americas tore apart families, communities, towns, and cities. Among the many losses and adaptations forced upon those who were captured and sold into slavery was the disruption of rites of passage. These rituals that mark birth, puberty, and death are central to many of the cultures of West and Central Africa that were a primary source for the slave trade. Throughout the diaspora, African descendants have long felt the losses from the Atlantic slave trade and the damage of rituals undone and names unknown, adding to the larger pain of separation. Memorials to those lost in the slave trade (or Maafa, as it is called by many Afro-centric scholars and community members) can be found from New York to Brazil. It did not take Ifá to bring the awareness of the ancestors to Trinidad. That has long been there. What Ifá brought was the spiritual technology, the ritual and guidelines for the use of ase and ẹbọ, needed to appease the spirits of those who died far from home, outside of the proper rituals.

In his article "Let Their Souls Be Perfectly Rested" (2007), Olóyè Ṣọlág-badé Pópóọlá argues for the need to address the missing death and burial rituals of those lost in the slave trade. Drawing on various ẹsẹ odu Ifá (the sacred verses of Ifá), Pópóọlá makes the case that neglect of those souls who died far from home may have serious consequences:

> With the rites not done for them, how could anyone expect peace and progress in its real sense on both sides of the Atlantic? It is my submission that without the performance of the appropriate rituals and rites for the souls of these twenty million Africans, there would never be progress and development in Africa. Those at the other side of the Atlantic also will never know peace and contentment. The souls of all these departed ones will continue to haunt these lands. . . . For how long should we wait before we decide to act appropriately on both sides of the Atlantic and lay the souls of these African ancestors to proper and deserved rest? (2007 35)

Given the immense scale of how many people were taken from Africa during the slave trade, with upwards of twenty million people, a solution that depends on addressing each soul individually presents a seemingly insurmountable problem. However, there is a solution that involves collective recognition of those travelers who were lost and never properly put to rest.

The responsibility to those who have come before, and those who will come after, is a core principle of spiritual citizenship, alongside the building of community in the present moment that follows principles of social justice, equality, liberation, and a moral code as informed by Ifá. The model of spiritual citizenship that I am proposing here is not a static fundamentalist reading of Ifá's sacred verses. Certainly, as with any corpus of sacred text, whether oral or written, readings can strategically find messages that serve the ideology of the reader. I am advocating for a reading of the Ifá literary corpus (a term coined by Àwíṣẹ Abímbólá [2007]) that is open, progressive, and honoring of the humanity of all people. From this reading a mission of social justice can emerge (I discuss this further in the following section on Alásùwadà).

One way to address those souls lost in the Atlantic slave trade, as proposed by Olóyè Pópóọlá, is to invoke the power of the Orisha of travelers, Aṣẹ́wẹlẹ. Largely unknown in the diaspora and indeed little known in Yorubaland, "Aṣẹ́wẹlẹ is the Orisa of travellers. It is the Orisa that was used in the olden days and some very few parts of Yoruba land. Up till today, they pray for protection of travellers. It is also used today to turn evil to good" (2007, 35). Pópóọlá argues, "This means that Aṣẹ́wẹlẹ has three functions; one, to appease the souls of those who had died in transit; two, to use their souls to pray for protection and progress and three, to use it to ward off all curses of the enemy" (37). This informs a diasporic perspective, one that is focused not on linking nations but rather on recognizing the link of roots and routes created by the distance traversed by people (Gilroy 1993). By establishing shrines both in the Americas and in West Africa, the spiritual connection between the two becomes solidified and anchored. The Aṣẹ́wẹlẹ shrines, then, serve as a physical representation of our remembrance and of our greater connection across time (those who have gone before) and space (those who were far from home).

In 2010, I was fortunate enough to be present at the installation of Trinidad's first Asewele shrine (the first such shrine in the Americas, as far as I am aware). The spiritual intensity of engaging "lost" spirits can be witnessed in my recollections. I was surprised when we did not get on the road until somewhat after 9:00 AM, several hours past our original departure time. Anticipating our early start, I had woken up an hour before dawn, around 5:00 AM. Many things happened before we could leave, including waiting for the inevitable late arrivals (this was Trinidad, after all). And, to be fair, many folks were coming from the other side of town and had to make their way deep into the Santa Cruz Valley to meet the bus. There was also pre-ritual work to be done, including Ifá divination by the elders.

Once the required consultations had been conducted and everyone was finally gathered, we were ready to board the buses, with a few folks following in cars. Fortunately, I had spent the night up at the shrine, which explains my readiness for the early deadline. As we settled on the bus and headed down the road, I turned to the person next to me and asked, "What we doin' again?" The answer I received did not clarify much: "We goin' to honor those ancestors lost at sea, those lost on de way here." I knew that we were doing an ancestral ritual. I just did not understand why we needed to caravan to the northernmost point of Trinidad to do so. The shrine we had just left had an ancestor grove where much of that ritual work was typically done.

I did not know then (and was not told until much later) that we were building a specific shrine to a new energy for Trinidad, Asewele. As with much Ifá and Orisha ritual, knowledge is compartmentalized and is shared on a need-to-know basis. As I was not an initiate then, I was not responsible for conducting the ritual, there was little need for me to know. Also, to be fair and to provide a fuller picture, my initiation to Ifá was immanent (the starting moment was up in the air at that point and could have been the next hour or the next week). As such, my own status was liminal, putting me even farther out of the loop. This liminality also obscured my status as a "researcher," which the people I had known for several years would routinely overlook. (I had gotten into the habit of reminding people that I was doing research and often carried not only a camera but also a notebook and pen, both for taking notes and as a performative reminder.) Finally, to complicate things on a different level, I was seriously ill, requiring a large part of my focus to be on maneuvering the physical challenges of the journey.

What I eventually discovered was that we were going to the ocean to bring us closer to the spirits of those who had perished at sea, to those we were honoring. It was not until much later, during the hike down the road (which was so broken down and rocky that the bus was not able to continue), that I began to put two and two together. Beyond the road was a path, seeming to disappear into the "bush," that I was told led to the ocean. It was on that path, where I was being helped by visiting American researcher Ryan

Bazinet, that I started to understand: we were going to honor and appease those lost souls who perished during the Atlantic slave trade, both on land and at sea, but especially those who had lost their lives at sea.

This understanding helped give me the perspective to push back my own physical pain. I moved forward with a new resolve just as we turned a corner and I glimpsed the sea. Once at the beach, I sat on a log to catch my breath and ponder the horizon while others scouted for a site to build the shrine. I started to feel a sense of weight, as if the ritual about to take place was bearing down on me. Distracting myself, I gazed out at the horizon and mused that if I could see all the way beyond the horizon, that shore would be the coast of West Africa, the coast of Guinea. This thought brought a new valence to the idea of "diasporic horizons." As personal accounts from the other side of the Atlantic and memorial sites of the slave trade (like the "point of no return," whether in Elmina Castle, Ghana, or Badagry, Nigeria, among others) had conveyed the force of history, I could feel my location within it in a very tangible way.

After some time had passed, the elders confirmed a site by divination, past a bluff (figure 5.1). To reach it, we would have to cross the beachhead, where the surf was crashing down on the rocks. Most of the priests and practitioners had timed their dash across between the ebb and flow of the waves so as to not get completely soaked or, worse yet, risk getting washed away. Given my current mobility challenges, I had decided to sit out this part of the journey. I was clear that I would stay where I was and offer my personal prayers from there. From my log I could gaze at the sea and the horizon to pay my respects both to those souls who had found a home at the bottom of the ocean and to those buried in Trinidad when it was a strange and foreign land. I did so, all the while disquieted by a growing feeling of weight pushing down on me, the weight of loss.

"I'm good here, really I am," I mumbled to myself and to anyone nearby who cared to hear. And I meant it. Fiercely. I was quite good there. To say I was resistant to being more directly exposed to the energies of unsettled spirits was an understatement. Considerably later, feeling restless and hot from the sun, I got up and made my way down toward the bluff to welcome those coming back from the shrine. They had crossed the bluff, said their prayers, and made their offerings to seat the ase (spiritual power, here specifically dedicated to honoring the lost souls). And then the elders had confirmed that everything was accepted through divination. All this had been done during the time that I had waited, sitting on the log. I felt good on

FIGURE 5.1 Ifá/Orisha devotees on Cumana Beach, Toco are seen here returning from establishing Trinidad's first shrine to Asewele, the Orisha of lost travelers, in honor of those unable to receive proper burial rites, especially dedicated to the Africans who were lost in the Middle Passage, 2010. Photo by N. Fadeke Castor.

my side and was happy to stand with the few others who had not made the journey. Together we would welcome folks back.

Or so I thought. I began to feel the weight intensify into a physical pressure pushing down on me. Moving me. I had to go, to go across the beachhead, past the waves crashing on the boulders, to . . . ? I didn't know where. I found myself making my way across the beach and rocks, where I had said that I would not go. Pushed to overcome my fear of getting wet, or worse, slipping on the rocks. Then I was being pushed up an incline toward a tree that was near some rocks. I felt more than saw the elders standing there. For as I reached the shrine I was pushed, literally pushed, by the force of Spirit down onto the ground so that my head touched the stone in full prostration, or *dobale*. And then it came. A wave of sorrow washed over me. I felt their screams, the pain of the collective souls left to wander so far from home. And I screamed. I howled. I cried and writhed, bawling, knowing that this recognition was not enough. It could never be enough.

It was a start, though. Relieved, I felt hands help me up, even as the weight I had been feeling lifted, buoyed by my release (lighter but not gone, never gone). And I rose with my body covered in dirt and my face covered in salt, from the waves and from my tears. I knew then that we had made an important step in honoring those spirits who had felt forgotten and whose souls had never been put to rest.

When I talked with Olóyè Pópóọlá years later about Aséwẹlẹ, he spoke of plans to establish a shrine in Nigeria on land near Badagry, "so that both of them will be across the Atlantic. So that we will be able to use it for people to pray and do things that will keep their ancestors' souls at peace." This is an ambitious project, still in its early stages, which joins the other memorials, shrines, and commemorations that weave together sites across the Atlantic. Since my initial research, another Asewele shrine has been placed at IESOM to handle the pressing need to appease and elevate the many lost souls (plate 10). In many instances these sites echo the movements of peoples, languages, cultures, and religions that create and inform the African diasporic space. These, together with a shared history and political visions, have helped to inform the diasporic subjectivities and identities that form the heart of an African diasporic (or black) cultural citizenship. And the spirit of this cultural citizenship lies in the spiritual citizenship of ritual knowledge and movement that recognizes, reclaims, and reconnects the lost souls of the diaspora. For at one point were we not all travelers? To be clear, the "we" that I invoke here is a diasporic "we": the descendants of those not meant to survive, those Africans who crossed the Atlantic (and, in lesser numbers, in another oft-forgotten diaspora, the Pacific). Are we not all indebted to Aséwẹlẹ?

Alásùwadà: From Conference to Movement?

It is Irete and Ika that would guide and bring them together.
Children of those that were taken away,
long ago to the lands of the West.
Alásùwadà it is Irete Ika that shall open the way for us to come together,
to change the world forever.
It is Irete Ika.

Understood within the diasporic frame, with the ever-present historical memory of the slave trade "children of those that were taken away," the goals of Alásùwadà were clear: to bring together the children of those who survived to build community and "change the world forever." In July 2012, under the odu Ifá Ìrẹtẹ̀ Ìká, an Ifá conference was organized and hosted by Iya Sangowunmi, the IESOM shrine and their Irentegbe temple. The Alásùwadà conference was convened by a Nigerian babaláwo, Olóyè Sọlágbadé Pópóọlá, one of the shrine elders and the head initiating priest of numerous

Ifá lineages throughout the Americas. Invitations were sent throughout his networks and beyond to the larger Ifá/Orisha community. Demonstrating its wide circulation, one version of the invitation was published on the website of Ile Iwosan Orunmila, a temple in Phoenix, Arizona:

> You are all cordially invited to attend the Alasuwada Ifa and Orisa International Conference to be held in Santa Cruz, Trinidad and Tobago July 6th–9th 2012. The theme of the Conference is: The Diaspora in All Its Splendor and Legacy Meets the Ifa Tradition of Yoruba Land. The conference is being held at Ile Eko Sango Osun Mil'Osa and Iretegbe Temple with the leadership and spiritual guidance of Chief Solagbade Pópóọlá.
>
> This conference targets Ifa/Orisa practitioners and interested devotees from the countries of the representatives of the international steering committee Nigeria. The Caribbean, United States, Canada, United Kingdom, Central America and South America. For more questions please email alasuwadaifaorisa@gmail.com.
>
> The objective of the conference is to build a powerful international movement that would bring respect and awareness of the tradition with like minded practitioners; so as to strengthen the work of Ifa through "The Alasuwada Movement."

In response to this conference call, priests and practitioners from throughout the Americas gathered in Santa Cruz, Trinidad, to discuss, learn, and explore how Ifá informed their work in the world and to imagine how this could be organized as a social movement. Over three days (more if you include the various ritual events before and after the conference), the themes of Ifá and unity were addressed in presentations, workshops, and keynotes to a diverse audience from Venezuela, Colombia, Mexico, Canada, and across the United States—specifically Los Angeles, Chicago, and New York. All of these locations reflected the Ifá lineages that Olóyè Pópóọlá has established in his journeys from his home compound in Ogun State, outside Lagos, Nigeria. The conference languages were English and Spanish, with translation equipment (headsets) provided for all who wanted it. Translators were drawn largely from the bilingual conference participants, who provided real-time translation. Not evident in this brief overview here are the incredible energy, exchanges, and inspiration provided over the weekend, under the auspices of Alásùwadà. It was during Alásùwadà that I glimpsed the spiritual citizenship whose emergence I have tracked in these pages.

On the day before the conference began, the unexpected presence of divinity underscored that there were more intelligences at work than just the conference participants. This shaped the flow of space and time for the event as all were reminded that Ifá/Orisha time is not always congruent with human time. A sudden intervention of sacred energy brought preparations that had been in full swing (including setting up the stage and prepping rooms for some conference attendees) to an abrupt stop the day before the opening. The energy manifested even as the Ifá priests and devotees from Venezuela, Colombia, and Mexico were gathering on the shrine just as people from the States began to arrive.

Included in this latter group was Oba Adejuyigbe Adefunmi II, the oba (or king) of Oyotunji Village in Sheldon, South Carolina, a settlement built from the intersection of Black Nationalism and an interpretation of a traditional Yorùbá village (figure 5.2). Oyotunji Village was founded in the 1970s by Oba Osejiman Adefunmi I, the current king's father. "The Village," as it is known throughout the Ifá/Orisha community, is populated by African diasporic religious practitioners, with numbers ranging from approximately two hundred at its height in the late 1970s to a couple dozen in the contemporary moment (for more on Oyotunji Village, see K. Clarke 2004; Hucks 2014). Oba Adefunmi's presence at the Alásùwadà conference added an important facet to the diasporic representation of the Ifá/Orisha community and a layer of ritual formality, in accordance with his status.

My first awareness of Oba Adefunmi's participation in the conference was during an intervention of sacred energy. I had gone up to the IESOM shrine hoping to connect with Awo Fasegun, an Ifá priest and old friend of mine arriving from Los Angeles whom I had not seen in many years. I was waiting for his return from a tour of Trinidad when I saw a car pull up. I approached the car, curious to see if my friend had returned. At first no one came out. Then, suddenly, one of the shrine's priests emerged from the driver's side of the car. As I stepped forward to ask for Awo Fasegun, I realized that there was something different in the priest's countenance. Before I could figure out what had changed, another car door opened, and Iya Sangowunmi gestured for me to help her out of the car. As I moved to do so, I offered my ritual greetings of "Aboru aboye" and started to ask about Awo Fasegun.

"No, no." Iya shook her head. "It's Oshun there."

Aaah. That is when I understood that Iya Omilade, the driver of the car, was in possession by Oshun. (Oshun drives? Oshun drives!) And soon I would realize that Oshun had come with spiritual work to do. Iya Sangow-

FIGURE 5.2 Oba Adejuyigbe Adefunmi II of Oyotunji Village, South Carolina, U.S. presenting at the Alasuwada Ifá and Orisha International Conference held at Ile Eko Sango/Osun Mil'osa in Santa Cruz, Trinidad, 2012. Photo by N. Fadeke Castor.

unmi's call for people to come attend to Oshun brought together both the shrine members and visitors for the conference. Drummers appeared, as if from nowhere, and the *kang kang kang* of a cowbell rang out. A series of events followed, familiar to devotees from throughout the diaspora or the continent: Oshun's bell was brought forth, *oyin* (honey) was produced, and libations were poured to Esu with *oti* (alcohol). Startled by the sudden presence of Orisha (and with the thought "Oshun drives!" still running through my head), I started to videotape the scene.

Unexpectedly, another car door opened. "Eh, eh," ran my thought of surprise, there was someone else in the car?! I realized that Oba Adefunmi had traveled from Oyotunji Village, South Carolina for the Alásùwadà conference and now was stepping out of the car into sacred space cleared for him by the ministrations of Oshun (figure 5.3). Before his foot touched the earth, the ground had been cooled with *omi tutù* (literally "cool water" in the Yorùbá language) as befits the reception of Yorùbá royalty (whether of continental or diasporic provenance). Upon his emergence, Oba Adefunmi first greeted Esu: he called for oti and "sprayed" Esu with a mouthful of gin, followed by a ritual dance. Having observed this important greeting, as Esu is always greeted first, he turned his attention to Oshun. As ritual greetings were exchanged between the Orisha and Oba Adefunmi, the group sang a song of greeting. "*Aboru aboye, aboye abosise*" rang out as drums, shekere, and cowbell maintained an insistent rhythm in welcome. Oshun passed an obi (kola nut) over the heads of Oba Adefunmi and Iya Sangowunmi before passing it to a nearby babalawo. The Awo broke open the obi and "da the obi" (performed divination), getting a good sign after two throws.

The ritualized reception of Oba Adefunmi by the deity Oshun, manifesting on a priest of the shrine, would have been significant enough to comment on by itself, yet that was just the beginning of the ritual work to be done that day. Once the greetings had concluded between Oshun and Oba Adefunmi (including a protracted dance between the two), the energy moved toward the crowd, transitioning them from observers to participants. This shift had started earlier, with Oshun indicating that all should partake of some of her honey, and as the honey was brought around to each of us, she encouraged us all to dance. In response to our initial halfhearted movements, Oshun's voice became forceful and commanding as she informed us that blessings would be brought only to those who danced and that we must dance. "Everyone must be moving. Move your bodies!" Then her powerful gaze (akin to the beam from a lighthouse) swung around to all

FIGURE 5.3 On the day before the Alasuwada Conference convened Oshun greets Oba Adefunmi II, king of Oyotunji Village, South Carolina, U.S., while Iya Sangowunmi (on left in green) leads a song accompanied by Baba Menes de Griot (on her right) on the cowbell. Ile Eko Sango/Osun Mil'osa, Santa Cruz, Trinidad, 2012. Photo by N. Fadeke Castor.

the people holding up our phones to capture the scene on video, including myself. I knew what was coming and hastily stopped recording. Just as I put down my camera, water flew toward us in blessing.

As we focused on dancing, the energy continued to build. Oshun called for every person on the property to come and then gathered us all in an open space. During the previous ritual events, some shrine members had continued setting up for the next day, but were now called to join in. With all the people finally gathered, we were organized into a circle. Then we were shown how to ritually greet Oba Adefunmi, on this occasion by dancing with him in the center of the circle, where he waited. One by one we entered the circle to dance with Oshun and greet the oba, moving to the drums and cowbell, which had never stopped. The ritual dancing and drumming had built up the energy in the circle. The spiritual work of creating community from a group of strangers had begun. And this, it turned out, was largely the work that Oshun had come to do.

Once the performative ritualized greetings of dance were done, Oshun talked to us about difference, overcoming difference, and the need to come together. She told us that in the days to come there would be conflicts and contentions (there were) and that they would be overcome (they were). And right there, she gave us the medicine needed to make the conference a success. After some admonishment about the consequences of looking out only for oneself and not embracing the "Other," she had everyone join hands. Oshun then had us repeat after her, "Unity is strength, strength is power." At first our efforts to repeat her words were a mishmash of out-of-sync voices. "No," she said, "this must be all together." Slowing down, she had us repeat the phrases again and again until we were all together. In unison we declared over and over, "Unity is strength, strength is power." And with that, her work done, Oshun left. I looked around, amazed by this divine intervention, only to catch the gaze of my friend, Awo Fasegun (who had arrived during the impromptu ritual); together we smiled.

My ethnographic sketch of Oshun's visit ("Oshun drives!") is given here to convey the tone of the whole conference. Indeed, rather than calling it a conference, I should use another word that does not have the academic connotations of (at its worst) a staid, intellectual meeting with a full schedule of disembodied presentations. In contrast, the Alásùwadà gathering was infused with sacred energy and embodied ritual from its earliest moments. Over the next several days, people gathered in sacred space to give presentations and discussions that were centered on the intellectual and esoteric aspects of Ifá. There were also spontaneous and planned rituals with testimonials, witnessing, and reverence for the ancestors. And, as predestined by Oshun, there was the building of unity across difference.

The Alásùwadà conference informed (and was informed by) spiritual citizenship. It brought people together across different nations, languages, cultures, ethnicities, and races to form a singular community. If even just for those three or four days, the experience of being in a unified Ifá community further reinforced a sense of belonging to the often abstract or amorphous spiritual community. Beyond this, while gathered at the IESOM Shrine Gardens, the participants learned about Ifá and shared each other's experiences and visions of Ifá. Among the topics discussed were how Ifá can inform social change and social justice, how Ifá can contribute to decolonization, how Ifá supports the building of political and economic communities, and an important teaching on the meaning of Alásùwadà itself.

The divine energy of Alásùwadà comes from the sacred odu Ifá Ọ̀sá Ògúndá and is in the same section of verses that contains the Ifá creation story (see Appendix I). Alásùwadà, is the divine force that guides and looks over social organizations, the coming together of humans into groups. (If there was an Orisha of sociologists, this would be the one.) So what does Alásùwadà mean? According to Pópóọlá, Alásùwadà means "he who molds destinies together," from the Yorùbá-language cognates, which read as "Ala, owner; *Asu*, molder; *Iwa*, destiny, and *Dà*, together." In exploration of the term he and his student Awo Agboola continue:

> Ifá, which knows how nature functions, implores each and every living thing here to work together in harmony and respect each other's roles/destinies. Many scholars and academics who have studied African Culture and many Indigenous cultures from other parts of the world have discovered that most early humans lived according to something called Communalism or Communal living. In Ọ̀sá Ọ̀gúndá as well as many other Ifá verses, we can find that Communalism or Communal living was the basis of ethics, morals, values, and Ìwà-Pẹ̀lẹ́ for Ifá and Orisa followers and priests. This is a lifestyle of living that implores all devotees to learn how to coexist in harmony with all around them both animate and inanimate life.
>
> It is ONLY through working together, applying the teachings of Alasuwada, and imbibing the virtues of Ìwà-Rere or Ìwà-Pẹ̀lẹ́ that we will all achieve and maintain equilibrium here in the world and achieve not only our individual destinies but those of our family, community, nation, and the world. Alasuwada teaches us that through communal living, the individuality of a person does not disappear but actually emerges stronger because that person's role/destiny will be seen clearly by others and respected for the betterment of all. Let all followers and priests follow Alasuwada as their foundation for living so that each and every person's destiny and other creature's destinies will complement and be in balance with one another.[16]

In exploring the meaning of Alásùwadà together, we all experienced one highlight of the conference: the telling of Pópóọlá's version of the creation story, from the same Odù Ọ̀sá Ọ̀gúndá. Because Olóyè Pópoólá had been unable to secure a transit visa to travel from Nigeria to Trinidad for the conference, he asked one of his Ifá students, Awo Agboola, to read his talk. His version of the creation story unfolded for more than an hour, including recitations in Yorùbá from the Ọ̀sá Ọ̀gúndá verses. Through the story we were all introduced to Akámarà, the universal spirit that began the universe and the five stages of creation. When it was over, there was a moment of reverent silence, followed by a standing ovation. Everyone there had just learned something profound that they did not know previously about Yorùbá cosmology, including ontology and epistemology—from how the universe was created to how the different races came to be.

The Alásùwadà conference was successful despite the many challenges in bringing together Ifá initiates and practitioners across linguistic, national, and ethnic boundaries. Olóyè Ṣọlágbadé Pópóọlá was the unifying force (other than Alásùwadà) that brought everyone together even as his absence was a source of division. It was ironic that he was unable to attend due to problems obtaining a visa to transit through a third country (the United States, the United Kingdom, or the Netherlands) to come to Trinidad from Nigeria.[17] People who had come from Venezuela, Colombia, and Mexico specifically to meet with him and learn from their spiritual elder were visibly and vocally disappointed by his absence. Most of his students are lucky if they see him once a year due both to his obligations in Nigeria and to his large number of spiritual children (easily a thousand) throughout the Americas. Even though he regularly travels four to five months of the year, he cannot visit all of his shrines and meet with all of his godchildren in a single year. Many of his newer initiates study locally under his more senior priests. In his absence from the conference, friction began to manifest, as was foretold through both divination and the manifestation of Oshun.

During ritual work with the ancestors on the second day of the conference, frustrations became public over a lack of communication (even with the translation gear) between the Spanish- and English-speaking participants, those from Latin America and those from Trinidad and the United States, respectively. Encouraged by the shrine leaders, people gave voice to their frustration. And something amazing happened. New bridges were forged, facilitated by the chant, which invoked memories of Oshun's visit and her message ("Unity is strength, strength is power"). And aiding the new connections were instructions from the ancestors. All those present were to greet Iya Sangowunmi and Oba Adefunmi to receive their blessings, and then we were to hug each and every person present (figure 5.4). With the dozens of people present, this process took all morning and pushed back the scheduled presentations. However, barriers had been broken down by the courage of people who spoke on difference. And, facilitated by the intervention of divine energies (Oshun and Egúngún), everyone there engaged in spiritual praxis, an embodied and productive ritualistic coming together. It was through spiritual knowledge in action that the distance of difference was spanned.

This theme of unity across difference, a theme central to many postcolonial countries and certainly to the national culture of Trinidad, would arise over and over again during the conference. It was very clear that the work of

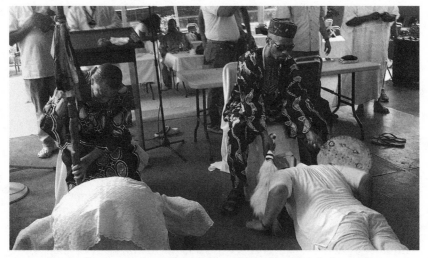

FIGURE 5.4 Iya Sangowunmi and Oba Adefunmi II give blessings during an Egungun ritual as members of the Alasuwada conference prostrate (dobale) in front of them. Ile Eko Sango/Osun Mil'osa, Santa Cruz, Trinidad, 2012. Photo by N. Fadeke Castor.

Alásùwadà was being conducted in the very act of coming together to learn about Alásùwadà. Drawing on spiritual epistemologies and ethical codes, utilizing forms of spiritual technology (divination, possession) to access sacred knowledge and solve problems—all to the end of acting together. Over and over again, we learned the theme from Alásùwadà—a single blade of grass is weak, but many blades of grass bound together are strong. By late Sunday night, the feeling of unity was palpable. Many hours past the planned end of the conference, people sang and danced together in joyous celebration of that unity.

Late Sunday night, in a separate meeting away from the celebration, the organizers and presenters considered options for creating a platform. They focused on crafting a set of declarations that called for people to work together across differences, to elevate their collective destinies with a focus on the development of iwa-pele (good character) on both individual and collective levels. Also included were support for families and children, collective economics, and other initiatives. The draft platform was then brought back to the gathered assembly, where it was passed by a majority vote. As the celebration progressed, vows were made to continue to build the movement under the banner of Alásùwadà and develop further social structures informed by Ifá principles. Very late Sunday night, the conference closed with music, dancing, and fellowship as all who were gathered felt the truth of Oshun's message: "Unity is strength, strength is power."

Localizing Ifà

How can the establishment of a new Ifá lineage in Trinidad and its consequent events (such as the Alásùwadà conference/movement) be viewed as spiritual citizenship? I find the possibility for a liberatory and decolonizing practice as spiritual knowledge is put into practice to reimagine identities and communities. To the extent that these identities are critically engaged and new forms of collectivity are constructed, I find the hope for social change. And as with any change, things can go either way—if a difference is made, it can be liberal (in the sense of open) or it can be conservative (reinforcing previously held beliefs and social structures). By no means do I think that we can chart these changes in a linear neo-evolutionary manner. In fact, quite the opposite! It is the visible dynamics that oscillate between these poles, and occasionally escape them altogether, that intrigue me.

One site where the new Ifá lineages are making an impact is on existing leadership structures. There have been changes with all the new priests along the lines of class (as discussed earlier, those with access to U.S. dollars can get initiated more easily in Nigeria or even in Trinidad), and as class is racialized, this also has an impact on the "color" and background of new leadership. On another level, Trinidad had been marked by the dominance of women in positions of spiritual leadership, as has been the case in many sites of the diaspora. The new Ifá lineages are privileging male leadership. Unlike in other places (notably Cuba), Ifá in Trinidad is not restricted only to men. However, those learning the rites, including memorizing the literary corpus of ẹsẹ odu Ifá, seem to be primarily men (reflected, for example, in the makeup of the Council of Traditional Afrikan Chiefs of Trinidad and Tobago). The new leadership that is emerging is predominantly male, with the leaders acting as priests and gatekeepers to spiritual knowledge and authority. This gendered dynamic continues to unfold in the contemporary moment as new devotees are initiated and as new initiates begin to train. There may yet again be a shift that moves this balance in a different direction. All of these dynamics certainly deserve our attention and continuing intersectional analysis.

An intriguing impact of the new Ifá lineage on Trinidad Orisha, emerging now as Trinidad Ifá/Orisha, has been the localization of Ifá practices and their adaptation by Trini Orisha shrines, both Yorùbá-centric and Trini-centric. Over a series of interviews in 2011, I brought up this issue of "local-ization" with the priests and devotees I talked with. In part, this was due to a conversation at Awo Ogunbowale's Shrine Ile Isokan, Ifebo Compound, Febeau Village, in Lower Santa Cruz on July 4, 2010. The issue that domi-nated our conversation after a Sunday Ifà service was how to both incorpo-rate the new knowledge from Nigeria and also respect the ancestral heritage that had been passed down to them. From that conversation, I took away a sense of the Ile members' deep commitment to Orisha and Ifá as a spiritual practice, beyond the national or cultural affiliation. More important than where the knowledge came from was whether it worked, the efficacy of that knowledge. Yet this was in tension with a deep commitment to honoring the ancestors and the way that they had done ritual alongside the pull of the implied authenticity of the imagined "Africa" (i.e., If it's from Nigeria, it must be from an ancestral practice going back over generations. And don't we all come from there anyway? Is that not also our ancestral practice?).

In 2011, I explored these issues further in a series of interviews, finding many diverse perspectives on localization and one resounding theme. The commonality in people's positions on the local implementation of Ifá was that, yes, there would be a Trinidadian element or interpretation put to the ritual practices. Local herbs are used in the *ewe* (a sacred mixture of herbs, liquids, and other ingredients) for consecration of ritual items and people in initiations (among other things). Local animals are given as ẹbọ offerings to Ifá and Orisha. And, finally, local fruits, vegetables, and other foodstuffs also feed the spirits. However, I found in my research that the drive to localize these new Ifá lineages, and their accompanying knowledge systems, goes even deeper. As highlighted in the section on Alásùwadà in this chapter we see an example of new verses (ẹsẹ) of odu Ifá being written in Trinidad, adding their story to the corpus of knowledge preserved in Ifá. On another level, spirits continue to manifest, both ancestral and Orisha, at great frequency in Trinidad, giving instructions on how things are to be done. "More drumming, more dancing, more joy!" These are the mes-sages coming through that counterbalance the very cerebral and intellectual teachings of Ifá (especially in the diaspora). As is the way in the Caribbean, and certainly in Trinidad, things are not "either/or." Rather, they are "both/and." Ultimately, it is not either Trinidad Orisha or Nigerian Ifá; it is both Orisha and Ifá in Trinidad emerging to find a new balance that honors both ancestral roots (those who have come before) and routes (those we have traveled from and returned to).

This new balance was very visible in the Alásùwadà conference and was one of its more remarkable contributions. A new verse of the odu Ifá for the conference, Ìrẹtẹ̀ Ìká, was written out of the intense energy produced from the coming together of Ifá priests and practitioners from throughout the Americas, literally an expression of Alásùwadà's energy. This contribution to the corpus of ẹsẹ odu Ifá (sacred Ifá verses) represents a paradigm shift as contributions are now being made from Trinidad. The text of odù is centered in Yorubaland and contains an expansive body of its oral history, medicine, philosophy, and theology. In writing a new verse for Ìrẹtẹ̀ Ìka, the Awo present at the conference were inscribing the diaspora experience into the historical narrative of odu Ifá. I return to the small sample of this new verse to illustrate this narrative arch:

> It is Irete and Ika that would guide and bring them together.
> Children of those that were taken away,
> long ago to the lands of the West.
> Alásùwadà it is Irete Ika that shall open the way for us to come
>   together,
> to change the world forever.
> It is Irete Ika.

Overcoming this legacy of the African diaspora, marked by the Atlantic slave trade and slavery, framed the recounting of experiences that weekend up in the hills of Santa Cruz. This historic dispersal of African people was the reason for the different cultures and languages gathered at the conference. This was the reason for the divisions of language and nationality, of race and ethnicity. And this was what Alásùwadà, together with Oshun and Egungun, through the vision and experience of spiritual citizenship, had provided us with the àṣẹ to overcome.

Iri tu wili tu wili
Iri tu wili tu wili
Iri tu wili-wili
Koo tu reke-reke
Dia fun Origun
Ti nloo s'eda ibu orun ati aye ni'gba ijinji
Iri tu wili tu wili
Iri tu wili tu wili
Iri tu wili-wili
Koo tu reke-reke
Dia fun Olu-Iwaye
Ti nloo p'ero si ibu orun ati aye in kutukutu owuro
Iri tu wili tu wili
Iri tu wili tu wili
Iri tu wili-wili
Koo tu reke-reke
Dia fun Baba-Asemu-Egun-Sunwon
Ti nloo yan ipa fun ibu orun ati aye ni'gba iwase
Iri tu wili tu wili
Iri tu wili tu wili
Iri tu wili-wili
Koo tu reke-reke
Dia fun Olofin-Otete
Ti yoo tuu iwa wa si'le aye
Ni'jo to nloo gba ado iwa l'owo Olodumare
Ni'jo ti won yoo tu iwa s'aye
Horo eepe kan soso
O wa di agbon eepe kan

Agbon eepe kan lo da aye
Iri tu wili tu wili
La fi da aye
Oun la bu da ile
Ki ire susu o waa su piripiri
Ire gbogbo wa d'asuwa
Origun lo bi Olu-Iwaye
Olu-Iwaye lo bi Baba-Asemu-Egun-Sunwon
Baba-Asemu-Egun-Sunwon lo bi Olofin-Otete
Olofin-Otete lo ru agbon eepe wa sile aye
Olofin-Otete gbe agbon eepe da Ile-Ife
Ire gbogbo wa d'asuwa
Sikan ni Mogun
Agiriyan ni Morere eerun
Asuwa ni Morere eeyan
Asuwa da Aye
Asuwa da Orun
Asuwa da s'ile
Asekun-Suwada ni'gba iwa a se
Asekun-Suwada ni'gba iwa a gun
Asuwada ni'gba iwa a ro
Irun pe susu won gb'ori
Irun agbon pe susu won a di ojontarigi
Omi pe susu won a d'okun
Odo pe susu won a d'osa
Igi pe susu, won a di'gbo
Eruwa pe susu, won a d'odan
Irawo pe susu, won a gb'orun
Agbon pe susu f'owo t'ile
Ita pe susu bo'le
Giri-giri o tan ni'le aladi
Giri-giri o tan l'agiyan eerun
Asuwa ni t'oyin
Asuwa ni t'ado
Asuwa l'eeran nhu ni'nu oko
Asuwa ni ti osusu owo
Asuwa l'eeran nhu ni'nu ahere
Asuwa ni ti Elegiiri

Opo eniyan tii la a pe l'ogun
Asuwa laa b'odan
Asuwa l'esu fii je'ko
Asu opo suu laa ba yindinyindin ni'nu ile e won
Asu opo suu laa ba yaya l'agiriyan
Asuwa opo suu laa ba ikan ninu ogan
Asuwa opo suu la ba ekunkun l'eti omi
Asuwa opo suu laa ba labelabe l'oko
Asuwa opo suu laa ba oore l'odo
Asuwa opo suu laa ba lamilami
Ewe adosusu kii duro l'oun nikan
Asuwa opo suu laa ba ebe
Asuwa opo suu laa ba Igi Erimi
Asuwa opo suu laa ba eja egbele l'okun
Asuwa opo suu laa ba egungun
Akaraba egungun
Bo ba si je l'odo
Gbogbo eja ni te lee
Alasuwada mo pe o o
Ki o ran iwa susu wa
Ki o ko ire gbogbo wa ba mi o
B'ori kan ba sunwon
A ran Igba o
Ori Origun-Aseda sunwon
O ran mi
B'ori kan sunwon
A ran igba
Ori mi to sunwon
Lo ran yin
Ori i yin to sunwon
Lo ran mi
B'ori kan ba sunwon
A ran igba

May the dew burst out quickly
May the dew burst out rapidly
May the dew burst out continuously
And be vast throughout the expanse

These were the declarations of Ifa for Origun
When going to coordinate the creation of the vast expanse of the
  universe during the dawn of time
May the dew burst out quickly
May the dew burst out rapidly
May the dew burst out continuously
And be vast throughout the expanse
These were the declarations of Ifa for Olu-Iwaye
When going to soothe and pacify the hotness of the universe during the
  dawn of life
May the dew burst out quickly
May the dew burst out rapidly
May the dew burst out continuously
And be vast throughout the expanse
These were the declarations of Ifa for Baba-Asemu-Egun-Sunwon
When going to assign roles and provide order to the vast expanse of the
  universe during the dawn of creation
May the dew burst out quickly
May the dew burst out rapidly
May the dew burst out continuously
And be vast throughout the expanse
These were the declarations of Ifa for Olofin-Otete
When going to steer the boat of existence to the earth
And when going to collect the miniature gourd of destiny from
  Olodumare
When going to steer the boat of existence to the earth
A grain of sand
Transformed into a basket full of sand
A basket full of sand is what was used to create the earth
May the dew burst out quickly
This was the command used to create the universe
It was also used to create the land
So that clusters of goodness and well being would gather henceforth
All goodness and well being clustered in harmony
Origun begot Olu-Iwaye
Olu-Iwaye begot Baba-Asemu-Egun-Sunwon
Baba-Asemu-Egun-Sunwon begot Olofin-Otete
It was Olofin-Otete who carried the basket of sand to the earth

Olofin-Otete created the land of Ife (for habitation)
[Olofin-Otete, primordial name for Oduduwa]
Indeed, all goodness and well-being clustered in harmony
Sikan insects swarm around Ogun shrines
The anthill is the abode of ants
Groups of human beings cluster together
The creation of the planets was manifested in clusters
Likewise that of the heavens
Likewise that of the earth
To multiply and arrange during the dawn of life
To multiply and organize from the very beginning of existence
All creations have been occurring in clusters since the beginning of time
Human hair clusters together and situates itself on the head
A man's facial hair clusters together and becomes thick and bushy
Drops of water cluster together to become mighty seas
Brooks cluster together to become lagoons
Trees cluster together to become forests
Grasses cluster together to become savannas
Stars cluster together and situate themselves in the heavens
Hornets cluster together to reside on the wall of a house
Red ants cluster together on the ground
The nests of Aladi insects are never bereft of occupants
An anthill is never bereft of ants
Bees cluster into swarms
Ado insects cluster into swarms
To act as a group is the character of the eeran grass on the farm
To act in multitude is the attitude of the broom
Eeran grass grows in clumps in the farmhouse
Elegiiri usually fly in flocks
A large number of people moving together is an army
Banyan plants are found in tufts
Esu [locusts] devour plants in swarms
Maggots are found clustered in their abodes
Yaya insects are found clustered in anthills
White ants are found clustered in large anthills
Ekunkun are found clustered in water
Blade grasses are found clustered on the farm
Oore plants are found clustered by the riverside

Dragonflies move in swarms
Adosusu plants do not grow in singles but in tufts
A heap of earth for planting is seen in clusters
In clusters do we find Erinmi trees
In clusters do we find baby fish in the ocean
In clusters do we find the Egungun [ancestors]
The Akaraba fish
When it eats in the water
All other fish will follow it in droves
Lo, the maker of this perfect order, Alasuwada, I beseech you
Please send a conglomerate of good essences
And bring abundant blessings and Ire to me
If one Ori is good
It will extend to two hundred others
The Ori of Origun the creator is blessed
And it affects me positively
If one Ori is blessed
It will extend to two hundred others
My Ori that is blessed
Has affected you positively
Your Ori that is blessed
Has affected me positively
If one Ori is blessed
It will affect two hundred others

The verse was provided for this book by Olóyè Ṣọlágbadé Pópóọlá, according to whom it "shares with us how each and every follower and priest should be interacting with all forms of life during this sojourn." (For further information on Ifá's moral and ethical code see Pópóọlá 2014.)

NAME	ASPECT OF NATURE	POWER
Olódùmarè	Supreme Being; God; creator and owner of all things	
Eshu/Èṣù	crossroads	possibilities; messenger
Òrúnmìlà	all living things	wisdom; knowledge; divination
Osain/Òsanyìn	herbs/plants	medicine; healing through herbs
Oshun/Òṣun	river/fresh water	creativity; women's power; fertility
Yemanja/Yemọja	ocean/salt water	motherhood
Oya	wind	storms; wind; thunder
Shango/Ṣàngó	thunder	justice; kingship
Ogun	iron	warrior; technology
Mama Latay/Onílè	earth	ground; stability
Shakpana/Ṣọ̀npọ̀nná	pestilence	illness; healing

Note: This brief sampling of Orisha is not meant to be exhaustive or illustrative. The number of orisha is said to 201 or 801 where the "1" represents infinity; for every aspect of Olódùmarè is sacred and represented by an Orisha. This chart is suggestive of the wide breadth and scope of Yorùbá deities.

I I I I I I I I	II II II II II II II II	II II I I I I II II	I I II II II II I I
1. ÈJÌ OGBÈ	2. ÒYÈKÚ MÉJÌ	3. ÌWÒRÌ MÉJÌ	4. ÒDÍ MÉJÌ
I I I I II II II II	II II II II I I I I	I I II II II II II II	II II II II II II I I
5. ÌROSÙN MÉJÌ	6. ÒWÓNRÍN MÉJÌ	7. ÒBÀRÀ MEJI	8. ÒKÀNRÀN MÉJÌ
I I I I I I II II	II II I I I I I I	II II I I II II II II	II II II II I I II II
9. ÒGÚNDÁ MÉJÌ	10. ÒSÁ MÉJÌ	11. ÌKÁ MÉJÌ	12. ÒTÚRÓPÒN MÉJÌ
I I II II I I I I	I I I I II II I I	I I II II I I II II	II II I I II II I I
13. ÒTÚRÁ MÉJÌ	14. ÌRÈTÈ MEJI	15. ÒSÉ MÉJÌ	16. OFUN MÉJÌ

Notes: 1. The remaining 240 permutations of odù Ifá are made by combining the right leg of one major odù with the left leg of another major odù.

EXAMPLE: I I
               II II
               I I
               I II
          ÒSÉ 'TÚRÁ

2. The order of the odù Ifá reflects their seniority, with number one being the highest. This order can be different based upon Ifá lineage.

For more on odù Ifá, including two verses of each odù Ifá, see Awo Salami's *Ifá: A Complete Divination* (2002).

Note on Orthography

1 Many thanks (*Ese pupo*) go to Chris Corcoran for her assistance with the ortho-graphic notes and linguistic terminology. Any mistakes or shortcomings in the text remain my own.

Preface

1 That state of in-betweenness that I would later study in the works of Victor Turner (1969, 1986) and a state that I viscerally recognized and knew well.

Introduction

1 Having received new titles in the past twenty years, including a kingship, he is now His Royal Majesty Oba Adébólú Fátunmise, the Àdàgbà of Iyánfowórogi.

2 See Peel (2001) for more on the ethnogenesis of the Yorùbá people.

3 The late 1960s up through the early 1970s was a long decade of social critique and transition across the globe marked by struggles for decolonization, civil rights, and Black Power. This was especially the case in the postcolonial world that expe-rienced waves of protest, social upheaval, and political pecarity. In Trinidad this time of social critique that spans the late 1960s into the mid-to-late 1970s has been locally constructed as the Black Power revolution (Oxaal 1971, Pantin 1990, Ryan and Stewart 1995). My concern in this book is with the religious, cultural, and so-cial movement that emerged from this period. As such, throughout this text I refer mainly to the 1970 Black Power movement, especially when referencing the concen-tration of events that occurred largely in 1970. Certainly these events were socially and politically presaged in previous years and had reverberations throughout the following decade. At times when wanting to emphasize the long durée beyond the events of 1970 I use the term 1970s Black Power movement. For the sake of brevity at times I also just write Black Power to refer to both the events of that time and the consciousness raised through the power of their social critique.

4 Now-for-now is a Trini term that indicates being present in the moment with little concern for the immediate past or the immediate future. The corollary in American culture would be the frequently invoked concept of mindfulness. See Birth's *Any Time Is Trinidad Time* (1999) for more on Trini time.

5 For more on African religious practices in Trinidad during the nineteenth century and the pre-independence twentieth century, see Trotman (1976, 2003).

6 This by no means represents an exhaustive or canonical list of literature on diaspora or more specifically the African diaspora.

7 This is also true of other global religious communities, from the various traditions or lineages within Christianity and Islam to lesser known religions. Though my ethnographic representations here are very specific to African diasporic religions, they may be recognizable to scholars and practitioners of other religions. I do not claim either universality or exceptionalism. Instead I hope that in my own observations there will be synergies, resonances, and conflicts that open spaces for dialogue and reflection.

8 I say this without dismissing the waves of African immigrants who have settled in the Americas over the last hundred-plus years. These immigrants are an often unrecognized addition to the African community in the Americas (with all the complexities of being interpolated into racial systems largely nonexistent in their home countries).

9 For Hindu and Orisha interpenetrations, see also Mahabir and Maharaj (1996). See M. McNeal (2007) for a comprehensive and insightful analysis of the interplay of Orisha and Hindu religions as two complementary facets of post-Creole multiculturalism.

10 For a rich religious history of Oyotunji Village, see Hucks (2014); for an ethnographically informed analysis of the community, see K. Clarke (2004).

11 *Canboulay*, from the French Creole *cannes brulees* for "burning cane," refers locally to the nineteenth-century gatherings that included drumming, singing, and dance held by freed Creole slaves, liberated Africans, and the descendants of both. Originally tied to celebrations of the harvest and the end of slavery in August, the celebrations became part of the pre-Lenten Carnival complex in the late 1800s.

12 See Castor (2009).

Chapter 1. The Spirit of Black Power

1 The historical narrative of 1970 Black Power that I present in this chapter is partial in two important aspects. First, the focus here is on the public events of a singular year, leaving out the larger historical frame of the long 1970s decade (from the late 1960s to the mid-to-late 1970s). Especially now as the fifty-year anniversary of Black Power approaches, this wider frame is a larger project that calls out to be done (while outside the scope of this book). And secondly, the voices of those who lived through those days of protest, and nights with police pounding on the doors, is a story that surely needs to be told. I extend many thanks to Attillah Springer (Tillah Willah, see https://tillahwillah.wordpress.com/) for her poignant evocation of Black Power memories. I hope that in calling attention to these absences this chapter will open the way for these stories to be shared in print.

2 It is clear that there was interchange and exchange culturally and spiritually throughout the West African region, going south into Central Africa and north toward Sierra Leone. Much has been written about the creolization of Sierra Leone,

whose particular colonial history as a location for settlement of numerous different peoples, many through repatriation, created an especially intensive environment of cultural contact. See Nunley (1987).

3 Here I am thinking of the circumambulation (see Aiyejina and Gibbons 1999, 202), the drum styles and rhythms, and the technique of placing the altars in the ground characteristic of both Trinidad Orisha and Haitian Vodou. These same characteristics are not as common or prevalent in other shared Yorùbá-based traditions in the diaspora such as Brazilian Candomblé or Cuban Santería. Noting the possible practice of Vodou by former slaves from the French Caribbean, Adderley writes of "Trinidad's vodun-like religion" (2006, 174).

4 The term "Orisha Work" is used in local circulation to address the practices of the leaders and members of and attendees to Orisha shrines, and upon occasion Spiritual Baptist churches. Academically the term has been utilized in the writings of J. D. Elder (1969), Kenneth Lum (2000, esp. 5), and Burton Sankeralli (2002).

5 See Adderley (2006, 92–125).

6 In his study of possession in both the Spiritual Baptist and Orisha religions, *Praising His Name in the Dance* (2000), Lum states, "The Spiritual Baptist Faith and Orisha Work in Trinidad use the same ontology as that of traditional religion," but he also, somewhat contradictorily, says that they "are neither African religions, nor finally Trinidadian versions of African religions" (16). Though he sees both religions as sharing an African (Yorùbá) religious base, Lum claims that their development in Trinidad makes them indigenous religions. I do not find that there is a substantial break, though I do agree that both traditions are highly indigenized. Additionally, as previously stated, I think that African diasporic religions in Trinidad draw on a wider purview than the Yorùbá people throughout West Africa.

7 See Munasinghe (2001a, 153), especially where she discusses the tensions described by scholars of the Caribbean as polarities (e.g., reputation/respectability; Wilson 1995) and finds, attributed to Trouillot (2002) that "the illuminating feature of these studies is that they attempt to capture intangible cultural dispositions that seem to characterize all Caribbean peoples, namely, the systematicity with which Caribbean people maintain multiplicity not only in the sense of movement between roles and types but in terms of types and roles that include movement."

8 Several sources also report the incorporation of Hindu ritual vessels, lithographs, and occasionally deities into the rituals and religious doctrine of Spiritual Baptist and Orisha practices (Houk 1993, 1995; Mahabir and Maharaj 1996).

9 The transition of community and church is poignantly illustrated in Earl Lovelace's novel *The Wine of Astonishment* (1984).

10 Stokely Carmichael was born in Port of Spain, Trinidad, on June 29, 1941; in 1952 he moved with his family to New York, where he attended the rigorous Bronx High School of Science. Though he is known for his leadership of the Black Power movement in the United States, his Trinidadian roots gave him particular salience and authority in the Caribbean. After speaking out against U.S. imperialism and the Vietnam War in 1969, Carmichael moved to Guinea and changed his name to Kwame Ture.

11 There were large riots in October 1968 at the University of West Indies, Mona campus in Jamaica after Walter Rodney's deportation from Jamaica. Pantin observes of Rodney that "his publication, 'Groundings With My Brothers' was considered required reading," which brought together academics with "brothers on the block" (1990, 29). The events in Jamaica were followed with considerable interest by Trinidadians and may have inspired, in part, reach out of university organizations, like NJAC, to community and labor organizations. For more on Black Power in Jamaica, see Nettleford (1972).

12 At the time, her arrest caused much consternation in the community and resulted in Valerie Belgrave's marginalization. Decades later, Belgrave remains a part of the Afro-Trinidadian middle-class community in good standing, as evidenced by her membership in several middle-class organizations.

13 More than thirty years later, in the new millennium, the Emancipation Support Committee (ESC) would incorporate all three colors in hand-painted flags that were handed out in its annual Kambule procession.

14 The Shanty Town mentioned here was moved and is now called the Beetham Gardens, after the highway that borders it on one side.

15 Much as the term "black" in the United Kingdom has been broadened to encompass people of South Asian descent, including Indians and Pakistanis, as a descriptive term (though less so as a term of self-identification). For more on this, see Baker, Diawara, and Lindeborg (1996); Carby (1999); Gilroy (1991); Hall (1996b); Hesse (2000); Mercer (1994).

16 However, Robinson would continue his successful political career. In fact, more than fifteen years later, in 1986, he would become prime minister as the political leader of the National Association for Reconciliation (NAR) government. Subsequent to this, Robinson would be president (1997–2003) in the PNM-led government, and in 2002 he cast the deciding vote for prime minister between the PNM and the United National Congress (UNC), breaking a parliamentary tie and changing the political direction of Trinidad's governance. For more on Robinson's politics, see Meighoo (2003).

17 Ironically, the tribunal was largely composed of African military officers who would be "suddenly recalled home to take up fresh appointment with a new government that had taken power by coup d'etat!" (Pantin 1990, 94).

18 "Overnight the 'curfew party' was born" as for weeks people gathered from 6:00 PM to 6:00 AM (Pantin 1990, 100). These parties would reemerge twenty years later, in 1990, during another state of emergency, resulting from the attempted coup led by Abu Bakr and the Jameet al Muslimeen.

19 For more on Carnival fetes as sorting mechanisms reinforcing social categories and stratification in the context of neoliberalism see Castor (2009).

Chapter 2. Multicultural Movements

1 This representation of events is based on a video of the Second Annual Orisha Family Day.

2 For more on Springer's role in the Orisha community, see Hucks (2006, 30–33).

3 The Ọòni is largely held to be the political and spiritual leader of the Yorùbá people on the continent and throughout the diaspora.

4 During this period, at the turn of the millennium, Orisha Family Day held a central place in the public calendar of the Orisha community. Following shifts in leadership, the passing of key Orisha elders, and the emergence of Ifá in the middle of the first decade of the twenty-first century, Orisha Family Day has fallen by the wayside.

5 Egúngún is an initiatory masquerade lineage, from the Yorùbá region of Nigeria that honors the ancestors, both familial and collective. For more on Egúngún in Nigeria, see Drewal (1992, esp. chap. 6).

6 Springer's comment was in the context of decades of broken promises by previous administrations and political leaders; for more with regard to Spiritual Baptists, see Henry (2003, 67).

7 For heuristic purposes, I refer to "Afro-Creoles" in general as a category of middle-class African descendants in Trinidad, specifically active in politics and cultural development. See Castor (2009) for further differentiation of the African middle class in Trinidad. For more on the Creole middle class in the Caribbean, specifically in Jamaica, see D. Thomas (2004).

8 In 1956, Dr. Eric Williams, a young Oxford-trained scholar, founded the People's National Movement (PNM) from a strong network of support formed in the Teacher's Union (and the earlier People's Education Movement, a branch of the Teachers Education and Cultural Association). The PNM, under the leadership of Dr. Williams, brought the country to independence in 1962 (after the brief and failed experiment of the West Indian Federation). Under the party slogan "Massa Day Done," the PNM ushered in a nearly thirty-year period of Afro-Trinidadian political, social, and economic dominance. This leadership in large part reinforced Indo-Trinidadian beliefs that they had been largely excluded from access to positions of political and economic power, especially highly coveted government and civil service jobs, under both colonial and postcolonial rule. For an analysis of Williams's rhetorical strategies, see especially Rohlehr (1998); Ryan (1972).

9 Two major works on East Indians and national identity in Trinidad call attention to this distinction with their titles: *Callaloo Nation: Metaphors of Race and Religious Identity among South Asians in Trinidad* (Khan 2004a) and *Callaloo or Tossed Salad? East Indians and the Cultural Politics of Identity in Trinidad* (Munasinghe 2001b). As Khan describes it, "A 'callaloo' society (literally, a multiple-ingredient stew, also the national dish) represents Trinidad, the callaloo nation, as profoundly cosmopolitan and democratic through a coexisting diversity that results in racial harmony and other marks of modernity" (2004b, 167).

10 For an overview of legislation criminalizing African religious practices in the Caribbean, see Paton (2009, 2015) and J. S. Handler and Bilby (2013).

11 The ordinance allowed persecution based on observation of the following practices: " a) binding the head with white cloth, b) holding of lighted candles with both hands, c) ringing of a bell at intervals during meetings, d) violent shaking of the body and limbs, e) shouting and grunting, f) flowers held in the hands of the per-

son present and g) white chalk marks about the door" (Herskovits and Herskovits 1947, 345).

12 Obeah is a largely pejorative term originating in British colonial rule and directed at non-Christian healing and spiritual practices utilized by Africans and their descendants. Bongo is an African diasporic funeral rite consisting of a ritual dance and music performed the night before the burial.

13 A major spiritual and political leader of Hindu Indo-Trinidadians, secretary-general of the Maha Sabha, Satnarayan Maharaj appealed in a letter to the editor for Prime Minister Patrick Manning to deny entrance to evangelist Benny Hill on the basis of the Summary Offences Act (chapter 11:02, S43. {1}; which legislates against obeah), which he quotes in full: "Any person who, by the practice of obeah or by any occult means or by any assumption of the supernatural power or knowledge intimidates or attempts to intimidate any person, obtains or endeavors to obtain any chattel money or valuable security from any other person, or to restore any person to health and any other person who procures, counsels, induces, or persuades or endeavors to persuade any person to commit any such offence, is liable to imprisonment for six month, and subject to the Corporal Punishment Acts, may be sentenced to undergo corporal punishment" (S. Maharaj 2006).

14 For a fictional account of this historical period and the persecution of Spiritual Baptists in Trinidad, see Earl Lovelace's novel *The Wine of Astonishment* (1984).

15 See Jean Comaroff and John Comaroff (2009) for more on the interplay of identity (ethnic and religious) with negotiations of legal entitlements and other forms of commodification in the neoliberal moment.

16 For the full text of the bill, see, http://www.ttparliament.org/legislations/b1999h10p.pdf, accessed March 30, 2016.

17 In 2001, the National Council of Elders was recognized under the Orisha Marriage Act. Then, in 2005, ten individuals, and the shrines they represented, registered as marriage officers under the auspices of the council. (*Trinidad and Tobago Gazette* 2001, 2005).

18 According to Hucks this act was "the first legal enactment to legitimize the status of African-derived religions in the diaspora world" (2006, 33).

19 "Orisa Community Repeats Call for Public Holiday," *Trinidad Guardian*, July 10, 2012. Years later, at the time this book went to press, advocates for an Orisha holiday were still organizing with no tangible results.

20 The NAR was a coalition of four groups representing different ethnic factions, including Indian and African populations that overwhelmingly won its general elections in 1986. However, within a year of taking power, external economic pressures and internal politics caused the coalition to fall apart along largely ethnic lines (see Premdas 1999).

21 See Munasinghe (2001b, 14–17).

22 Archbishop Burke's switch to the UNC has been linked to Panday's sponsorship of a national holiday for Spiritual Baptists (Henry 2003, 67).

23 It should be noted that in 2006, former prime minister Basdeo Panday was indicted for failure to disclose foreign bank account holdings in the millions while in office.

Having been tried, convicted, and sentenced to two years, he was released from the Port of Spain jail after one weekend because the jail did not have the facilities to keep a prisoner of his "standing."

24 The term "outside" refers here both to the common English usage of the term to indicate position relative to a boundary (as the opposite of inside) and to the Trinidadian English usage that refers to kinship relations outside of conventional legal unions—as in "his outside children," referring to a man's children with one woman (or more) while he is married (or cohabiting) with another woman.

25 For an overview of Black Nationalism that aims for a middle ground between "celebratory and hypercritical accounts of Black Power and black nationalism," see Glaude (2002), especially the introduction; quotation on p. 2. Hucks (2012) is a masterful historical study of the Yorùbá religion and Black Nationalism in the United States.

Chapter 3. Around the Bend

1 The edited transcription that I provide here is a selection from Baba Erinfolami's prayer and comes from a video I recorded at IESOM on June 24, 2011. Baba graciously helped to clarify some audio that was unclear but any mistakes are my own.

2 See Chief F.A.M.A.'s *Fundamentals of the Yoruba Religion (Orisa Worship)* for an insightful essay on the use of Ìbà for prayer in the diaspora versus its use in Yorubaland (1993, 1–8).

3 Iya Sangowunmi's birth name is Pat McLeod. Her name change came from her initiation as an Orisha priest or *Iyalorisha*, to the Orisha Shango in Oyo, Nigeria.

4 In Trinidadian terms, a description of African clothes often visible in Trinidad during the annual Emancipation celebrations.

5 In August 1999, though I had been in Trinidad for only a couple of days, I had seen mainly "Western" clothes of suits, blouses, and jeans on the street. I had yet to go to an Emancipation celebration, where large numbers of Trinidadians would be wearing African clothes on the streets.

6 For the link between the World Congress of Orisha Tradition and Culture and Black Nationalist politics in Brazil, see Matory (2005, 171–72). For another perspective on the connection between Black Nationalist politics and the Orisha religion in the United States, see K. Clarke (2004); Hucks (2012).

7 Among the volunteers was Keith McNeal, at that time a U.S. graduate student conducting ethnographic fieldwork in Trinidad. His perspective on his time working in the Congress Secretariat can be found in K. E. McNeal (2011, 281–84).

8 President A. N. R. Robinson and his wife hold honorary Yorùbá chieftaincy titles from his 1991 visit to Nigeria, given to them by the Ọ̀ọ̀ni of Ilé-Ifẹ̀.

9 This study uses the exchange rate of roughly TT$6 = $US1.

10 It is important to remember that the racial topography of African descendants in Trinidad includes categories ranging from "Trini white" to "Spanish" to "red" to "brown" to "black." For more on the particularities of ethnicity and race in Trinidad, see Yelvington's important edited collection *Trinidad Ethnicity* (1993).

11 Frances Henry, longtime researcher of Orisha in Trinidad and conference participant, shared my ethnographic observations. She notes: "From the outset and looking only at this arrangement, it seemed clear that there would be very local observation. Orisha practitioners and devotees are largely drawn from the working class and are not accustomed to attending events at one of the country's most prestigious hotels. Moreover, the TT$500 registration fee was felt to be excessive; most practitioners would find it a hardship to pay that fee. In addition, many of them live out of the city and would either have to find accommodation with friends and relatives or alternatively travel back and forth each day, incurring more expenses" (2003, 148).

12 Scholars have long noted this focus on connecting with West African, more specifically Yorùbá, religious practices, including Aiyejina and Gibbons (1999); Henry (1999, 2000, 2003); Houk (1993, 1995, 1999); Hucks (2006); Lum (2000); K. E. McNeal (2011); Scher (1997). This dynamic is not limited to Trinidad. It can be found to differing extents throughout African religious traditions in the diaspora, specifically in North America Orisha/Ifá and Santería lineages (see Palmié 1995; K. Clarke 2004).

13 Though I prefer this term, it is not without problems. While more specific than "Africanization," the use of the term "Yorùbá" here runs the risk of eliding the many cultures of West and Central Africa that have contributed to these religious practices, both in Yorubaland and especially in the diaspora. See the opening section in chapter 1 for more on the many cultures that inform what is commonly referenced as the "Yorùbá" tradition or Yorùbá-based religions in the diaspora.

14 This asset, alongside others, has been sold off over the past decade (2005–15) to support the shifting fortunes of the family.

15 See Hucks and Stewart (2003, 179–81) for a concise history of the importance of Carnival to Trinidad's culture.

16 This public debate would echo previous (and recurring) ones about the role of religious and/or spiritual representation in Carnival mas'. For example, Peter Minshall's mas' band, Hallelujah, sparked one such controversy, as have the incorporation of Hindi themes and images in mas' designs. Interestingly enough, the recurrent use of Spiritual Baptist "costuming," dance modes, and other motifs in calypso and soca performances in competitions and fetes has caused little or no controversy.

17 Interestingly, in 2015, the the queen of Carnival title went to a presentation entitled "Sweet Waters of Africa," which was performed to Ella Andall's song "Oshun Karele." (This title goes to the best large masquerade in the women's division, parallel to the men's division and king of Carnival title.) Both the presentation and the choice of song were inspired by the Orisha Oshun.

18 See the Trinidad Tourism Development Company's festival brochure, 26–27, at http://www.gotrinidadandtobago.com/resources/documents/13/tnt-festivals.pdf (accessed March 12, 2016). Also note that the Yorùbá-centric trend in Trinidad Orisha is not represented by a singular unified approach to Orisha practices and issues of lineage authority. In this chapter, I focus on one other path, that of Iya Sangow-

unmi and her shrine. Different positions could also be followed by close study of other Yorùbá-centric shrines and priests, such as the previously mentioned Egbe Onisin Eledumare and its leader, Babalorisa Oludari Massetungi (for a profile of Baba Oludari, see Henry 2003, 96), or Eniyan Wa and its leader, Iya Amoye (now deceased, iba). Both of these shrines organize their activities around a series of annual festivals (rather than an ẹbọ).

19 I attended the Rain Festival over the span of a decade (most recently in 2012), with extensive photo and video documentation. The Rain Festival presented here is a composite except where specified.

20 More recently, the Rain Festival has been preceded or followed by initiations timed to take advantage of visiting priests, including in 2007 and 2010 a group of Ifá initiates.

21 For a profile of LeRoy Clarke and his relationship to the Orisha religion, see Henry (2003, 93–94).

22 Henry (2003) views this as part of a larger trend that she labels "secularization" of Trinidad Orisha. I would not go this far because this presupposes a Western definition of religion that privileges codified and circumscribed appeals to the divine (Asad 1993).

Chapter 4. Trini Travels

1 Kabala or kabbalah in Trinidad refers to a mystical system of knowledge and ritual grounded in European esoteric religious orders, such as the School of Solomon. The powers invoked on the Kabala side draw from various esoteric texts, including the Sixth and Seventh Book of Moses, and the Lesser and Greater Keys of Solomon; for more on the Kabala in Trinidad see Lum 2000, Chapter 9 and Houk 1993, 90ff.

2 Here I have placed the word "original" in quotes to indicate the imagined and constructed nature of a Yorùbá culture or religion that exists ahistorically and statically outside of time to be discovered or connected with. The people that I worked with in Trinidad, including Baba Erinfolami, are aware of the futility of searching for such an imagined Yorùbá. This chapter and to some extent the next track the impact and tension points of contemporary diaspora meeting contemporary Yorubaland. A similar process for an American Yoruba community of Oyotunji Village is mapped out and wonderfully analyzed in Clarke (2004) and visible in the more U.S.-focused religious history of Hucks (2014).

3 Awo Oluwole Ifakunle Adetutu has an extensive history of study and initiations, with ritual lineage ties ranging from Oyotunji Village in South Carolina to Ejigbo, Ọsun State, Nigeria.

4 Ilé-Ifẹ̀ is a city in Ọsun State, Nigeria, that is the ancestral home for all Yoruba. According to myth, ancient Ilé-Ifẹ̀ is the source of all humanity.

5 On a visit to Trinidad in mid-2015, a friend told me of an upcoming trip to Nigeria, Benin, and Togo being planned for a group from Belmont known as the Rada area, after the Rada family that settled there in the mid-nineteenth century.

6 For more on this, see Castor (2009).

7 See the story "Pssst, Reds" in the opening of Castor (2009) for how I discovered on the streets of Trinidad that I was a red woman.

8 For an excellent discussion of the dynamics between class and color in Haiti, see Trouillot (1994).

9 This relationship is evidenced in his full ritual name, Awo Eniola Orisagbemi Ifagbamila Aworeni Adelekan, after his subsequent initiation to Ifá (Ìtefá) in Ilé-Ifẹ̀ under the direction of Chief Adelekan.

10 For an insightful and informative ethnographic exploration of when the diaspora meets the "homeland," see K. Clarke (2004, chap. 2).

11 In the Oshun sailout, offerings to the water deity are assembled on trays that literally sail into the ocean.

12 The notable individuals referenced here include, among others, Jeffrey Biddeau, Dr. Molly Ahye, Dr. Maureen Warner-Lewis, and Dr. J. D. Elder.

13 The mechanics of obì divination are clearly laid out by Baba Osundiya in *Awo Obi: Obi Divination in Theory and Practice* (2001).

14 Well documented by linguist Maureen Warner-Lewis in her pathbreaking work *Trinidad Yoruba* (1996).

15 *Àlàáfíà* refers to all lobes of the obì falling up and indicates a positive answer or resolution. In the diaspora it is also used as a greeting, synonymous with "Hi, how are you?" By contrast, in the Yorùbá language *àlàáfíà* means "peace"—often used in the greeting "Se àlàáfíà ni?," meaning "Is everything at peace?"

16 For further details on mourning, see Glazier's *Marchin' the Pilgrims Home* (1983, 51–58).

17 In past times, especially at the Christian end of the Spiritual Baptist spectrum, the receipt of ikin or other symbols associated with the African path would be met with dismay or denial. The seeker either would be directed toward another path by the "pointer" (the person acting as a guide on the ancestral journey) or would be referred to an Orisha yard or Spiritual Baptist church more closely associated with the African path (Burton Sankeralli, personal communication).

18 *Oludari* is a title of spiritual leadership in Egbe Onisin Eledumare that Olakela Massetungi held for so long (decades) that his name became synonymous with the title in Trinidad. Recently, EOE elected a new Oludari, and Olakela has received a new title of Oloye Ọrawale Ọranfẹ.

19 I do not provide specific names in the remainder of this section to preserve the anonymity of my contacts due to the sensitive nature of the discussion. For this reason I have also used plural pronouns (they, their, them).

Chapter 5. Ifá in Trinidad's Ground

1 Oyotunji Village was founded in 1970 by Oba Ofuntola Oseijeman Efuntola Adelabu Adefunmi I. In June 2016, his son Oba Adejuyigbe Adefunmi II prepared the village for the visit of the new Ọọ̀ni of Ilé-Ifẹ̀, Prince Adeyeye Enitan Ogunwusi six months after his enthronement. For accounts of the Yorùbá religious (trans)nationalism of Oyotunji, see K. Clarke (2004); Hucks (2012).

2 For more on Maria Lionza and her mountain, see Nichols (2006); Taussig (1996).

3 This is notable as up until roughly 2000 the majority of Orisha lineages in Venezuela were Cuban based and devotees self-identified as Lucumi/Santería. Babalawo

Fatalami (aka Santos Lopez) was one of the pioneers who traveled to West Africa and adopted continental Ifá/Orisha practices (Santos Lopez, personal communication, 1999).

4 The privileging of Ife titles above the analogous title in other towns across Yoruba- and is not without its politics. This construction that positions Ife titles as "Ag- báyé" and above all others has lately been contested as an imagined and recently constructed history. Interestingly, in recent years these politics have played out on social media and have been newly visible to the diaspora (at least in part). An analysis of these politics is both needed and outside the scope of the current volume. As it pertains to Trinidad, status and hierarchy are largely accepted as transmitted by the visiting elder. Where sections of my analysis are read as being Ife-centric (to some), they reflect, to the best of my ability, the politics of the people I worked with. I certainly make no claim to being comprehensive or universal in my portrayal of the Orisha/Ifá community in Trinidad. On the contrary, the community is complex, multifaceted, and rhizomatic. By necessity, any representation is partial and contingent on the ethnographer's gaze and path through the social and political landscape of the spiritual community (spiritscape if you will, with a nod to Appadurai).

5 For more on the ethnogenesis of the Yorùbá, especially in relation to religion, see Peel (2001). And also see Apter (1992) for an insightful analysis of the complex ritual dynamics evident in the politics of Yorùbá towns and their complex lineages and histories.

6 I am in no way advocating for a static, original, authentic, primeval idea of the Ifá corpus. Certainly, the knowledge contained within Ifá is fluid and dynamic, and it changes over time in relation to the social, political, and cultural currents of the larger environment (to a large extent Nigeria). Yet I would insist that attention needs to be paid to the wealth of knowledge tied to histories of those same dynamic social, political, and cultural currents. This became clear to me on a very concrete level in my research trips to Yorubaland in 2013 and 2014, solidifying what previously had been abstractions. One level that begs for further investigation is the impact that diasporic currents are having within Yorubaland, specifically in the spiritual economies and knowledge production of Ifá.

7 Okè Itaṣe is the Ifá temple in Ilé-Ifè, built on a sacred mound where Orunmila is said to have spent much time.

8 Òkànràn'sá and Èjì Ogbè are both Odù, 2 of the 256 different signs marking primal energy patterns. Òkànràn'sá is the "Odù that carries ẹbọ to heaven," and Èjì Ogbè is the "King of all 256 Odù" (Taiwo Thompson, personal communication, December 28, 2015).

9 Often this tension is resolved in favor of what works. This practicality is a core component in the adaption of African diasporic religions throughout the diaspora.

10 Personal communication via facebook chat with Iya Ifasina Agbede (May 2, 2015). Thanks go to Iya Ifasina Agbede for her contribution (*A dupe Iya!*). Iyanifa Fasina has made significant contributions to Orisha and Ifá in Trinidad during the early 1990s. Her contributions in the United States date from before that and continued up to her passing in 2015.

11 *Aṣẹ* (or in Diasporic Yoruba spelled ase, and pronounced ashay) is a Yorùbá word that has many meanings, from a verbal performative, "it shall be so," to the spiritual force of creation that flows through all natural things (from stones to humans). For a wonderful exploration of its meaning in the diaspora, specifically Brazil, see Boyce Davies (2013, 72–75).

12 Here I am using the Yorùbá marking of ẹbọ to distinguish the term for ritual offering from the Trinidad "ebo," which is one local name of the annual Orisha ritual of propitiation that lasts five to seven days, and is marked by drumming, dancing, sacrifice and possession.

13 See Beliso-De Jesús (2015, chap. 5), on the controversy regarding initiating women to Ifá in Cuba.

14 I do not want to imply or be read as saying that there are not layers of spiritual eldership in Trinidad. Certainly, there are elders with decades of experience among the ancestral Trinidad Orisha community. Since the turn of the millennium, some important national elders have passed (Ìbà'e), leaving a leadership gap even as the community is in flux with the new Ifá lineages and their initiates. As this work goes to press, while new councils regularly emerge (e.g., the Isese Council), people were not able to answer when I asked, "Who is the national leader of Trini Orisha?" This atomization of African diasporic religious practice and leadership is characteristic of much of Trinidad's history. I expect that a national leader (or leaders) will emerge again for a time, reflecting the historical ebb and flow of the religion.

15 For the connection of Carnival and calypso to the Orisha religion in Trinidad, see Henry (2003, chap. 7); Warner-Lewis (1991, chap. 8). These important works only touch on the surface of this topic, which deserves further investigation.

16 Personal communication, note posted on Facebook (April 2015) written by Olóyè Ṣọlágbadé Pópóọlá and Awo Agboola Jose Rodriguez.

17 This issue of the inaccessibility of a transit visa between Nigeria and Trinidad brings to the forefront the everyday obstacles facing Ifá and Orisha devotees in their efforts to travel between the two countries. There have long been calls for a direct flight between the two countries, which have not materialized. Rumors of new air bridges are routinely reported in Trinidadian and Nigerian newspapers. This issue was most recently addressed on a governmental level during the 2005 visit of then Nigerian president Olúṣẹgun Ọbásanjọ̀ and again, in 2012, with President Goodluck Jonathon. Those governmental discussions focused on a consummation of the existing Bilateral Air Services Agreement signed between the two countries. There is now excitement around workarounds to the long-promised Nigeria-Trinidad air bridge (which as of 2017 has not materialized). For example, in 2015 an Ifá initiate contacted me from Trinidad to excitedly share news of a new direct flight route between São Paolo, Brazil, and Tobago (paired with flights between Togo and Brazil) that had the advantage of not requiring often difficult-to-obtain transit visas from the the United States, the United Kingdom, or other European nations.

GLOSSARY

Note: Unless otherwise noted, entries are in Continental Yorùbá first, followed by a slash and the Diasporic Yoruba. Where the Diasporic Yoruba is not indicated, it is the same as the Continental Yorùbá, without diacritical marks. Other languages are indicated as they appear, such as Trinidad Creole and Cuban Lucumí.

Many thanks for the assistance of Taiwo Thompson, Eniola Adelakan, and Chris Corcoran with the Yorùbá tonal markings (here and throughout the text) and many of the definitions. Adewale-Somadhi (2001) was a useful reference. Any mistakes or tonal mismarkings are my own.

àború àboyè, àboyè àbosíse̩: greeting to babaláwo asking that all prayers and sacrifices be accepted
Adó: Yoruba town, capital of È̩kìtì State, Nigeria; also known as Adó-È̩kìtì
Àgbà: elder
Àgbáyé: global, worldwide; used as appellation in chieftaincy titles from Ilé-Ifè̩
Akámarà: the universal spirit that began the universe; primordial divinity responsible for creation of the material universe
aláàfià (also alaafia/alfia): peace; used as a greeting, from Arabic meaning 'health, good health' probably by way of Hausa
Alagbàá/Alagba: chieftaincy title for the head priest of the Egúngún society
Alájogun/ajogun: misfortune; the militant hosts of the spiritual realms; negative forces of nature that oppose the work of òrìs̩à and life of mankind, such as death (ikú), sickness (àrùn), loss (òfò), litigation (e̩jó̩), fight (ìjà), etc.
Alásùwadà: he who molds destinies together; from the sacred odù Ifá Ò̩sá Ògúndá
Àpènà: the secretary of the secret Ògbóni society
Àràbà: the chief Ifá priest of a town; highest title for a babaláwo in Ifá hierarchy; also the Silk Cotton tree (one of the tallest, most preeminent trees in the forest)
às̩e̩/ase/ashe: sacred life force energy; the power/ability/authority to make things happen, which is owned by Olódùmarè (the Supreme Being) and shared with all other beings; affirmative performative interjection meaning "May it be so!/ So be it!/ It *is* so!/ It must be so!"

Aséwele: Òrìṣà of lost travelers

Àwíṣe: title in the Ifá religion; someone who says things and it comes to pass

Awo: title for Ifá priest; also refers to sacred mystery

Awoméríndínlógún: title of the sixteen major Ifá priests in Òkè'tasè, Ilé Ifè, Òṣun State, Nigeria

àyèwò: searching; spiritual investigation: used as a euphemism for yet-to-be determined source of negativity during Ifá consultation in order to avoid manifestation through explicit naming

bàbálàwo: father of the mysteries; title for male priest of Ifá

babalórìṣa: father of Orisha; title for male Orisha initiate; priest

bembe: used in Santería for a ritual gathering where people make offerings, sing, and dance to drumming for the Oricha (Lu.)

bongo (Trini.): an African diasporic funeral rite consisting of a ritual dance and music performed the night before the burial

bùbá: man's shirt

Candomblé: African diasporic religion in Brazil, mainly Yorùbá-derived

chapelle (Trini.): consecrated inner sanctum of a *palais*, reserved for altars, shrines, and special ritual activities; usually reserved for initiates

da: in Trinidad, to divine; to throw (particularly obì seeds, for divination)

Dada: Orisha who is brother to the Orisha Shango; associated with children born with matted hair or dreadlocks.

desayanne/desien/désonu/désonnu (Trini.): an initiation to Orisha involving head washing and consecration to a specific energy

dòòbálè/dòbálè/dobale: full-length prostration on ground, a sign of respect to an elder, priest, or deity

ebo: in Trinidad, used as name for feast, multiday celebration of Orisha

Egun (Diasporic): ancestors

Egúngún: masquerade of collective ancestors

èjè: blood

Èjì Ogbè: the first of the sixteen major sacred odù Ifá in the Ifá divination system

epo: palm oil

Erinlè: hunter Orisha; sometimes known as Inle; in Trinidad known as Erinlè Ajaja

Èṣù/Eshu: Orisha of communication, choices, crossroads, custodian of àṣe

Èṣù Òdàrà: the Èṣù close to Ifá that transmits supplicants prayers to Olódùmarè

ewe: leaf, herb; a sacred mixture of herbs, liquids, and other ingredients used in Ifá/Orisha ritual cleansings, blessings, and consecrations; originally used in Cuban Lucumí this meaning has come to be used throughout African diasporic religions

ẹbọ: sacrifice or offering

ẹgbé: group of people; an association or organization; society of coequals; age-mates

Ẹgbé Òrun: spiritual comrades from the spiritual realms, a group of all people on earth left behind when born; also heavenly mate

ẹ kú iṣẹ́/ekuse/eku ise: well done; also greeting to someone who is working

Ẹlẹ́gán: initiation to Ifá without seeing Odù

ẹsẹ̀ odù Ifá: verses of odù Ifá

feast (Trini.): an annual ritual gathering over several days to pray, sing, dance, and make offerings, including sacrifices, to Orisha; also called ebo

fìlà: traditional Yorùbá brimless hat

gèlè: fabric headwrap whose cloth, style and height can connote status and affiliation

Gẹ̀lẹ̀dẹ́: masquerade in Yorubaland, initiatory lineage that incorporates a corpus of prayers, music and dance designed to appease the mothers.

goat-mouth (Trini.): calling something into being by saying it (or the opposite) (e.g., saying "Not a drop of rain in sight," and then it pours)

ìbà: homage, prayer of respect; often included along with mention of a person who is deceased

Ìbejì: twins; Orisha of twins

ibi: opposite of ire; negativity, imbalance

Ifá: wisdom of Olódùmarè, the message of Òrúnmìlà

Ìjèbú: Yorùbá town in Ogun State, Nigeria

Ìká Méjì: one of the sixteen major sacred Odù of Ifá

ikin Ifá: palm nut kernels, when consecrated used in Ifá divination; voice of Orunmila

ilé: house, congregation, or lineage of Ifá/Orisha devotee

Ilé-Ifẹ̀: a city in Òsun State, Nigeria; historic ancestral home for all Yorùbá, also known as Ifé Oòdáyé; according to myth, ancient Ilé-Ifẹ̀ is the source of all humanity

ìlẹ̀kẹ̀: consecrated necklace of beads worn by Orisha/Ifá devotees; each pattern of colored beads represents a different Orisha or spiritual energy; can also indicate lineage

iná: light, fire

ire: blessing of good or positive energy; balance, alignment

Ìrèntegbè: alias for Ìrẹtẹ̀ Ogbè; one of the 256 sacred chapters of odù Ifá

Ìrẹtẹ̀ Méjì: one of the sixteen major sacred odù Ifá

ìróké Ifá: wooden carving, with rattle inside; staff of authority of Ifá priests used in prayer and to tap the divination tray (ọpọ́n Ifá) during preliminary invocations in a consultation

Irúnmọlẹ̀: divine spiritual energies that came from the spiritual realms (Òrun) to inhabit and create the earth; includes many, but not all Orisha.

ìta: divination reading received during initiation; serves as a road map for life, providing things to avoid (taboos) and goals to strive for.

Ìtènífá/Ìtẹfá: a process of Ifá initiation

ìwà: character; also destiny or fate

ìwà-pẹ̀lẹ́: good character; gentle and noble character; someone who has patience

iwà-rere: good character

ìyá: literally "mother," also honorific title for female priest

Ìyálóde Awo Àgbáyé: women's leadership title in Yorùbá culture; chief of all women; literally meaning Mother of the Mysteries Worldwide

ìyàwó: wife, bride; term used for new initiate in Cuba Lucumi

jhandi (Trini.): flag to mark site of Hindu prayer ritual

jouvay, j'ouvert (Trini): literally opening of the way; the opening ritual of Carnival in the late night hours of Dimanche Gras/Carnival Sunday where covered in mud, paint or oil people dance through the streets to loud sounds systems and steel bands in a masquerade to exorce their "demons" from the past year.

jumbie (Trini.): derogatory term for a spirit, usually understood as an evil spirit

Kambule, also Canboulay, Cannes-Brulees (Trini.): nineteenth-century creole term for burning cane, used for celebration to mark the sugarcane harvest; in contemporary Trinidad used as label for festive cultural practices associated with Carnival, including stick fighting and old-style masquerades

kí nkan má ṣe/kin kin mase/kin kan mashe: literally, may nothing bad happen to; a protective verse, used in incantation prior to calling and giving praise to living lineage of priests

limin'/liming (Trini.): a form of hanging out, often involving a combination of storytelling, music, drink, all in an open-ended manner of "now for now"

Lucumí: in Cuba, language derived from a mixture of Spanish and Yorùbá; also used to refer to Yorùbá-derived religion, often interchangeable with Santería

mas' (Trini.): short for "masquerade"; used to refer to masquerading traditions ranging from full-body costumes, say Dragon mas', or the contemporary beaded and feathered bikinis that parade during Carnival

mourning (Trini.): ritual of fasting and prayer while lying on earthen ground over days in search of spiritual visions; practice in Spiritual Baptist and sometimes Orisha religions

obeah: a largely pejorative term directed at non-Christian healing and spiritual practices utilized by Africans and their descendants; used throughout the former British West Indies by members of the colonial governance and plantocracy, especially in legislation directed at policing and criminalizing non-Christian practices; reclaimed by some Afro-Caribbean people as a term of pride and power for African sacred science

obì: kola nuts, often used in divination; also edible food with high level of caffeine

obì àbàtà: usually four-lobed (also three-, four-, five-, and six-lobed) kola nuts used for divination, also used as offering to Orisha and Ifá

Odù: deity at the core of Ifá's awo

odù: one of 16 major sacred geomantic binary signs of Ifá that when combined in pairs forms 256 figures also known as odù Ifá

Ogbè Atẹ̀: nickname for Ogbè Ìrẹtẹ̀; one of 256 sacred odù Ifá

Ògbóni: secret society of elders in Yorùbá society

Ògún: Orisha of iron, technology, war, and kingship

Ògúndá Méjì: one of sixteen major sacred odù Ifá

òkè: mountain

Òkè Ìtaṣè/Òkè'taṣè: one of the sacred compounds in Ilé-Ifẹ̀ where Òrúnmìlà spent time

Olódùmarè: supreme being; God

Olókun: in Nigeria and Benin Republic, literally, owner of the ocean: an Òrìṣà most often associated with the ocean (and sometimes with rivers), sometimes considered male and at other times female; in the diaspora, owner of the bottom of the ocean, an òrìṣà

Olóyè: in Ifá, title for a person who holds a chieftaincy title

Olúorogbo: an Orisha, original scribe for the Orisha, said to be the originator of written language; an Orisha funfun and brother to Obatala, mainly venerated in Ilé-Ifẹ̀; note, separate from the son of Morèmi (also named Olúorogbo).

Olúwo: in Ifá, a title of hierarchy to someone who has achieved a "master" status

omi tutù: cool water

Onílẹ̀: owner of the earth, Ilẹ̀, aka in Trinidad as: Mama la Terre/Mama Lata/Mama Latay

Onírè: a Yorùbá town; also a chieftaincy title; owner of blessings/good luck, praise name for Òrìṣà Ògún

Orí: personal divine consciousness; head

oríkì: praise poem

Òrìṣà/Orisha: deities; divine emissaries of Olódùmarè (God); often seen as forces of nature or historical figures; also used as name for Yoruba-based religion in Trinidad

Òrúnmìlà: one of the Irúnmolẹ̀ from the spiritual realms (Òrun); deity of wisdom; chief custodian of Ifá

Oṣé Ṣàngó: sacred double-headed ax of Ṣàngó/Shango

Òṣogbo: town in Òṣun State, Nigeria dedicated to Òṣun and home to the Sacred Òṣun Grove

otí: clear alcohol, often gin; used as offering to Orisha and Ifá

oyin: honey

òyìnbó: foreigner or stranger; term often used for "white person," which may apply to any non-African, or even any European/American cultured non-Yorùbá-speaking African

ọba: king, ruler

Ọbàtálá: Orisha of clarity and creator of humans; known as molder of heads in the spiritual realms

Òkànràn'sá: short for Òkànràn Ọ̀sà; one of the 256 odù Ifá; carries ẹbọ or sacrifice to the spiritual realms (Òrun)

ọmọ: child; used to indicate spiritual child (disciple/protégé) of an elder priest

Ọmọ Awo: student of Ifá

Ọ̀òni: title of kingship in Ilé-Ifẹ̀

Ọ̀pá òrìrè: the staff of Ifá; also known as Osùn

ọpọ́n Ifá: Ifá divination tray, usually carved from wood

Òrun: heavenly realm, spiritual realms

Ọsá Méjì: One of the sixteen major sacred odù Ifá

Ọsá Ògúndá: one of the 256 sacred odù Ifá, which contains one version of the Yoruba creation story.

Ọsanyìn/Osain: Orisha of herbs and medicine

Ọṣọ́ọ̀sì/Oshosi: Orisha of the forest; tracker and hunter

Ọṣun/Oshun: Orisha of love, fertility, creativity, and fresh water; associated with women's power; one of the Irúnmọlẹ̀

Ọ̀ṣun: the staff of Ifá; also known as Ọ̀pá òrìrẹ̀

ọwọ́ Ifá kan: one hand of Ifá made up of sixteen to twenty consecrated ikin; a preliminary initiation to Ifá where the person is introduced to Ifá and placed under his protection

Ọ̀yẹ̀kú Méjì: one of the sixteen major sacred odù Ifá

Ọ̀yọ́túnjí/Oyotunji: in the Yorùbá language, literally means "Ọ̀yọ́ awakes" or "Ọ̀yọ́ returns"; also used to refer both to a village of the same name outside Sheldon, South Carolina, in the United States, and the initiatory lineage based in that village

Ọ̀yọ́: city in Oyo State, Nigeria; former seat of the Ọ̀yọ́ Kingdom

palais (Trini.): a consecrated "set-apart" space, often with half-high walls, a roof, and earthen floor where devotees gather to praise and honor Orisha through prayer, drumming, song, and dance; benches often occupy three sides

Rada: in Trinidad, creole term for the Arada people of the West African kingdom of Dahomey (now the Republic of Benin, west of Nigeria); also a nation of lwa (dieties) in Haitian Vodoun

Ṣàngó/Shango: Orisha of kingship, justice, lightning

singbare/synbere: in Trinidad, an initiation to Orisha that involves cuts to the head or body in which sacred medicines are rubbed

sòkòtò: pants

tambor: drum; also used in Cuban Santería for a ritual gathering where people make offerings, sing, and dance to drumming for the Orisha

Yemọja/Yemaya: Orisha of water, motherhood; associated with the ocean in the diaspora

Yorùbá: ancient peoples largely in contemporary southwest Nigeria; also spread throughout West Africa across at least five other postcolonial nations; also refers to their language, culture, and religion

Yorubaland: geographic and imagined cultural area encompassing the Yorùbá people in West Africa, cutting through parts of at least five postcolonial nations, from Nigeria to Sierra Leone

Abimbola, Wande. 1997a. *IFÁ: An Exposition of Ifá Literary Corpus*. New York: Athelia Henrietta Press.

———. 1997b. *Ifá Will Mend Our Broken World: Thoughts on Yoruba Religion and Culture in Africa and the African Diaspora*. Roxbury, MA: Aim Books.

Abrahams, Roger. 1983. *The Man-of-Words in the West Indies: Performance and the Emergence of Creole Culture*. Baltimore: Johns Hopkins University Press.

Abrahams, Roger, and John Szwed. 1983. "After the Myth: Studying Afro-America Cultural Patterns in the Plantation Literature." In *The Man-of-Words in the West Indies: Performance and the Emergence of Creole Culture*, edited by Roger Abrahams, 40–54. Baltimore: Johns Hopkins University Press.

Abu-Lughod, Lila. 1991. "Writing against Culture." In *Recapturing Anthropology: Working in the Present*, edited by Richard G. Fox, 137–62. Santa Fe, NM: School of American Research Press.

Aching, Gerard. 2002. *Masking and Power: Carnival and Popular Culture in the Caribbean*. Minneapolis: University of Minnesota Press.

Adderley, Rosanne Marion. 2006. *"New Negroes from Africa": Slave Trade Abolition and Free African Settlement in the Nineteenth-Century Caribbean*. Bloomington: Indiana University Press.

Adéwálé-Somadhi, Chief FAMA Àìná. 1993. *Fundamentals of the Yorùbá Religion (Orisa Worship)*. San Bernadino, CA: Ilé Òrúnmìlà Communications.

———. 2001. *FAMA's ÈDÈ AWO (Òrìṣà Yorùbá Dictionary)*. San Bernadino, CA: Ilé Òrúnmìlà Communications.

Ahye, Molly. 2000. "Parade and Expressive Votive Dancing in Trinidad Carnival: Epiphany of Dionysos/Bacchus." PhD diss., New York University.

Aiyejina, Funso, and Rawle Gibbons. 1999. "Orisa (Orisha) Tradition in Trinidad." In *Proceedings of the 6th World Congress of Orisha Tradition and Culture*, 180–209. Port of Spain, Trinidad: Secretariat of the 6th World Congress of Orisa Tradition and Culture. Reprinted in *Caribbean Quarterly* 45 (4): 35–50.

Aiyejina, Funso, Rawle Gibbons, and Baba Sam Phills. 2009. "Context and Meaning in Trinidad Yoruba Songs: *Peter Was a Fisherman* and *Songs of the Orisha Palais*." *Research in African Literatures* 40 (1): 127–36.

Alexander, M. Jacqui. 2006. *Pedagogies of Crossing: Meditations on Feminism, Sexual Politics, Memory, and the Sacred*. Durham, NC: Duke University Press.

Allahar, Anton. 1999. "Popular Culture and Racialisation of Political Consciousness in Trinidad and Tobago." In *Identity, Ethnicity and Culture in the Caribbean*, edited by Ralph R. Premdas, 246–81. St. Augustine: University of the West Indies.

———. 2002. "'Race' and Class in the Making of Caribbean Political Culture." *Transforming Anthropology* 10 (2): 13–29.

———, ed. 2005. *Ethnicity, Class, and Nationalism: Caribbean and Extra-Caribbean Dimensions*. Lanham, MD: Lexington Books.

Allen, Jafari Sinclaire. 2011. *¡Venceremos? The Erotics of Black Self-Making in Cuba*. Durham, NC: Duke University Press.

———. 2012. "A Conversation 'Overflowing with Memory' on Omise'eke Natasha Tinsley's 'Water, Shoulders, into the Black Pacific.'" *GLQ: A Journal of Lesbian and Gay Studies* 18 (2–3): 249–62.

———. 2015. "Erotics in Medias Res: Topping Caribbean Studies from the Bottom?" *Small Axe* 19 (1 46): 159–68.

Allen, Jafari Sinclaire, and Ryan Jobson. 2016. "The Decolonizing Generation: (Race and) Theory in Anthropology since the Eighties." *Current Anthropology* 57 (2): 129–40.

Anderson, Benedict. 1991 [1983]. *Imagined Communities: Reflections on the Origin and Spread of Nationalism*. London: Verso.

Anthony, Michael. 1998. "The First Emancipation Day." *Trinidad Guardian*, August 27.

Appadurai, Arjun. 1997. *Modernity at Large: Cultural Dimensions of Globalization*. Minneapolis: University of Minnesota Press.

Apter, Andrew. 1991. "Herskovits' Heritage: Rethinking Syncretism in the African Diaspora." *Diaspora* 1 (3): 235–60.

———. 1992. *Black Critics and Kings: The Hermeneutics of Power in Yorùbá Society*. Chicago: University of Chicago Press.

———. 2002. "On African Origins: Creolization and *Connaissance* in Haitian Vodou." *American Ethnologist* 29 (2): 233–60.

———. 2005. *The Pan-African Nation: Oil and the Spectacle of Culture in Nigeria*. Chicago: University of Chicago Press.

———. 2016. "Beyond Négritude: Black Cultural Citizenship and the Arab Question in FESTAC 77." *Journal of African Cultural Studies* 28 (3): 313–26.

———. Forthcoming. Introduction to *Oduduwa's Chain: Locations of Culture in the Yoruba-Atlantic*. Chicago: University of Chicago Press.

Asad, Talal. 1973. *Anthropology and the Colonial Encounter*. London: Ithaca Press.

———. 1993. *Genealogies of Religion: Discipline and Reasons of Power in Christianity and Islam*. Baltimore: Johns Hopkins University Press.

Ashby, Glenville C. 2012. *The Believers: The Hidden World of West Indian Spiritualism in New York*. Hertfordshire, UK: Hansib Publications.

Ashcroft, B. 2009. "Alternative Modernities: Globalization and the Post-colonial." *ARIEL: A Review of International English Literature* 40 (1): 81–105.

Austin-Broos, Diane J. 1997. *Jamaica Genesis: Religion and the Politics of Moral Orders*. Chicago: University of Chicago Press.

Back, Les, and John Solomos. 2000. "Introduction: Theorising Race and Racism." In *Theories of Race and Racism: A Reader*, edited by Les Back and John Solomos, 1–32. London: Routledge.

Baker, Houston A., Jr., Manthia Diawara, and Ruth H. Lindeborg, eds. 1996. *Black British Cultural Studies*. Chicago: University of Chicago Press.

Bakhtin, Mikhail. 1981. *The Dialogic Imagination: Four Essays*. Translated by Caryl Emerson and Michael Holquist. Austin: University of Texas Press.

———. 1984 [1968]. *Rabelais and His World*. Translated by Helene Iswolsky. Bloomington: Indiana University Press.

Balibar, Etienne, and Immanuel Wallerstein. 1991. *Race, Nation, Class: Ambiguous Identities*. London: Verso.

Barber, Karin. 1981. "How Man Makes God in West Africa." *Africa* 51(3): 724–45.

Barnes, Sandra, ed. 1997. *Africa's Ogun*. 2nd ed. Bloomington: Indiana University Press.

Bascom, William. 1972. *Shango in the New World*. Austin: Occasional Publication, African and Afro-American Research Institute, University of Texas, Austin.

Bastide, Roger. 1971 [1967]. *African Civilisations in the New World*. Translated by Peter Green. New York: Harper and Row.

———. 1978. *African Religions in the New World: Toward a Sociology of the Interpretation of Civilizations*. Translated by H. Sabba. Baltimore: Johns Hopkins University Press.

Behar, Ruth, and Deborah A. Gordon, eds. 1995. *Women Writing Culture*. Berkeley: University of California Press.

Belgrave, Valerie. 1995. "The Sir George Williams Affair." In *The Black Power Revolution of 1970: A Retrospective*, edited by Selwyn Ryan and Talmoon Stewart, 119–31. St. Augustine: Institute for Social and Economic Research, University of the West Indies.

Beliso–De Jesús, Aisha M. 2015. *Electric Santeria: Racial and Sexual Assemblages of Transnational Religion*. New York: Columbia University Press.

Benitez-Rojo, Antonio. 2001 [1992]. *The Repeating Island: The Caribbean and the Postmodern Perspective*. 2nd ed. Translated by James E. Maraniss. Durham, NC: Duke University Press.

Bernabé, J., P. Chamoiseau, and R. Confiant. 1993 [1989]. *Eloge de la Créolité/In Praise of Creoleness*. Bilingual edition. Translated by M. B. Khyar. Paris: Gallimard.

Best, Lloyd. 2004. "Race, Class and Ethnicity: A Caribbean Interpretation." *The Third Annual Jagan Lecture Presented at York University*. March 3, 2001, 1-28. CERLAC Colloquia Papers Series, April.

Bhabha, Homi. 1992. *The Location of Culture*. London: Routledge.

Birth, Kevin K. 1999. *Any Time Is Trinidad Time: Social Meaning and Temporal Consciousness*. Gainesville: University Press of Florida.

———. 2008. *Bacchanalian Sentiments: Musical Experiences and Political Counterpoints in Trinidad*. Durham, NC: Duke University Press.

Bisnauth, Dale. 1996. *History of Religions in the Caribbean*. Trenton, NJ: Africa World Press.

Blanes, Ruy, and Diana Espirito Santo, eds. 2013. *The Social Life of Spirits*. Chicago: University of Chicago Press.

Boddy, Janice. 1989. *Wombs and Alien Spirits*. Madison: University of Wisconsin Press.

———. 1994. "Spirit Possession Revisited." *Annual Review of Anthropology* 23: 407–34.

Bourdieu, Pierre. 1977. *Outline of a Theory of Practice*. Cambridge: Cambridge University Press.

———. 1984. *Distinction: A Social Critique of the Judgement of Taste*. Cambridge, MA: Harvard University Press.

———. 1990. *The Logic of Practice*. Stanford, CA: Stanford University Press.

Boyce Davies, Carole. 2007. *Left of Karl Marx: The Political Life of Black Communist Claudia Jones*. Durham, NC: Duke University Press.

———. 2013. *Caribbean Spaces: Escapes from Twilight Zones*. Urbana: University of Illinois Press.

Boyce Davies, Carole, and Babacar M'Bow. 2007. "Towards African Diaspora Citizenship: Politicizing an Existing Global Geography." In *Black Geographies and the Politics of Place*, edited by Katherine McKittrick and Clyde Woods, 14–45. Toronto, Ontario: Between the Lines; Cambridge, MA: South End Press.

Braithwaite, Lloyd. 1953. *Social Stratification in Trinidad*. Mona: ISER.

———. 1973. "The Problem of Cultural Integration in Trinidad." In *Consequences of Class and Color: West Indian Perspectives*, edited by David Lowenthal and Lambros Comitas, 241–60. New York: Anchor Books.

Brandon, George. 1993. *Santeria from Africa to the New World: The Dead Sell Memories*. Bloomington: Indiana University Press.

Brathwaite, Edward Kamau. 1971. *The Development of Creole Society in Jamaica, 1770–1820*. Oxford: Clarendon Press.

Brereton, Bridget. 1989 [1981]. *A History of Modern Trinidad, 1783–1962*. Kingston: Heinemann.

———. 2002 [1979]. *Race Relations in Colonial Trinidad*. Cambridge: Cambridge University Press.

Brown, David H. 1993. "Thrones of the Orichas: Afro-Cuban Altars in New Jersey, New York, and Havana." *African Arts* 26 (4): 44–59, 85–87.

———. 2003. *Santeria Enthroned: Art, Ritual, and Innovation in an Afro-Cuban Religion*. Chicago: University of Chicago Press.

Brown, Karen. 1991. *Mama Lola*. Berkeley: University of California Press.

Burton, Richard D. 1997. *Afro-Creole: Power, Opposition and Play in the Caribbean*. Ithaca, NY: Cornell University Press.

Carby, Hazel. 1999. *Cultures in Babylon*. London: Verso.

Carr, Andrew. 1989 [1955]. *A Rada Community in Trinidad*. Port of Spain, Trinidad: Paria Publishing.

Castor, Nicole. 1999. "Virtual Community: The Orisha Tradition in the New World and Cyberspace." In *Proceedings of the 6th World Congress of Orisa Tradition and Culture*, 87–92. Port of Spain, Trinidad: Secretariat of the 6th World Congress of Orisa Tradition and Culture.

———. 2009. "Invoking the Spirit of Canboulay: Pathways of African Middle Class Cultural Citizenship in Trinidad." PhD diss., University of Chicago.

Castor, N. Fadeke. 2013. "Shifting Multi-Cultural Citizenship: Trinidad Orisha Opens the Road." *Cultural Anthropology* 28 (3): 475–89.

———. n.d. "Our Collective Ancestors: Spiritual Ethnicity in Ifá Devotion across the Americas" in *Embodiment and Relationality in Religions of Africa and its Diasporas,* Yolanda Covington-Ward and Jeanette S. Jouili, editors. Forthcoming.

Césaire, Aimé. 1972. *Discourse on Colonialism. Slavery and Beyond.* Edited by D. Davis. New York: Monthly Review Press.

Chatterjee, Partha. 1993. *The Nation and Its Fragments.* Princeton, NJ: Princeton University Press.

Clarke, Kamari. 1997. "Genealogies of Reclaimed Nobility: The Geotemporality of Yoruba Belonging." PhD diss., University of California, Santa Cruz.

———. 2004. *Mapping Yoruba Networks: Power and Agency in the Making of Transnational Communities.* Durham, NC: Duke University Press.

———. 2013. "Notes on Cultural Citizenship in the Black Atlantic World." *Cultural Anthropology* 28 (3): 464–74.

Clarke, Kamari, and Deborah Thomas. 2006. *Globalization and Race: Transformations in the Cultural Production of Blackness.* Durham, NC: Duke University Press.

Clarke, LeRoy. 2005. Opening address at Sango Annual Rain Festival, June 9–25. In *Ile Eko Sango Osun Mil'osa, Opening Address at Sango' Annual Rain Festival,* edited by Iya Sangowunmi. Unpublished brochure.

Clifford, James. 1994. "Diasporas." *Cultural Anthropology* 9 (3): 302–38.

Clifford, James, and George Marcus. 1986. *Writing Culture: The Poetics and Politics of Ethnography.* Berkeley: University of California Press.

Cohen, Colleen Bellerino. 1998. "'This is De Test': Festival and the Cultural Politics of Nation Building in the British Virgin Islands." *American Ethnologist* 25 (2): 189–214.

Cohen, Peter. 2009. "The Orisha Atlantic: Historicizing the Roots of a Global Religion." In *Transnational Transcendence: Essays on Religion and Globalization,* edited by Thomas J. Csordas, 231–62. Berkeley: University of California Press.

Coker, Natasha. 1999. "Rituals of Orisa Marriage." *Trinidad and Tobago Express,* August 7.

Comaroff, Jean. 1985. *Body of Power, Spirit of Resistance.* Chicago: University of Chicago Press.

Comaroff, Jean, and John Comaroff. 1991. *Of Revelation and Revolution.* Vol. 1, *Christianity, Colonialism and Consciousness in South Africa.* Chicago: University of Chicago Press.

———. 1992. *Ethnography and the Historical Imagination.* Boulder, CO: Westview Press.

———, eds. 1993. *Modernity and Its Malcontents: Ritual and Power in Postcolonial Africa.* Chicago: University of Chicago Press.

———. 1997. *Of Revelation and Revolution.* Vol. 2, *The Dialectics of Modernity on a South African Frontier.* Chicago: University of Chicago Press.

———. 2000. "Millennial Capitalism: First Thoughts on a Second Coming." *Public Culture* 12 (2): 291–343.

———. 2003a. "Ethnography on an Awkward Scale." *Ethnography* 4 (2): 147–79.

————. 2003b. "Reflections on Liberalism, Policulturalism, and ID-Ology: Citizenship and Difference in South Africa." *Social Identities* 9 (4): 445–73.

————. 2009. *Ethnicity, Inc*. Chicago: University of Chicago Press.

Comaroff, John L. 1996. "Ethnicity, Nationalism and the Politics of Difference in the Age of Revolution." In *The Politics of Difference*, edited by Edwin Wilmsen and Patrick McAllister, 162–83. Chicago: University of Chicago Press.

Conquergood, Dwight, 2002. "Performance Studies: Interventions and Radical Research." *Drama Review* 46 (2): 145–56.

Cooper, Carolyn. 1995. *Noises in the Blood: Orality, Gender and the "Vulgar" Body of Jamaican Popular Culture*. Durham, NC: Duke University Press.

————. 2004. *Soundclash*. New York: Palgrave Macmillan.

Coronil, Fernando. 1997. *The Magical State: Nature, Money and Modernity in Venezuela*. Chicago: University of Chicago Press.

Cowley, John. 1998. *Carnival, Canboulay and Calypso: Traditions in the Making*. Cambridge: Cambridge University Press.

Daniels, Donna. 1997. "When the Living Is the Prayer: African-Based Religious Reverence in Everyday Life among Women of Color Devotees in the San Francisco Bay Area." PhD diss., Stanford University.

Darbeau, Dave. n.d. "The Chains Are Bursting." East Dry River Speaks. mimeograph (reprinted in Oxaal 1971).

Delgadillo, Theresa. 2011. *Spiritual Mestizaje: Religion, Gender, Race, and Nation in Contemporary Chicana Narrative*. Durham, NC: Duke University Press.

Derby, Lauren. 1994. "Haitians, Magic and Money: Raza and Society in the Haitian-Dominican Borderlands, 1900–1937." *Comparative Studies in Society and History* 36 (3): 488–526.

Deren, Maya. 1953. *Divine Horsemen: The Living Gods of Haiti*. New York: Thames and Hudson.

Drewal, Margaret. 1991. "The State of Research in Performance in Africa." *African Studies Review* 34 (3): 1–64.

————. 1992. *Yoruba Ritual: Performers, Play, and Agency*. Bloomington: Indiana University Press.

Du Bois, W. E. B. 1994 [1903]. *Souls of Black Folk*. New York: Dover.

Dudley, Shannon. 2004. *Carnival Music in Trinidad: Experiencing Music, Expressing Culture*. New York: Oxford University Press.

————. 2008. *Behind the Bridge*. Oxford: Oxford University Press.

Duncan, Carol B. 2008. *This Spot of Ground: Spiritual Baptists in Toronto*. Waterloo, ON: Wilfrid Laurier University Press.

Dunham, Katherine. 1969. *Island Possessed*. Chicago: University of Chicago Press.

Durkheim, Émile. 1995 [1912]. *Elementary Forms of Religious Life*. Translated by Karen E. Fields. New York: Free Press.

Eastman, Rudolph. 2008. *The Fight for Dignity and Cultural Space: African Survivals and Adaptations in Trinidad*. Bloomington, IN: Xlibris Corporation.

Elder, J. D. 1969. *Yoruba Ancestor Cult in Gasparillo: Its Structure, Organization and So-*

cial Function in Community Cohesion. St. Augustine, Trinidad: University of the West Indies.

———. 1988. *African Survivals in Trinidad and Tobago*. London: Karia Press.

———. 2004. "Cannes Brûlées." In *Carnival: Culture in Action*, edited by Milla Riggio, 48–52. New York: Routledge.

Epega, Afolabi A., and Philip John Neimark. 1995. *The Sacred Ifá Oracle*. New York: HarperCollins.

Fabian, Johannes. 2002 [1983]. *Time and the Other: How Anthropology Makes Its Other*. New York: Columbia University Press.

Fanon, Frantz. 1963 [1961]. *The Wretched of the Earth*. New York: Grove Press.

———. 1967. *Black Skin, White Masks*. New York: Grove Press.

Forte, Maximilian. 2005. *Ruins of Absence, Presence of Caribs: (Post)colonial Representations of Aboriginality in Trinidad and Tobago*. Gainesville: University Press of Florida.

Gaomkar, D. P., ed. 2001. *Alternative Modernities*. Durham, NC: Duke University Press.

Gates, Henry Louis, Jr. 1988. *The Signifying Monkey: A Theory of Afro-American Literary Criticism*. New York: Oxford University Press.

———. 1989. *Figures in Black: Words, Signs, and the Racial Self*. Cary, NC: Oxford University Press.

Geertz, Clifford. 1973. *The Interpretation of Cultures*. New York: Basic Books.

Gellner, Ernest. 1983. *Nations and Nationalism*. Ithaca, NY: Cornell University Press.

Gibbons, Rawle. 2007. "Trinidad Sailor Mas." In *Just below South: Intercultural Performance in the Caribbean and the U.S. South*, edited by Jessica Adams, Michael P. Bibler and Cecile Accilien, 146–66. Charlottesville: University of Virginia Press.

Gilroy, Paul. 1991. *"There Ain't No Black in the Union Jack": The Cultural Politics of Race and Nation*. Chicago: University of Chicago Press.

———. 1993. *The Black Atlantic: Modernity and Double Consciousness*. Cambridge, MA: Harvard University Press.

———. 1994. *Small Acts: Thoughts on the Politics of Black Cultures*. New York: Serpent's Tail.

Glaude, Eddie, Jr. 2002. *Is It Nation Time? Contemporary Essays on Black Power and Black Nationalism*. Chicago: University of Chicago Press.

Glazier, Stephen D. 1983. *Marchin' the Pilgrims Home: A Study of the Spiritual Baptists of Trinidad*. Salem, MA: Sheffield.

———. 2001a. "The Orisha (Shango) Movement in Trinidad." In *Encyclopedia of African and African-American Religions*, edited by Stephen D. Glazier, 221–23. New York: Routledge.

———. 2001b. "Spiritual Baptists." In *Encyclopedia of African and African-American Religions*, edited by Stephen D. Glazier, 315–19. New York: Routledge.

———. 2008. "Demanding Dieties and Reluctant Devotees: Belief and Unbelief in the Trinidadian Orisa Movement." *Social Analysis* 52 (1): 19–38.

Glissant, Édouard. 1989 [1981]. *Caribbean Discourse. Selected Essays*. Translated and with an introduction by J. Michael Dash. Charlottesville: University Press of Virginia.

———. 1997. *Poetics of Relation*. Translated by Betsy Wang. Ann Arbor: University of Michigan Press.

Goldberg, David. 2002. *The Racial State*. London: Blackwell.

Gomez, Michael A. 1998. *Exchanging Our Country Marks: The Transformation of African Identities in the Colonial and Antebellum South*. Chapel Hill, NC: University of North Carolina Press.

Granger, Geddes. n.d. "Corruption." East Dry River Speaks. mimeograph (reprinted in Oxaal 1971).

Grant, Lennox. 2005a. "Old Soldier of Ogun to Lead E-Day March." *Trinidad Guardian*, July 31.

———. 2005b. "A Souvenir Something from Soca Safari." *Trinidad Guardian*, August 7.

Gray-Burke, Barbara. n.d. "A Brochure for Teachers on Spiritual Shouter Religion in Trinidad and Tobago." www.n2consulting.com/brochure.htm/ (accessed March 30, 2001).

Green, Garth L., and Philip W. Scher. 2007. *Trinidad Carnival: The Cultural Politics of a Transnational Festival*. Bloomington: Indiana University Press.

Greenfield, Sidney M., and Andre Droogers, eds. 2001. *Reinventing Religions: Syncretism and Transformation in Africa and the Americas*. New York: Rowman and Littlefield.

Gregory, Steven. 1999. *Santería in New York City: A Study in Cultural Resistance*. New York: Garland.

Guilbault, Jocelyne. 2005. "Audible Entanglements: Nation and Diasporas in Trinidad's Calypso Music Scene." *Small Axe* 17 (9 1): 40–63.

———. 2007. *Governing Sound: The Cultural Politics of Trinidad's Carnival Musics*. Chicago: University of Chicago Press.

Gupta, Akhil, and James Ferguson. 1992. "Beyond 'Culture': Space, identity and the politics of difference." *Cultural Anthropology* 7 (1): 6–23.

Guss, David M. 2000. *The Festive State: Race, Ethnicity and Nationalism as Cultural Performance*. Berkeley: University of California Press.

Hall, Stuart. 1977. "Pluralism, Race and Class in Caribbean Society." In *Race and Class in Post Colonial Societies: A Study of Ethnic Group Relations in the English-Speaking Caribbean, Bolivia, Chile and Mexico*, 150–81. Paris: UNESCO.

———. 1989. "Cultural Identity and Cinematic Representation." *Framework* 36:68–82.

———. 1993. "What Is This 'Black' in Black Popular Culture?" Reprinted in the Special Issue "Rethinking Race." *Social Justice* 20 (1–2).

———. 1995. "Negotiating Caribbean Identities." *New Left Review* 209 (January/ February): 3–14.

———. 1996a. "Ethnicity: Identity and Difference." In *Becoming National*, edited by Geoff Eley and Roland Grigor Suny, 339–49. New York: Oxford University Press.

———. 1996b. "New Ethnicities." In *Stuart Hall: Critical Dialogues in Cultural Studies*, edited by David Morley and Kuan-Hsing Chen, 441–49. London: Routledge.

———, ed. 1997. *Representation: Cultural Representations and Signifying Practices*. London: Sage.

———. 1999. "Thinking the Diaspora: Home-Thoughts from Abroad." *Small Axe* 6: 1–18.

————. 2003. "Cultural Identity and Diaspora." In *Theorizing Diaspora*, edited by Jana Evans Braziel and Anita Mannur, 233–46. Oxford: Blackwell.

Hall, Stuart, David Held, and Tony McGrew, eds. 1992. *Modernity and Its Futures*. Cambridge: Polity Press.

Hanchard, Michael. 2004. Black Transnationalism, Africana Studies, and the 21st Century. *Journal of Black Studies* 35 (2): 139–53.

Handler, Jerome S., and Kenneth M. Bilby. 2013. *Enacting Power: The Criminalization of Obeah in the Anglophone Caribbean, 1760–2011*. Kingston, Jamaica: University of the West Indies Press.

Handler, Richard. 1988. *Nationalism and the Politics of Culture in Quebec*. Madison: University of Wisconsin Press.

Harding, Rachel. 2003. *A Refuge in Thunder: Candomblé and Alternative Spaces of Blackness*. Bloomington: Indiana University Press.

Harewood, Susan. 2005. "Masquerade Performance and the Play of Sexual Identity in Calypso." *Cultural Studies <–>Critical Methodologies* 5 (2): 189–205.

Harris, Max. 2003. *Carnival and Other Christian Festivals: Folk Theology and Folk Performance*. Austin: University of Texas Press.

Harris, Wilson. 1995. *History, Fable and Myth in the Caribbean and Guianas*. Wellesley, MA: Calaloux Publications.

Harrison, Faye V., ed. 1991. *Decolonizing Anthropology: Moving Further toward an Anthropology of Liberation*. Washington, DC: American Anthropological Association.

————. 2008. *Outsider Within: Reworking Anthropology in the Global Age*. Urbana: University of Illinois Press.

Hegel, Georg Wilhelm Friedrich. 1956. *The Philosophy of History*. New York: Dover.

Henry, Frances. 1999. "African Religions in Trinidad: The Legitimation and Acceptance of the Orisha Religion Today." Paper presented at the 6th World Congress of Orisha Culture and Tradition, August 15–22, Port of Spain, Trinidad (reprinted in Henry 2000).

————. 2000. *Beliefs, Doctrines and Practices of the Orisha Religion in Trinidad, 1958–1999*. Port of Spain: self-published by author.

————. 2003. *Reclaiming African Religions in Trinidad: The Socio-political Legitimation of the Orisha and Spiritual Baptist Faiths*. Kingston, Jamaica: University of the West Indies Press.

Herskovits, Melville. 1958. *The Myth of the Negro Past*. Boston: Beacon Press.

Herskovits, Melville J., and Frances S. Herskovits. 1947. *Trinidad Village*. New York: Knopf.

Hesse, Barnor. 2000. "Introduction: Un/settled Multiculturalisms." In *Un/settled Multiculturalisms: Diasporas, Entanglements, Transruptions*, edited by Barnor Hesse, 1–30. London: Zed Books.

Hiepko, Andrea Schweiger. 2011. "Europe and the Antilles: An Interview with Édouard Glissant." Translated by Julin Everett. In *The Creolization of Theory*, edited by Françoise Lionnet and Shu-mei Shih, 255–61. Durham, NC: Duke University Press.

Higman, B. W. 1984. *Slave Populations of the British Caribbean 1807–1834*. Baltimore: Johns Hopkins University Press.

Hill, Errol. 1997 [1972]. *Trinidad Carnival: Mandate for a National Theatre*. London: New Beacon Books.

Hintzen, Percy. 1997. "Reproducing Domination Identity and Legitimacy Constructs in the West Indies." *Social Identities* 3 (1): 47–76.

———. 2001. "Rethinking Democracy in the Postnationalist State." In *New Caribbean Thought: A Reader*, edited by Brian Meeks and Folke Lindahl, 104–24. Kingston, Jamaica: University of West Indies Press.

———. 2002. "The Caribbean: Race and Creole." In *A Companion to Racial and Ethnic Studies*, edited by David Goldberg and John Solomos, 475–94. Oxford: Blackwell.

Hobsbawm, Eric J., and Terence Ranger. 1992 [1983]. *The Invention of Tradition*. Cambridge: Cambridge University Press.

Hoetink, H. 1985. "Race and Color in the Caribbean." In *Caribbean Contours*, edited by Sidney Mintz and Richard Price, 55–84. Baltimore: Johns Hopkins University Press.

Holbraad, Martin. 2012. *Truth in Motion: The Recursive Anthropology of Cuban Divination*. Chicago: University of Chicago Press.

Houk, James. 1993. "Afro-Trinidadian Identity and the Africanisation of the Orisha Religion." In *Trinidad Ethnicity*, edited by Kevin Yelvington, 161–79. Knoxville: University of Tennessee Press.

———. 1995. *Spirits, Blood, and Drums: The Orisha Tradition in Trinidad*. Philadelphia: Temple University Press.

———. 1999. "Chaos, Compromise, and Transformation in the Orisha Religion in Trinidad." In *Religion, Diaspora and Cultural Identity*, edited by John Pulis, 295–310. Amsterdam, Netherlands: Gordon and Breach.

Howard, Rosalyn. 2004. "Yoruba in the British Caribbean: A Comparative Perspective on Trinidad and the Bahamas." In *The Yoruba Diaspora in the Atlantic World*, edited by Toyin Falola and Matt D. Childs, 157–76. Bloomington: Indiana University Press.

Hucks, Tracey E. 1998. "Approaching the African God: An Examination of African American Yoruba History from 1959 to the Present." PhD diss., Harvard University.

———. 2001. "Trinidad, African-Derived." In *Encyclopedia of African and African-American Religions*, edited by Stephen D. Glazier, 338–43. New York: Routledge.

———. 2006. "'I Smoothed the Way, I Opened Doors': Women in the Yoruba-Orisha Tradition of Trinidad." In *Women in Religion in the African Diaspora*, edited by Ruth Marie Griffith and Barbara Diane Savage, 19–36. Baltimore: Johns Hopkins University Press.

———. 2012. *Yoruba Traditions and African American Religious Nationalism*. Albuquerque: University of New Mexico Press.

Hucks, Tracey E., and Diane Stewart. 2003. "Authenticity and Authority in the Shaping of Trinidad Orisha Identity: Toward an African-Derived Religious Theory." *Western Journal of Black Studies* 27 (3): 176–85.

Hurston, Zora. 1990 [1938]. *Tell My Horse: Voodoo and Life in Haiti and Jamaica*. New York: Harper and Row.

IESOM. 2005. "Brief History of Ile Eko SANGO/OSUN Mil'Osa & The SANGO Holy Rain Festival." In *Ile Eko Sango Osun Mil'osa, Opening Address at Sango' Annual Rain Festival*, edited by Iya Sangowunmi. Unpublished brochure.

———. 2006. "Sango/Osun Rain Festival." Ile Eko Sango Osun Mil'osa. Unpublished brochure.

Jackson, John L., Jr. 2013. *Thin Description: Ethnography and the African Hebrew Israelites of Jerusalem*. Cambridge, MA: Harvard University Press.

Jackson, Shona N. 2012. *Creole Indigeneity: Between Myth and Nation in the Caribbean*. Minneapolis: University of Minnesota Press.

James, C. L. R. 1973 [1962]. "The Middle Classes." In *Consequences of Class and Color: West Indian Perspectives*, edited by David Lowenthal and Lambros Comitas, 79–92. New York: Anchor Books.

———. 1989 [1963]. *The Black Jacobins: Toussaint L'Ouverture and the San Domingo Revolution*. New York: Vintage Books.

———. 1992. "Lincoln, Carnival, George Padmore: Writings from *The Nation*." In *The C. L. R. James Reader*, edited by Anna Grimshaw, 281–95. London: Blackwell.

———. 1993. *Beyond a Boundary*. Durham, NC: Duke University Press.

Jelly-Schapiro, Joshua. 2005. "'Are We All Creoles Now?': Ethnicity and Nation in a Heterogeneous Caribbean Diaspora." In *Ethnicity, Class, and Nationalism: Caribbean and Extra-Caribbean Dimensions*, edited by Anton L. Allahar, 23–55. Lanham, MD: Lexington Books.

Johnson, E. Patrick. 2003. *Appropriating Blackness*. Durham, NC: Duke University Press.

———. 2005. "Black Performance Studies: Genealogies, Politics, Futures." In *The Sage Handbook of Performance Studies*, edited by Soyini D. Madison and Judith Hamera, 446–63. California: Sage.

Johnson, Paul Christopher. 2007. *Diasporic Conversions: Black Carib Religion and the Recovery of Africa*. Berkeley: University of California Press.

———. 2011. "An Atlantic Genealogy of 'Spirit Possession.'" *Comparative Studies in Society and History* 53 (2): 393–425.

———. 2012. "Religion and Diaspora." *Religion and Society: Advances in Research* 3:95–114.

Jones, Joni L. 1997. "Performing Osun without Bodies: Documenting the Osun Festival in Print.: *Text and Performance Quarterly* 17 (1): 69–93.

Joseph, Peniel. 2007. *Waiting 'til the Midnight Hour: A Narrative History of Black Power in America*. New York: Owl Books.

———. 2014. Stokely: A Life. New York: Basic Civatas Books.

Kachun, Mitch. 2003. *Festivals of Freedom: Memory and Meaning in African American Emancipation Celebrations, 1808–1915*. Amherst: University of Massachusetts Press.

Kamugisha, Aaron. 2007. "The Coloniality of Citizenship in the Contemporary Anglophone Caribbean." *Race & Class* 49 (2): 20–40.

Kantrowitz, Stephen. 2012. *More Than Freedom: Fighting for Black Citizenship in a White Republic, 1829–1889*. New York: Penguin.

Kelley, Robin. 2000. "How the West Was One: On the Uses and Limitations of Diaspora." *Black Scholar* 30 (3–4): 31–35.

Khambon, Khafra. 1995a. "Black Power in Trinidad and Tobago: February 26–April 21, 1970." In *The Black Power Revolution of 1970: A Retrospective*, edited by Selwyn Ryan and Talmoon Stewart, 215–42. St. Augustine: Institute for Social and Economic Research, University of the West Indies.

———. 1995b. "The Vibrations of 1970." In *The Black Power Revolution of 1970: A Retrospective*, edited by Selwyn Ryan and Talmoon Stewart, 243–60. St. Augustine: Institute for Social and Economic Research, University of the West Indies.

Khan, Aisha. 1993. "What Is 'a Spanish'? Ambiguity and 'Mixed' Ethnicity in Trinidad." In *Trinidad Ethnicity*, edited by Kevin Yelvington, 180–207. Knoxville: University of Tennessee Press.

———. 2000. "On the 'Right Path': Interpolating Religion in Trinidad." In *Religion, Diaspora and Cultural Identity*, edited by John Pulis, 247–76. Amsterdam, Netherlands: Gordon and Breach.

———. 2001. "Journey to the Center of the Earth: The Caribbean as Master Symbol." *Cultural Anthropology* 16 (3): 271–302.

———. 2004a. *Callaloo Nation: Metaphors of Race and Religious Identity among South Asians in Trinidad*. Durham, NC: Duke University Press.

———. 2004b. "Sacred Subversions? Syncretic Creoles, the Indo-Caribbean, and 'Culture's In-between.'" *Radical History Review* 89:165–84.

———. 2007. "Good to Think? Creolization, Optimism and Agency." *Current Anthropology* 48 (5): 653–73.

Knauft, Bruce M. 2002. *Critically Modern: Alternatives, Alterities, Anthropologies.* Bloomington: Indiana University Press.

Korom, Frank J. 2003. *Hosay Trinidad: Muharram Performances in an Indo-Caribbean Diaspora*. Philadelphia: University of Pennsylvania Press.

Laitinen, Maarit. 2002. *Marching to Zion: Creolisation in Spiritual Baptist Rituals and Cosmology*. Helsinki: University of Helsinki.

Lamming, George. 1998. "The Legacy of Eric Williams." *Callaloo* 20 (4): 731–36.

Landes, Ruth. 1994 [1947]. *City of Women*. 2nd ed. Albuquerque: University of New Mexico Press.

Lawal, Babatunde. 1995. "A Ya Gbo, A Ya To: New Perspectives on Edan Ogboni." *African Arts* 28 (1): 37–49, 98–100.

Layne, Niasha. 2000. "Lancelot Layne, Papa Was a Loyal Son." *Trinidad Express*, August 11.

Lewis, Rupert. 2001. "Reconsidering the Role of the Middle Class in Caribbean Politics." In *New Caribbean Thought: A Reader*, edited by Brian Meeks and Folke Lindahl, 127–43. Kingston, Jamaica: University of the West Indies Press.

Lieber, Michael. 1981. *Street Life: Afro-American Culture in Urban Trinidad*. Cambridge, MA: Schenkman.

Lionnet, Françoise, and Shu-mei Shih, eds. 2011. *The Creolization of Theory*. Durham, NC: Duke University Press.

Liverpool, Hollis. 2001. *Ritual of Power and Rebellion: The Carnival Tradition in Trinidad and Tobago, 1763–1962*. Chicago: Research Associates School Times Publications/ Frontline Distribution International.

Loomba, Ania, Suvir Kaul, Matti Bunzl, Antoinette Burton, and Jed Esty eds. 2006. *Postcolonial Studies and Beyond*. Durham, NC: Duke University Press.

Lord, Richard. 2000. "Orishas Get Land Deeds from PM." *Trinidad Guardian*, August 3.

Lorde, Audre. 2007 [1984]. *Sister Outsider*. Berkeley, CA: Crossing Press.

Love, Velma. 2012. *Divining the Self: A Study in Yoruba Myth and Human Consciousness.* University Park: Pennsylvania State University Press.

Lovelace, Earl. 1984. *The Wine of Astonishment.* New York: Aventura/Vintage Books.

———. 1997. *Salt.* New York: Persea Books.

———. 1998 [1979]. *The Dragon Can't Dance.* New York: Persea Books.

———. 2003. *Growing in the Dark (Selected Essays).* Edited by Funso Aiyejina. San Juan: Lexicon Trinidad.

———. 2004. "The Emancipation-Jouvay Tradition and Almost Loss of Pan." In *Carnival: Culture in Action,* edited by Milla Riggio, 187–94. New York: Routledge.

Lum, Kenneth Anthony. 2000. *Praising His Name in the Dance: Spirit Possession in the Spiritual Baptist Faith and Orisha Work.* Amsterdam: Harwood Academic.

Lux, William R. 1972. "Black Power in the Caribbean." *Journal of Black Studies* 3 (2): 207–25.

Magid, Alvin. 1988. *Urban Nationalism: A Study of Political Development in Trinidad.* Gainesville: University of Florida Press.

Mahabir, Noorkumar and Ashram Maharaj. 1996. "Hindu Elements in the Shango/Orisha Cult of Trinidad." In *Across the Dark Waters: Ethnicity and Indian Identity in the Caribbean,* edited by D. Dabydeen and B. Samaroo, 90–107. London: MacMillan Caribbean.

Maharaj, Kathleen. 2000. "The Obeah Man Who Wasn't: The True Story of Papa Nezer." *Trinidad Express,* March 21, Features.

Maharaj, Satnarayan. 2006. Letter to the editor. *Trinidad Guardian,* April 13.

Makalani, Minkah. 2011. *In the Cause of Freedom: Radical Black Internationalism from Harlem to London, 1917–1939.* Chapel Hill: University of North Carolina Press.

Marcus, George E. 1998. *Ethnography through Thick and Thin.* Princeton, NJ: Princeton University Press.

Martin, Tony. 1998. *The Progress of the African Race since Emancipation and Prospects for the Future.* Trinidad: Emancipation Support Committee.

Mason, John, and Gary Edwards. 1985. *Black Gods: Òrìsà Studies in the New World.* Brooklyn: Yoruba Theological Archministry.

Mason, Michael Atwood. 2002. *Living Santeria: Rituals and Experience in an Afro-Cuban Religion.* Washington, DC: Smithsonian Institution Press.

Matory, James Lorand. 1994. *Sex and the Empire That Is No More: Gender and the Politics of Metaphor in Oyo Yorùbá Religion.* Minneapolis: University of Minnesota Press.

———. 2005. *Black Atlantic Religion: Tradition, Transnationalism and Matriarchy in the Afro-Brazilian Candomblé.* Princeton, NJ: Princeton University Press.

———. 2009. "The Many Who Dance in Me: Afro-Atlantic Ontology and the Problem with 'Transnationalism.'" In *Transnational Transcendence: Essays on Religion and Globalization,* edited by Thomas J. Csordas, 231–62. Berkeley: University of California Press.

Maugé, Conrad E. 1996. *The Lost Orisha.* Mount Vernon, NY: House of Providence.

Mbembe, Achille. 2001. *On the Postcolony.* Berkeley: University of California Press.

McClaurin, Irma, ed. 2001. *Black Feminist Anthropology: Theory, Politics, Praxis, and Poetics.* New Brunswick, NJ: Rutgers University Press.

McLeod, Patricia. 1999. "World Congress: Caribbean Report." In *Proceedings of the 6th World Congress of Orisa Tradition and Culture,* 17–37. Port of Spain, Trinidad: Secretariat of the 6th World Congress of Orisa Tradition and Culture.

McNeal, Keith E. 2008. "Performing Divinity with a Difference: Iconopraxis and Dual-Embodiment in African and Hindu Traditions of Spirit Mediumship in the Southern Caribbean." Paper presented at the Linguistic Anthropology Laboratory, University of California, San Diego, March 10.

———. 2011. *Trance and Modernity in the Southern Caribbean: African and Hindu Popular Religions in Trinidad and Tobago.* Gainesville: University Press of Florida.

McNeal, Meida. 2007. "Choreographing Citizenship in the 'Gayelle': Performing Trinidadian Cultural Nationalisms." PhD diss., Northwestern University.

Meeks, Brian. 1996. *Radical Caribbean: From Black Power to Abu Bakr.* Barbados: The Press of the University of the West Indies.

Meighoo, Kirk. 2003. *Politics in a Half-Made Society.* Kingston, Jamaica: Ian Randle.

Mercer, Kobena. 1994. *Welcome to the Jungle: New Positions in Black Cultural Studies.* New York: Routledge.

Mignolo, Walter. 2000. *Local Histories/Global Designs: Coloniality, Subaltern Knowledges and Border Thinking.* Princeton, NJ: Princeton University Press.

Miller, Daniel. 1994. *Modernity: An Ethnographic Approach.* New York: Berg.

Mintz, Sidney. 1971. "The Caribbean as a Socio-cultural Area." In *Peoples and Cultures of the Caribbean: An Anthropological Reader,* edited by Michael M. Horowitz, 17–46. Garden City, NY: Natural History Press.

———. 1974. *Caribbean Transformations.* Chicago: Aldine.

———. 1985. *Sweetness and Power: The Place of Sugar in Modern History.* New York: Viking Press.

Mintz, Sidney, and Richard Price. 1992 [1976]. *The Birth of African American Culture.* Boston: Beacon Press.

Mintz, Sidney, and Sally Price, eds. 1985. *Caribbean Contours.* Baltimore: Johns Hopkins University Press.

Mischel, Frances. 1957. "African Powers in Trinidad: The Shango Cult." *Anthropological Quarterly* 30:45–59.

Mohammed, Patricia. 2002. "Taking Possession: Symbols of Empire and Nationhood." *Small Axe* (6 1): 31–58.

Mohanty, Chandra Talpade. 2006 [2003]. *Feminism without Borders: Decolonizing Theory, Practicing Solidarity.* Durham, NC: Duke University Press.

Moonsammy, Patricia A. 2009. "Rapso Warriors: Poetic Performance, Revolution, and Conscious Art Music in Trinidad and Tobago." PhD diss., University of Michigan.

Moran, Patricia. 2000. "Experiencing the Pan-African Dimensions of Carnival." In *Ah Come Back Home,* edited by Ian Isidore Smart and Kimani S. K. Nehusi, 163–78. Washington, DC: Original World Press.

Mordecai, Rachel L. 2014. *Citizenship under Pressure: The 1970s in Jamaican Literature and Culture.* Kingston, Jamaica: University of the West Indies Press.

Mudimbe, V. Y. 1988. *The Invention of Africa.* Bloomington: Indiana University Press.

———. 1994. *The Idea of Africa.* Bloomington: Indiana University Press.

Munasinghe, Viranjini. 2001a. *Callaloo or Tossed Salad? East Indians and the Cultural Politics of Identity in Trinidad*. Ithaca, NY: Cornell University Press.

———. 2001b. "Redefining the Nation: The East Indian Struggle for Inclusion in Trinidad." *Journal of Asian American Studies* 4 (1): 1–34.

———. 2002. "Nationalism in Hybrid Spaces: The Production of Purity Out of Impurity." *American Ethnologist* 29 (3): 663–92.

Murphy, Joseph M. 1994. *Working the Spirit: Ceremonies of the African Diaspora*. Boston: Beacon Press.

———. 2006. "Don't Confuse Spiritual Baptist with Orisha." *Trinidad and Tobago Express*, March 30.

Nettleford, Rex M. 1972 [1970]. *Identity, Race, and Protest in Jamaica*. New York: Morrow.

Nichols, Elizabeth G. 2006. "The Power of the Pelvic Bone: Breaching the Barriers of Social Class in Venezuela." *Frontiers: A Journal of Women Studies* 27 (3): 71–105.

Nunley, John. 1987. *Moving with the Face of the Devil: Art and Politics in Urban West Africa*. Urbana: University of Illinois Press.

———. 1988. "Masquerade Mix-Up in Trinidad Carnival: Live Once, Die Forever." In *Caribbean Festive Arts*, edited by John Nunley and Judith Bettleheim, 85–118. Seattle: University of Washington Press.

Nunley, John, and Judith Bettleheim, eds. 1988. *Caribbean Festive Arts: Each and Every Bit of Difference*. Seattle: University of Washington Press.

Nurse, Keith. 1999. "Globalisation and Trinidad Carnival: Diaspora, Hybridity and Identity in Popular Culture." In *Identity, Ethnicity and Culture in the Caribbean*, edited by Ralph R. Premdas, 80–114. St. Augustine: University of the West Indies.

Nurse, Keith, and Christine Ho, eds. 2005. *Globalization and Popular Culture in the Caribbean*. Kingston, Jamaica: Ian Randle.

Ofosu, Natasha. 2000. "'Shango' Gives New Light to Orisha Faith." *Trinidad Guardian*, July 22.

Ogbar, Jeffrey Ogbanna Green. 2005. *Black Power: Radical Politics and African American Identity*. Baltimore: Johns Hopkins University Press.

Olmos, Margarite Fernandez and Lizabeth Paravisini-Gebert, eds. 1997. *Sacred Possessions: Vodou, Santería, Obeah and the Caribbean*. New Brunswick, NJ: Rutgers University Press.

Olupona, Jacob Kehinde. 2011. *City of 201 Gods: Ilé-Ifè in Time, Space, and the Imagination*. Berkeley: University of California Press.

Olupona, J. K., and R. O. Abiodun, eds. 2016. *Ifá Divination, Knowledge, Power, and Performance*. Bloomington: Indiana University Press.

Olupona, Jacob Kẹhinde, and Terry Rey, eds. 2008. *Òrìṣà Devotion as World Religion: The Globalization of Yorùbá Religious Culture*. Madison: University of Wisconsin Press.

Omi, Michael, and Howard Winant. 1994. *Racial Formation in the United States: From the 1960s to the 1990s*. New York: Routledge.

Ong, Aihwa. 1999a. "Cultural Citizenship as Subject Making: Immigrants Negotiate Racial and Cultural Boundaries in the United States." In *Race, Identity, and Citizenship: A Reader*, edited by Rodolfo D. Torres, Louis F. Mirón, and Jonathon Xavier Inda, 262–93. Oxford: Blackwell.

———. 1999b. *Flexible Citizenship: The Cultural Logics of Transnationalism*. Durham, NC: Duke University Press.

———. 2006. *Neoliberalism as Exception: Mutations in Citizenship and Sovereignty*. Durham, NC: Duke University Press.

Ortner, Sherry. 1994. "Theory in Anthropology since the Sixties." In *Culture/Power/ History*, 372–411, edited by N. Dirks, G. Eley, and S. Ortner. Princeton, NJ: Princeton University Press.

Osundiya, Baba. 2001. *Awo Obi: Obi Divination in Theory and Practice*. New York: Athelia Henrietta Press.

Oxaal, Ivar. 1971. *Race and Revolutionary Consciousness: A Documentary Interpretation of the 1970 Black Power Revolt in Trinidad*. Cambridge, MA: Schenkman.

Palmer, Colin. 2000. "Defining and Studying the Modern African Diaspora." *Journal of Negro History* 85 (1/2): 27–32.

———. 2006. *Eric Williams and the Making of the Modern Caribbean*. Raleigh: University of North Carolina Press.

Palmié, Stephan. 1995. "Against Syncretism: 'Africanizing' and 'Cubanizing' Discourse in North American Òrìsà Worship." In *Counterworks: Managing the Diversity of Knowledge*, edited by R. Fardon, 80–104. London: Routledge.

———. 2002. *Wizards and Scientists: Explorations in Afro-Cuban Modernity and Tradition*. Durham, NC: Duke University Press.

———. 2006. "Creolization and Its Discontents." *Annual Review of Anthropology* 35:433–56.

———. 2013. *The Cooking of History: How Not to Study Afro-Cuban Religion*. Chicago: University of Chicago Press.

Panday, Basdeo. 1999. Second Annual Orisha Family Day address. African Ancestral Site, Lopinot Road, Arouca, Trinidad, March 21 (link no longer active).

———. 2000. "Presentation of the Deed to Land at Maloney to the Council of Elders Spiritual Baptist Faith of Trinidad and Tobago." Maloney, Trinidad. March 30 (link no longer active).

Pantin, Raoul. 1990. *Black Power Day: The 1970 February Revolution, a Reporter's Story*. Santa Cruz, Trinidad: Hatuey Productions.

———. 2005. Emancipation Day 1990. *Trinidad and Tobago Express*. July 31.

Paquet, Sandra Pouchet, Patricia J. Saunders, and Stephen Stuempfle, eds. 2007. *Music, Memory, Resistance: Calypso and the Caribbean Literary Imagination*. Kingston, Jamaica: Ian Randle.

Paton, Diana. 2009. "Obeah Acts: Producing and Policing the Boundaries of Religion in the Caribbean." *Small Axe* 13 (1): 1–18.

———. 2015. *The Cultural Politics of Obeah: Religion, Colonialism and Modernity in the Caribbean World*. Cambridge: Cambridge University Press.

Paton, Diana, and Maarit Forde, eds. 2012. *Obeah and Other Powers: The Politics of Caribbean Religion and Healing*. Durham, NC: Duke University Press.

Peel, J. D. Y. 2001. *Religious Encounter and the Making of the Yoruba*. Bloomington: Indiana University Press.

Perez, Elizabeth. 2016. *Religion in the Kitchen: Cooking, Talking, and the Making of Black Atlantic Traditions*. New York: New York University Press.

Piot, Charles. 1999. *Remotely Global: Village Modernity in West Africa*. Chicago: University of Chicago Press.

Pitts, Walter F., Jr. 1993. *Old Ship of Zion: The Afro-Baptist Religion in the African Diaspora*. New York: Oxford University Press.

Placido, Barbara. 1998. "Spirits of the Nation: Identity and Legitimacy in the Cults of Maria Lionza and Simon Bolivar." PhD diss., University of Cambridge.

———. 2001. "'It's All to Do with Words': An Analysis of Spirit Possession in the Venezuelan Cult of Maria Lionza." *Journal of the Royal Anthropological Institute* 7 (2): 207–24.

Pópóọlá, Sọlágbadé. 2007. "Let Their Souls Be Perfectly Rested." *Elérìi Ìpín: A Magazine of the International Council for Ifá Religion* 3:31, 34–35, 37.

———. 2014. *Ọmọlúàbí: The Description of a Complete Human Being*. Phoenix, AZ: Ifa-Works, LLC.

Premdas, Ralph R. 1996. "Ethnicity and Elections in the Caribbean: A Radical Realignment of Power in Trinidad and the Threat of Communal Strife." Working Paper no. 224. Helen Kellogg Institute for International Studies, University of Notre Dame.

———. 1999. "The Ascendance of an Indian Prime Minister in Trinidad and Tobago: The 1995 Elections." In *Identity, Ethnicity and Culture in the Caribbean*, edited by Ralph R. Premdas, 323–58. St. Augustine, Trinidad: University of the West Indies.

Price, Richard. 1985. "An Absence of Ruins? Seeking Caribbean Historical Consciousness." *Caribbean Review* 14 (3): 24–29, 45.

———. 2006. "On the Miracle of Creolization." In *Afro-Atlantic Dialogues: Anthropology in the Diaspora*, edited by Kevin Yelvington, 115-150. Santa Fe, NM: School of American Research Press.

Price, Richard, and Sally Price. 1997. "Shadowboxing in the Mangrove." *Cultural Anthropology* 12 (1): 3–36.

Pulis, John W., ed. 1999. *Religion, Diaspora and Cultural Identity*. Amsterdam, The Netherlands: Gordon and Breach.

Puri, Shalini. 1999. "Canonized Hybridities, Resistant Hybridities: Chutney Soca, Carnival and the Politics of Nationalism." In *Caribbean Romances: The Politics of Regional Representation*, edited by Belinda Edmonson, 12–38. Charlottesville: University of Virginia Press.

———. 2003. "Beyond Resistance: Notes Towards a New Caribbean Cultural Studies." *Small Axe* 7 (2): 23–38.

———. 2004. *The Postcolonial Caribbean: Social Equality, Post-nationalism and Cultural Hybridity*. New York: Palgrave Macmillan.

Reddock, Rhoda, ed. 1996. *Ethnic Minorities in Caribbean Society*. St. Augustine, Trinidad and Tobago: I.S.E.R., The University of the West Indies.

Regis, Louis. 1999. *The Political Calypso: The Opposition in Trinidad and Tobago 1962–1987*. Gainesville: University Press of Florida.

———. 2004. "Reflections on the Imaging of Africa in the Calypso of Trinidad and Tobago." Paper presented at "Cross Culturalism and the Caribbean Canon: A Cultural Studies Conference." University of the West Indies, St. Augustine, Trinidad and Tobago, January 7–10.

Riggio, Milla Cozart, ed. 2004. *Carnival: Culture in Action*. New York: Routledge.

Robothom, Dan. 1998. "Transnationalism in the Caribbean: Formal and Informal." *American Ethnologist* 25 (2): 307–21.

Rodney, Walter. 1969. *The Groundings with My Brothers*. London: Bogle-L'Ouverture Publications.

Rohlehr, Gordon. 1992. *My Strangled City and Other Essays*. Port of Spain: Longman Trinidad.

———. 1998. "The Culture of Williams: Context, Performance, Legacy." *Callaloo* 20 (4): 849–88.

———. 1999. "The State of Calypso Today." In *Identity, Ethnicity and Culture in the Caribbean*, edited by Ralph R. Premdas, 29–46. St. Augustine: University of the West Indies.

———. 2004a [1990]. *Calypso and Society in Pre-independence Trinidad*. Port of Spain: Lexicon.

———. 2004b. "Calypso Reinvents Itself." In *Carnival: Culture in Action, the Trinidad Experience*, edited by Milla Riggio, 213–27. New York: Routledge.

Rosenthal, Judy. 1998. *Possession, Ecstasy and Law in Ewe Voodoo*. Charlottesville: University Press of Virginia.

Ryan, Selwyn. 1972. *Race and Nationalism in Trinidad and Tobago: A Study of Decolonization in a Multiracial Society*. Toronto: University of Toronto Press.

———. 1995. "1970: Revolution or Rebellion?" In *The Black Power Revolution of 1970: A Retrospective*, edited by Selwyn Ryan and Talmoon Stewart, 691–708. St. Augustine: Institute for Social and Economic Research, University of the West Indies.

———. 1999. *The Jhandi and the Cross: The Clash of Cultures in Post-Creole Trinidad and Tobago*. St. Augustine: Sir Arthur Lewis Institute of Social and Economic Studies.

Ryan, Selwyn, and Talmoon Stewart, eds., with the assistance of Roy McCree. 1995. *The Black Power Revolution of 1970: A Retrospective*. St. Augustine: Institute for Social and Economic Research, University of the West Indies.

Salami, Ayọ̀. 2002. *Ifá: A Complete Divination*. Lagos: NIDD.

Sangowunmi, Iya. 2011. *Esu: Personifications of Essences*. Chaguanas, Trinidad: Sangowunmi Publishers.

Sangowunmi, Iya, ed. 2005. *Ile Eko Sango Osun Mil'osa, Opening Address at Sango' Annual Rain Festival*. Unpublished brochure.

Sankeralli, Burton, ed. 1995. *At the Crossroads: African Caribbean Religion and Christianity*. Trinidad: Caribbean Conference of Churches.

———. 1999a. "Of Obeah and Sacrifice: The Demonizing of African Traditions." *Trinidad Guardian*, August 9.

———. 1999b. "Ogun in the 21st Century." *Trinidad Guardian*, July 19.

———. 1999c. "Orisha: A World Religion." *Trinidad Guardian*, August 2.

———. 1999d. "Orisha, Defining Our Caribbean Culture." *Trinidad Guardian*, July 26.

———. 1999e. "Orisha Represents a Coherent Pattern of Work." *Trinidad Guardian*, June 28.

———. 1999f. "Salutation to Eshu." *Trinidad Guardian*, July 12.

———. 1999g. "Use Orisha to Guide in Time of Crisis." *Trinidad Guardian*, July 5.

———. 2002. "Pan-African Discourse and the Post-Creole: The Case of Trinidad's Yoruba." Paper presented at the "Conference on Caribbean Culture," University of the West Indies, St. Augustine, January 9–13. Unpublished manuscript.

———. 2004. "Indian Presence in Carnival." In *Carnival: Culture in Action*, edited by Milla Cozart Riggio, 76–84. New York: Routledge.

Schechner, Richard. 2004. "Carnival (Theory) after Bakhtin." In *Carnival: Culture in Action*, edited by Milla Cozart Riggio, 3–12. New York: Routledge.

Scher, Philip W. 1997. "Unveiling the Orisha." In *Africa's Ogun*, edited by Sandra Barnes, 315–31. 2nd ed. Bloomington: Indiana University Press.

———. 1999. "West Indian American Day." In *Religion, Diaspora and Cultural Identity*, edited by John Pulis, 45–66. Amsterdam, Netherlands: Gordon and Breach.

———. 2003. *Carnival and the Formation of a Caribbean Transnation*. Gainesville: University Press of Florida.

———. 2005. "From the Metropole to the Equator: Carnival Consciousness between New York and Trinidad." In *Globalization and Popular Culture in the Caribbean*, edited by Keith Nurse and Christine Ho, 45–63. Kingston, Jamaica: Ian Randle.

Scott, David. 1991. "That Event, This Memory: Notes on the Anthropology of African Diasporas in the New World." *Diaspora* 1 (3): 261–84.

———. 1999. *Refashioning the Future: Criticism after Postcoloniality*. Princeton, NJ: Princeton University Press.

Scott, James C. 1990. *Domination and the Arts of Resistance: Hidden Transcripts*. New Haven, CT: Yale University Press.

Segal, Daniel. 1989. "Nationalism in a Colonial State: A Study of Trinidad and Tobago." PhD diss., University of Chicago.

———. 1993. "'Race' and 'Colour' in Pre-independence Trinidad and Tobago." In *Trinidad Ethnicity*, edited by Kevin Yelvington, 81–115. Knoxville: University of Tennessee Press.

———. 1994. "Living Ancestors: Nationalism and the Past in Postcolonial Trinidad and Tobago." In *Remapping Memory: The Politics of Timespace*, edited by J. Boyarin, 221–39. Minneapolis: University of Minnesota Press.

Sheller, Mimi. 2012. *Citizenship from Below: Erotic Agency and Caribbean Freedom*. Durham, NC: Duke University Press.

Simpson, George Eaton. 1962. "The Shango Cult in Nigeria and in Trinidad." *American Anthropologist* 64 (6): 1204–19.

———. 1965. *The Shango Cult in Trinidad*. Rio Piedras, Puerto Rico: Institute of Caribbean Studies, University of Puerto Rico.

———. 1970. *Religious Cults of the Caribbean*. Rio Piedras: University of Puerto Rico.

———. 1978. *Black Religions in the New World*. New York: Columbia University Press.

Slocum, Karla, and Deborah Thomas. 2003. "Rethinking Global and Area Studies: Insight from Caribbeanist Anthropology." *American Anthropologist* 105 (3): 553–65.

Smart, Ian Isidore, and Kimani S. K. Nehusi, eds. 2000. *Ah Come Back Home: Perspectives on the Trinidad and Tobago Carnival*. Washington, DC: Original World Press.

Smith, M. G. 1965. *The Plural Society in the British West Indies*. Berkeley: University of California Press.

———. 1984. *Culture, Race, and Class in the Commonwealth Caribbean*. Mona Jamaica: Department of Extra-mural Studies, University of West Indies.

Smith, M. G., and Norman Paul. 1963. *Dark Puritan*. Mona Jamaica: Department of Extra-mural Studies, University of the West Indies.

Smith, Raymond. 1982. *Racism and Colonialism: Essays on Ideology and Social Structure*. Edited by R. Ross. The Hague: Leiden University Press.

———. 1996. *The Matrifocal Family: Power, Pluralism, and Politics*. New York: Routledge.

Springer, Pearl Eintou. 1995. "Orisa and the Spiritual Baptist Religion in TT." In *At the Crossroads: African Caribbean Religion and Christianity*, edited by Burton Sankeralli, 85–108. Trinidad: Caribbean Conference of Churches.

Stallybrass, Peter, and Allon White, eds. 1986. *The Politics and Poetics of Transgression*. Ithaca, NY: Cornell University Press.

Stephens, Rev. Patricia. 1999. *The Spiritual Baptist Faith: African New World Religious Identity, History and Testimony*. London: Karnak House.

Stephenson-Lee Chee, Valerie. 1999. "Our Ancestral Heritage: The influence of the Yoruba Tradition on African Spirituality in Trinidad and Tobago." Paper presented at *the 6th World Congress of Orisa Tradition and Culture*. Port of Spain, Trinidad, August 15–22, 1999.

Stewart, Charles. 2007. *Creolization: History, Ethnography, Theory*. Walnut Creek, CA: Left Coast Press.

Stewart, Charles, and Rosalind Shaw, eds. 1994. *Syncretism and Anti-syncretism: The Politics of Religious Synthesis*. London: Routledge.

Stewart, Dianne M. 2005. *Three Eyes for the Journey: African Dimensions of the Jamaican Religious Experience*. Oxford: Oxford University Press.

Stewart, John O. 1989. *Drinks, Drummers and Decent Folk: Ethnographic Narratives of Village Trinidad*. Albany: State University of New York Press.

Stuempfle, Stephen. 1995. *The Steelband Movement: The Forging of a National Art in Trinidad and Tobago*. Philadelphia: University of Pennsylvania Press.

Taitt, Ria. 1999. "PM Promises More Rights for Orishas." *Trinidad and Tobago Express*, March 22.

Taussig, Michael T. 1980. *The Devil and Commodity Fetishism in South America*. Chapel Hill: University of North Carolina Press.

———. 1986. *Shamanism, Colonialism, and the Wild Man: A Study in Terror and Healing*. Chicago: University of Chicago Press.

———. 1996. *The Magic of the State*. New York: Routledge.

Taylor, Patrick. 2001. *Nation Dance: Religion, Identity and Cultural Difference in the Caribbean*. Bloomington: Indiana University Press.

Teish, Luisah. 1985. *Jambalaya*. New York: HarperCollins.

Thomas, Bert J. 1992. "Caribbean Black Power: From Slogan to Practical Politics." *Journal of Black Studies* 22 (3): 392–410.

Thomas, Deborah. 2002. "Modern Blackness: 'What We Are and What We Hope to Be.'" *Small Axe* 6 (2): 25–48.

———. 2004. *Modern Blackness: Nationalism, Globalization, and the Politics of Culture in Jamaica*. Durham, NC: Duke University Press.

———. 2011. *Exceptional Violence: Embodied Citizenship in Transnational Jamaica*. Durham, NC: Duke University Press.

Thomas, Deborah A., and M. Kamari Clarke. 2013. "Globalization and Race: Structures of Inequality, New Sovereignties, and Citizenship in a Neoliberal Era." *Annual Review of Anthropology* 42:305–25.

Thomas, Eudora. 1987. *A History of the Shouter Baptists in Trinidad and Tobago*. Ithaca, NY: Calaloux Publications.

Thompson, Robert Farris. 1984. *Flash of the Spirit: African and Afro-American Art and Philosophy*. New York: Random House.

———. 1988. "Recapturing Heaven's Glamour: Afro-Caribbean Festivalizing Arts." In *Caribbean Festive Arts*, edited by John Nunley and Judith Bettleheim, 17–29. Seattle: University of Washington Press.

———. 1993. *Face of the Gods: Art and Altars of Africa and the African Americas*. New York: Prestel Publishers.

Triandafyllidou, Anna. 1998. "National Identity and the 'Other.'" *Ethnic and Racial Studies* 21 (4): 593–612.

Trinidad and Tobago Express. 1999. "Come leh we dance Shango." March 22.

Trinidad and Tobago Gazette. 2001. (40) 240. December 20. Port of Spain: Government Printer. (link no longer active).

———. 2005. (44) 23. February 14. Port of Spain: Government Printer. (link no longer active).

Trinidad Guardian. 1999a. "Culture Ministry Helps with Orisha Congress."

———. 1999b. "Orisha Weddings Now Legal." August 17.

———. 2000. "Equality for Baptists." April 1.

Trotman, David V. 1976. "The Yoruba and Orisha Worship in Trinidad and British Guinea: 1838–1870." *African Studies Review* 19 (2): 1–17.

———. 1999a. "The Children of Shango." *Trinidad Guardian*, August 31.

———. 1999b. "1870–1970: A Century of Debilitation." *Trinidad Guardian*, September 3.

———. 2003. "Africanizing and Creolizing the Plantation Frontier of Trinidad, 1797–1838." In *Trans-Atlantic Dimensions of Ethnicity in the African Diaspora*, edited by Paul E. Lovejoy and David V. Trotman, 218–39. London: Continuum.

———. 2007. "Reflections on the Children of Shango: An Essay on a History of Orisha Worship in Trinidad." *Slavery and Abolition* 28 (2): 211–34.

Trouillot, Michel-Rolph. 1991. "Anthropology and the Savage Slot: The Poetics and Politics of Otherness." In *Recapturing Anthropology: Working in the Present*, edited by Richard Fox. Santa Fe, NM: School of American Research.

———. 1992. "The Caribbean Region: An Open Frontier in Anthropological Theory." *Annual Review of Anthropology* 21:19–42.

———. 1994. "Culture, Color and Politics in Haiti." In *Race*, 146–174, edited by Stephen Gregory and Roger Sanjek. New Brunswick, NJ: Rutgers University Press.

———. 1995. *Silencing the Past: Power and the Production of History*. Boston: Beacon Press.

———. 1998. "Culture on the Edges: Creolization in the Plantation Complex." *Plantation Society in the Americas* 5 (1): 8–28.

———. 2001. "The Anthropology of the State: Close Encounters of a Deceptive Kind: Forum on Theory in Anthropology." *Current Anthropology* 42 (1): 125–38.

———. 2002. "The Otherwise Modern: Caribbean Lessons from the Savage Slot." In *Critically Modern: Alternatives, Anthropologies, Alterities*, edited by Bruce M. Knauft, 220–40. Bloomington: Indiana University Press.

———. 2003. *Global Transformations: Anthropology and the Modern World*. New York: Palgrave Macmillan.

Ture, Kwame, and Charles V. Hamilton. 1992 [1967]. *Black Power: The Politics of Liberation in America*. New York: Vintage Books.

Turner, Victor. 1967. *The Forest of Symbols*. Ithaca, NY: Cornell University Press.

———. 1969. *The Ritual Process: Structure and Anti-structure*. Chicago: Aldine.

———. 1982. *From Ritual to Theatre: The Human Seriousness of Play*. New York: Performing Arts Journal Publications.

———. 1986. *The Anthropology of Performance*. New York: Performing Arts Journal Publications.

Vertovec, Stephen. 1992. *Hindu Trinidad: Religion, Ethnicity and Socio-economic Change*. London: MacMillan Caribbean.

Walcott, Derek. 1974. "The Caribbean: Culture or Mimicry?" *Journal of Interamerican Studies and World Affairs* 16(1): 3–13.

———. 1998. *What the Twilight Says: Essays*. New York: Farrar, Straus and Giroux.

Warner, Keith Q. 1993. "Ethnicity and the Contemporary Calypso." In *Trinidad Ethnicity*, edited by Kevin Yelvington, 275–91. Knoxville: University of Tennessee Press.

Warner-Lewis, Maureen. 1991. *Guinea's Other Sons*. Dover: Majority Press.

———. 1994. *Yoruba Songs of Trinidad*. Dover: Majority Press.

———. 1996. *Trinidad Yoruba: From Mother Tongue to Memory*. Tuscaloosa: University of Alabama Press.

———. 2009. "Affirming the Subaltern: The Contribution of JD Elder." *Research in African Literatures* 40 (1): 1–7.

Weber, Max. 1963. *The Sociology of Religion*. Boston: Beacon Press.

West, Michael O., William G. Martin, and Fanon Che Williams, eds. 2009. *From Toussaint to Tupac: The Black International since the Age of Revolution*. Chapel Hill: University of North Carolina Press.

Wilder, Gary. 2015. *Freedom Time: Negritude, Decolonization, and the Future of the World*. Durham, NC: Duke University Press.

Williams, Brackette. 1989. "A Class Act: The Race to Nation across Ethnic Terrain." *Annual Review of Anthropology* 18:401–44.

———. 1990. "Nationalism, Traditionalism, and the Problem of Cultural Authenticity." In *Nationalist Ideologies and the Production of National Cultures*, edited by Richard Fox, 112–29. Washington, DC: American Anthropological Association.

———. 1991. *Stains on My Name, War in my Veins: Guyana and the Politics of Cultural Struggle*. Durham, NC: Duke University Press.

———. 1995. Review of Paul Gilroy, *The Black Atlantic*. *Social Identities* 1: 175–92.

Williams, Eric Eustace. 1962. *The History of the People of Trinidad and Tobago*. New York: Praeger.

———. 1970. *From Columbus to Castro: The History of the Caribbean, 1492–1969*. London: Deutsch.

———. 1981. *Forged from the Love of Liberty: Selected Speeches of Dr. Eric Williams*. Compiled by Paul K. Sutton. Trinidad: Longman Caribbean.

———. 1993. *Eric E. Williams Speaks: Essays on Colonialism and Independence*. Edited by Selwyn Reginald Cudjoe. Wellesley, MA: Calaloux Publications.

———. 1994 [1944]. *Capitalism and Slavery*. Chapel Hill: University of North Carolina Press.

———. 1998 [1961]. "Massa Day Done (Public Lecture at Woodford Square, 22 March 1961)." *Callaloo* 20 (4): 725–30.

Wilson, Peter J. 1995 [1973]. *Crab Antics: A Caribbean Case Study of the Conflict between Reputation and Respectability*. Prospect Heights, IL: Waveland Press.

Yelvington, Kevin, ed. 1993. *Trinidad Ethnicity*. Knoxville: University of Tennessee Press.

———. 1995. *Producing Power: Ethnicity, Gender, and Class in a Caribbean Workplace*. Philadelphia: Temple University Press.

———. 2001. "The Anthropology of Afro-Latin America and the Caribbean: Diasporic Dimensions." *Annual Review of Anthropology* 30: 227–60.

———, ed. 2006a. *Afro-Atlantic Dialogues: Anthropology in the Diaspora*. Santa Fe, NM: School of American Research Press.

———. 2006b. "The Invention of Africa in Latin America and the Caribbean: Political Discourse and Anthropological Praxis, 1920–1940." In *Afro-Atlantic Dialogues: Anthropology in the Diaspora*, edited by Kevin Yelvington, 35–82. Santa Fe, NM: School of American Research Press.

Zane, Wallace W. 1999. *Journeys to the Spiritual Lands: The Natural History of a West Indian Religion*. London: Oxford University Press.

Note: page numbers followed by *f* and *n* indicate figures and endnotes, respectively.

IESOM shrine. *See* Ile Eko Sango/Osun
  Mil'osa (IESOM) shrine
Ifá established in Trinidad: 2007 priest visits,
  128–29, 131–33; Alásùwadà Ifá conference/
  movement and, 128, 156–66, 159f, 161f,
  165f; Àséwélé ritual and shrines, 151–56,
  155f, *Plate 10*; gender and, 142–43; historical
  roots, 129; Ifá/Orisha Worldview Practitioners Conference, 145–50; initiations
  and, 130, 131, 138, 141–43; new lineage established, 137–40; Pópóolá lecture, 137–43;
  priesthood–initiation distinction and,
  144–45; ritual variations and conflicts,
  133–37; spiritual citizenship, social change,
  and, 166–68; Venezuela connections, 130–31
Ifagbola, Agba (Charles Castle), 81, 108, 109
Ifakunle Adetutu, Awo Oluwole, 101, 105,
  109, 116–17, 146, 187n3
Ifá/Orisha religion: associated with "poor
  folks in the country," 80; black internationalism and, 11–12; esoteric aspects, 120–21;
  explicit link between the two, 140; gender
  and, 140; Haitian Vodou, common characteristics with, 28, 181n3; Indo-Trinidadian
  participation in, 14; saints in, 116–17;
  Spiritual Baptists, relationship with, 30–32,
  181n6. *See also* divinations; festive practices; initiation to Ifá; public sphere, emergence of Orisha in; ritual; transnational
  spiritual networks
Ifá/Orisha Worldview Practitioners Conference, 145–50
Ifáyomi, Awo, 109
ikin, receiving, 120–21
Ile Eko Sango/Osun Mil'osa (IESOM) shrine,
  113f; Alásùwadà Ifá conference, 14–17, 128,
  156–66, 159f, 161f, 165f; Carnival mas' band,
  91–94; Ifá/Orisha Worldview Practitioners
  Conference, 145–50; Odun Ojo Orisha,
  112; Rain Festival, 25, 71–79, 94–97, *Plates
  1–2, Plates 6–7*; raising of Shango's double-
  headed ax, 8–9, 9f, 112, *Plate 9*; as sacred
  ground, *Plate 8*
Ilé-Ifè, Nigeria: about, 187n4; chieftaincy
  titles of, 132, 189n4; king's representatives
  sent to Sixth World Congress, 84; ritual

variation across zones of, 134–35; Sacred
  Journey to (2004), 110, 121–26; spiritual
  economies in, 122–25; travels to Orisha
  World Congress in, 105–8. *See also* Oòni of
  Ilé-Ifè
Ile Isokan, Ifebo Compound, Febeau Village,
  167
Ile Iwosan Orunmila, 157
Indo-Trinidadians: at Ifá/Orisha Worldview
  Practitioners Conference, 149; March to
  Caroni and, 47; participation in "African"
  Orisha tradition, 14; UNC and, 63, 66. *See
  also* Panday, Basdeo
initiate–priest distinction, 144–45
initiation to Ifá: of author, 3; definition of
  an initiate, 144; first in Trinidad, 130, 141;
  importance of, 141–43; Ìtènífá vs. Elégán,
  136; Pópóolá on, 138, 141–43; at Rain Festival, 187n20; reinitiation, 135–36; on Sacred
  Journey to Ilé-Ifè (2004), 123–25
insider/outsider boundaries, 124
International Festival of African Tradition
  and Culture, 131
Inter-Religious Organization (IRO), Trinidad,
  149
invocations, 75–77, 114–15, 137–38
Irentegbe temple, 156–57
Ìretè Ìká, 156, 168
itefa. See initiation to Ifá
Iwori, 79
Iyewa, Yeye, 146

Jackson, John, 114
Jamaica, 182n11
Jambalaya (Teish), xiii
Jameet al Muslimeen, 182n18
Ji, Ravi, 149
Johnson, Paul Christopher, 10, 77
Jones, Omi Oshun Joni L., 133

Kabala (Kabbalah), 100, 187n1
Keita, Awo Ifawole, 16
Kenny Cyrus Alkebulan Ile Ijebu shrine, 84,
  107f, 131–32
Khambon, Khafra (Dave Darbeau), 25, 41, 42,
  46, 47, 52

Khan, Aisha, 183n9
Khan, Noble, 149
knowledge dissemination, politics of, 124, 138
Kolade, Baba, 78
kola nut (obi) divinations, 78–79, 117–20, 119f, 134, *Plate 1*
Korede, Awo Ifá, 109, 146

LaSalle, Rex, 50–51
legislation, 32–33, 59–61, 183n11
"Let Their Souls Be Perfectly Rested" (Pópóọlá), 151
liberation, national/black, 12
liminality, xiv, 153
Lindsay, Isaac, 26
lineages: Cuban, 142, 143; establishing new lineage in Trinidad, 137–40, 141; gender bias in, 143; multiplicity of, 135. *See also* Ilé-Ifè̩, Nigeria; initiation to Ifá
Lionza, Maria, 131
Liverpool, Hollis ("Chalkdust"), 146, 148
localization, 166–67
local knowledge, 138
lookmen, 129
Lopez, Santos (Bablawo Fatalami), 188n3
Lorde, Audre, xi, 12
Lord Shango Day, 61
Lum, Kenneth, 30, 181n6

Maharaj, Satnarayan, 184n13
majoritarianism, 63
Makanjuola, Agba, 132
Manning, Patrick, 184n13
Maracas Youth Group, 95
Maraj, Bhdase Sagan, 47
masquerade (mas') bands, 91–94
Massetungi, Babalorisa Oludari Olakela, 36, 92, 122, 187n18, 188n18, *Plate 3*
Maugé, Conrad (Awo Ifayomi Epega-Agbede), 116
McLeod, Curt, 8
McLeod, I. T., 8, 84
McLeod, Pat. *See* Sangowunmi, Iya
McNeal, Keith, 185n7
Medahochi, Baba, 16
Meeks, Brian, 47–48, 51

Meighoo, Kirk, 58
men in leadership, privileging of, 166. *See also* gender
Michener, Roland, 43
middle class: Black Power movement and, 35; complication of label, 103; national culture and, 52–53; political leadership by Afro-Creole middle class, 57, 61, 64–65; trans-national spiritual networks and, 102–3
Middle Passage, 77, 151–56
Minshall, Peter, 186n16
Mishra, Malay, 148
mourning ceremony and receiving *ikin*, 120–21
multiculturalism: Afrocentric perspective and, 90; Black Nationalism vs., 67–68; difference and, 85; ideological shift and, 58–59; Panday compared to Williams on, 62–63, 65–66; religious, 13–14
Munasinghe, Viranjini, 58–59
mutinies, 50–53
mystical experiences, 120–21

Nannee, Papa, 129
National Action Cultural Committee, 52
National Alliance for Reconstruction (NAR), 62, 182n16, 184n20
National Council of Orisha Elders, 84–85, 184n16
national councils, 64
National Joint Action Committee (NJAC), 42, 44–46, 51–53
Neezer, Papa, 119
networks, spiritual. *See* transnational spiritual networks
Nigeria: exchanges with, 100, 109–11, 121–26; finances of travel to, 123, 138; icons for new lineage brought from, 141; imagined "Africa" and, 167; initiations in, 109, 123–25; languages of, ix; Ọ̀ṣun Ọ̀ṣogbo Festival (Òṣun State), 133; Pópóọlá's plans for shrine near Àséwélé near Badagry, 156; priests and officials visiting from, 16–17, 84, 95, 121, 131–32, 137–43, 147; spiritual economy and, 123–24; Yorubaland, imagined community of, 4, 108, 115; Yorùbá language, 120, 133, 188n15;

Nigeria, (*continued*)
  Yorùbá religion of, in tension with
    Trinidad-centric perspective, 85–87, 91–95.
    See also Ifá/Orisha religion; Illé-Ifè, Nigeria;
    transnational spiritual networks
Nigeria-Trinidad air bridge, 190n17

Obatala, 3, 73
Obba, 74
obeah, 60, 184nn12–13
obi (kola nut) divinations, 78–79, 117–20,
  119f, 134, *Plate 1*
Odéyẹmí, Ìdòwú, 115
Odù, 141
odù Ifá, 92–93, 112, 113f, 142, 151–52, 162–63,
  168, 177
offerings, 139, 167
Ogun, 1–2, 5
Ogunkeye, Baba, 96f
ole talk, 88
Olúbàse, Ọọ̀ni Ọba Okùnadé Síjúwadé, 55, 84,
  85, 106, 132, 185n8
Oludari, Babalorisa. *See* Massetungi, Babalo-
  risa Oludari Olakela
Olukayode, Aina, 106
Oluorogbo, 73
Omilade, Iya, 158
Ong, Aihwa, 6
Onile, 73–74
Ọọ̀ni of Ilé-Ifè (Ọba Okùnadé Síjúwadé
  Olúbàse), 55, 84, 85, 106, 132, 185n8
Orisha (deities): associated with saints,
  116–17; attributes, 175. *See also specific
  Orisha by name, such as* Oshun
Orisha Family Day festival, 54–57, 83, 101,
  183n4
Orisha Marriage Act (1999), 60–61, 184n16
Orisha religion. *See* Ifá/Orisha religion
Orunmila, 116–17, 133, 135, 189n7
Osayin, 14, 73, 116–17
Oshosi, 73
Oshun: about, xv, 5; at Alásùwadà confer-
  ence, 128, 158–62, 161f; initiation in Trin-
  idad and, 141; multiple narratives of, 133;
  odu Ifá and, 92–93; possession by, xiv–xv,
  1–2, 158–60; Rain Festival invocation of,

74; Salybia Bay Oshun Festival, *Plate 4*;
  shrine to, 31f
Ọsun (holy staff of Ifá), 134–36
Osunyemi, Iya, 92, 140
Oxaal, Ivar, 39–40
Oya, 74
Oyeku Meji, 78
Oyotunji Village, South Carolina, 16, 128, 158,
  187nn2–3, 188n1

Pan-Africanism, 89–91
Panday, Basdeo, 54–59, 60–68, 84, 85, 101,
  184n23
Pantin, Raoul, 37–39, 44–49
Pegasus, 44, 51
People's National Movement (PNM): Black
  Power movement and, 38, 49–50, 52;
  March to Caroni and, 46; Robinson and, 49,
  182n16; Williams and, 183n8
persecution, 32–33, 59–60
Peters, Winston ("Gypsy"), 146, 148–49
Phills, Baba Sam, 111
political consciousness and religious consciousness, 36
political recognition. *See* public sphere, emergence of Orisha in
Pópóọlá, Olóyè Ṣọlágbadé: 2007 lecture,
  137–43; Alásùwadà Ifá conference and,
  156–57, 164; on Àséwélé, 151, 156; creation
  story, 162–63; Ifá/Orisha Worldview Practitioners Conference and, 146, 147, 150; impact of 2007 visit of, 128–29; International
  Festival of African Tradition and Culture
  and, 131; "Let Their Souls Be Perfectly
  Rested," 151; prayers for, 78
possession by Oshun, xiv–xv, 1–2, 158–60
praxis, sacred, 77
praxis, spiritual, 5–7, 114, 136, 144, 164
priest–initiate distinction, 144–45
Protestantism, colonial struggles over, 29–30
public sphere, emergence of Orisha in: Afro-
  Creole middle-class leadership and, 61,
  64–65; ethnic party politics and, 58; Ifá/
  Orisha Worldview Practitioners Conference
  and, 149; legislative persecution and recognition, 59–61; multicultural rhetoric of

Teish, Luisah, xiii–xv
Teteron National Defense Force Base, 50
Thomas, Deborah A., 12
Tobago, 87–88
Toussaint, Mother, 140
transnational spiritual networks: Baba
 Erinfolami's movement to Ifá, 99–101; class
 and, 102–5; defined, 6; festivals and, 77,
 97–98; festivals in Trinidad seen through
 lens of Ifá, 110–14; Ifá recognized in earlier
 Trinidad Orisha practices, 115–21; initiations in Yorubaland, 109–10; invocations
 and, 114–15; new knowledge incorporated
 with old systems, 126–27; points of conver-
 gence, 102; Sacred Journey to Ilé-Ifè (2004)
 and spiritual economies, 110, 121–26;
 Saints and Orisha, 116–17; travel to Orisha
 World Congress in Ilé-Ifè, 105–8; turn of
 millennium and, 101, 105. See also diaspora
Trinidad: about, 6; African ethnicities set-
 tling in, 28–29; as "callaloo nation," 183n9.
 See also Ifá established in Trinidad; Ile Eko
 Sango/Osun Mil'osa (IESOM) shrine
Trinidad-centric vs. Yorùbá-centric approach,
 85–87, 91–95
Trouillot, Michel-Rolph, 181n7

United National Congress (UNC), 55, 58,
 62–63, 65–66, 85, 182n16, 184n22
unity-across-difference theme, 164–65
University of Trinidad and Tobago, 146

Venezuela, 130–31
Viranjini, Munasinghe, 181n7
visions, 120–21
Vodou, Haitian, 28, 181n3
voice: of black women, xiii; of God/dess,
 hearing, xiii–xv

Warner-Lewis, Maureen, 102
Weekes, George, 47
Williams, Eric: Black Power movement
 and, 37, 38, 49; Carnival caricature of, 40;
 ethnic party politics and, 58; Granger
 and, 44; Panday compared to, on multi-
 culturalism, 62–63, 65–66; PNM and,
 183n8
women, leadership role of, 140, 142
Woodford Square march, 44–46
World Congress of Orisha Tradition and
 Culture, Sixth (1999), 16, 67, 79–86, 102
World Congress of Orisha Tradition and
 Culture, Seventh (2001), 105–8

Yemoja, 74
Yorùbá, meaning of term, 4
Yorùbá-centric vs. Trinidad-centric approach,
 85–87, 91–95
Yorubaland, imagined community of, 4, 108,
 115. See also Ilé-Ifè, Nigeria
Yorùbá language, 120, 133, 188n15
Yorùbá religion. See Ifá/Orisha religion